EXPANDING SUBURBIA

Polygons: Cultural Diversities and Intersections
General Editor: **Lieve Spaas**, *Professor of French Cultural Studies, Kingston University*

Volume 1: *Reynard the Fox: Social Engagement and Cultural Metamorphoses in the Beast Epic from the Middle Ages to the Present*
Edited by Kenneth Varty

Volume 2: *Echoes of Narcissus*
Edited by Lieve Spaas in association with Trista Selous

Volume 3: *Human Nature and the French Revolution: From the Enlightenment to the Napoleonic Code*
Xavier Martin, translated from the French by Patrick Corcoran

Volume 4: *Secret Spaces, Forbidden Places: Rethinking Culture*
Edited by Fran Lloyd and Catherine O'Brien

Volume 5: *Relative Points of View: Linguistic Representation of Culture*
Edited by Magda Stroinska

Volume 6: *Expanding Suburbia: Reviewing Suburban Narratives*
Edited by Roger Webster

EXPANDING SUBURBIA

Reviewing Suburban Narratives

Edited by Roger Webster

Berghahn Books
New York • Oxford

First published in 2000 by

Berghahn Books
www.BerghahnBooks.com

© 2000 Roger Webster

Library of Congress Cataloging-in-Publication Data

Expanding suburbia: reviewing suburban narratives / edited by Roger Webster.
  p.cm
  Includes bibliographical references and index.
  ISBN 1-57181-790-5 –ISBN 1-57181-791-3 (alk paper)
  1. Suburban life 2. Suburbs in literature. I. Webster, Roger

HT351 .E96 2000
307.74—dc21   00-049350

British Library Cataloguing in Publication Data

A catalogue record for this book is available
from the British Library.

Printed in the United States on acid-free paper.

ISBN 1-57181-790-5 (hardback)
ISBN 1-57181-791-3 (paperback)

CONTENTS

Acknowledgements   vii

Introduction: Suburbia Inside Out   1
Roger Webster

1. From William Morris to the Morris Minor: 15
   an Alternative Suburban History
   Simon Dentith

2. 'The New Suburbanites' and Contested Class Identities   31
   in the London Suburbs, 1880–1900
   Lynne Hapgood

3. The Riddle of Suburbia: Suburban Fictions at the *fin*   51
   de siècle
   Gail Cunningham

4. Poisoned Minds: Suburbanites in Postwar British Fiction   71
   Dominic Head

5. Suburban Values and Ethni-Cities in Indo-Anglian   91
   Writing
   Peter Childs

6. An Incident in the Neighbourhood: Crime,   109
   Contemporary Fiction and Suburbia
   Linden Peach

7. Between Subdivisions and Shopping Malls: Signifying   125
   Everyday Life in the Contemporary American South
   Joanna Price

8. Urban Thrall: Renegotiating the Suburban Self in   141
Nick Hornby's *Fever Pitch* and *High Fidelity*
Daniel Lea

9. The Sound of the Suburbs: the Idea of the Suburb in   161
English Pop
D.J. Taylor

10. Kitsch on the Fringe: Suburbia in Recent Australian   173
Comedy Film
Nicole Matthews

Notes on Contributors   187

Select Bibliography   191

Index   193

ACKNOWLEDGEMENTS

I would like to thank the following for their support and help in producing this volume of essays: Lieve Spaas for the original suggestion, Jean Stephenson and Fiona McCullough for their help in preparing the manuscript, John Freeman for lightening my administrative load, and, as always, Glenda, Annie and Duncan. A special debt is due to colleagues and students at Liverpool John Moores University who have pursued a truly interdisciplinary approach to study, which has been to the benefit of myself and many others. Finally, but most importantly, I would like to thank the contributors, who have been so generous with their ideas and time in producing this volume.

INTRODUCTION:
SUBURBIA INSIDE OUT

Do you know the road I live in – Ellesmere Road, West Bletchley? Even if you don't, you know fifty others like it.

You know how these streets fester all over the inner-outer suburbs. Always the same. Long, long rows of little semi-detached houses…. The stucco front, the creosoted gate, the privet hedge, the green front door. The Laurels, the Myrtles, the Hawthorns, Mon Abri, Mon Repos, Belle Vue. At perhaps one house in fifty some anti-social type who'll probably end in the workhouse painted his front door blue instead of green….

When you've time to look about you, and when you happen to be in the right mood, it's a thing that makes you laugh inside to walk down these streets in the inner-outer suburbs and to think of the lives that go on there. Because after all, what *is* a road like Ellesmere Road? Just a prison with cells in a row. A line of semi-detached torture chambers where the poor little five-to-ten-pound-a-weekers quake and shiver, every one of them with the boss twisting his tail and the wife riding him like the nightmare and the kids sucking his blood like leeches.[1]

George Orwell's caricature of suburbia in *Coming up for Air* (1939), serves as a defining illustration of the myths and stereotypes that have arisen around suburban culture. Orwell's depiction is articulated through the 1930s character of George Bowling, a traditional middle-Englander undergoing a series of crises from mid-life to intimations of the rise of fascism and impending war. His attitudes expressed towards suburbia stem from a tradition that can be traced back to the nineteenth century and earlier[2], and which became particularly pronounced in a number of twentieth-century literary depictions. One phrase that is significant for its precision, or perhaps its imprecision, 'inner-outer suburbs', raises a series of questions about where we locate suburbia, how do we view it as a geographical, social or cultural zone? What is evident is that suburbia is inevitably viewed against or from a backdrop, against an 'other' zone – for example geographical (country or city) or social class (working or upper). It occupies a space as much defined by what it is not as by what it is, constructed by difference and imitation rather than possessing innate and original features. Its identity then, insofar as it can be ascribed one, is shifting and insecure; a borderline and liminal space which, in spite of the myths and stereotypes attaching to it, may be more helpfully characterised by a recognition of contradiction and flux than of conformity and stability.

The dominant stereotypes of suburbia have generally relegated it to a geographical region existing on the margins of city and country, at or beyond the edges of cultural sophistication and tradition, a surface where the mundane and monotony prevail, consumerism and commodification determine lifestyles and time and space are reduced to the garden or television screen. Suburbia has no 'history'; its archives are empty. There is no depth from which archaeology might exhume its artefacts. Frequently represented as outcast colony or gulag, a community of the historically semi-detached, there are important parallels to be drawn between the growth of suburbia and that of colonialism, which are explored later in this volume. Paradoxically, suburbia's decentredness and depthlessness – its apparent lack of any profound cultural signifying status – are at one level where the potency of suburbia lies. It has become a sterile zone, devoid of cultural and aesthetic value so that the very absence of signification becomes a haunting presence – a cultural and geographical 'other'.

However, beyond or behind this simulacrum there are alternative versions of suburbia. The superficial myth of homogeneity can mask a range of tendencies from the discordant and bizarre to the comic and tragic, as repeated portrayals of suburban life have stressed. The dysfunctional family, for example, is as much a product of suburbia as it is of city or country, from Chekov and Ibsen to Mike Leigh's *Abigail's Party* (1977) and Sam Mendes' recent film, *American Beauty* (1999). It can be argued too that some television soap dramas such as Phil Redmond's *Brookside* have pushed back the frontiers of television orthodoxy, approaching a number of hitherto taboo subjects utilising the setting of suburban life. As Roger Silverstone has commented in his groundbreaking volume, *Visions of Suburbia* (1997), 'An understanding of how suburbia was produced, and continues to be both produced and reproduced, is an essential precondition for an understanding of the twentieth century, an understanding above all of the emerging character and contradictions of our everyday lives'.[3]

There has been a discernible and highly significant change in the modes and perspectives of representations of suburbia from the external to the internal; from the outside to the inside. This has coincided with the critical revolution arising from the growth and influence of cultural and interdisciplinary studies, which has spurred the questioning of, and a departure from, canonical and narrow literary traditions. This profound shift in critical approaches and the resulting re-evaluation of high and popular culture has affected the situating of suburbia. Just as suburbia's geographical position has become more centralised and contested, so its representations have been modified, becoming increasingly complex, particularly in literary and cinematic portrayals. Critical assessments have begun to respond to these changes, and views from outside have tended to accentuate suburbia in relation to the country or the city. As Raymond Williams has argued, representations of the city and the country have been in a dialectical relationship since at least the sixteenth century.[4] These interlinked centres of experience have dominated English spatial and cultural imagination for several centuries, and the rise of suburbia has challenged and repositioned this hegemony.

The city/country dualism is often manifest in travel and documentary writing, for example H. V. Morton's *In Search of England* (1927):

> But London is too big: by the time you reach the fringe of her there is no London to be seen; and you cannot waste sentiment on suburban gasworks.... In a line with the public-house were new shops. In a field some way off the high road were scared-looking, pink and white villas, each one possessing a bald garden and a brand new galvanised dustbin at the back door. Wives as new as the gardens and the houses busied about their work and took frequent peeps through the front windows to make sure that the baby was still on the safe side of the garden fence. The most significant item on the landscape was an empty omnibus

standing in a weary attitude opposite the public house. There
were London names on the indicator board, but they seemed as
unlikely as the Italian names on the French express at Calais.

The history of London is the moving on of that red omnibus
another mile along the road; more pink and white houses;
more shops; more wives; more babies.[5]

As in Morton's description, suburbia is frequently used as a
backcloth against which to identify values of uniqueness and
tradition, of a desired or threatened identity. Suburbia
assumes a position of otherness, discursively represented as an
unattractive zone against which normative individuality and
subjectivity can be defined. Interestingly, Bill Bryson describes
a similar vista some seventy years later in his travelogue *Notes
from a Small Island* (1995):

> Goodness me, but isn't London big? It seems to start about
> twenty minutes after you leave Dover and just goes on and on,
> mile after mile of endless grey suburbs with their wandering
> ranks of terraced houses and stuccoed semis that always look
> more or less identical from a train, as if they've been squeezed
> out of a very large version of one of those machines they use to
> make sausages. How, I always wonder, do all the millions of
> occupants find their way back to the right boxes each night in
> such a complex and anonymous sprawl? [6]

There is a remarkable degree of consistency, indeed uniformity, in such external perspectives on suburbia. Their defining characteristics, whether viewed from the country or the
city, tend to be reducible to unimaginative conformist design
and behaviour determined by imitation rather than origi-
nality; a lack of individuality combined with excessive social
homogeneity; spatially cramped and confined conditions,
and a neglect for, or the undermining of, traditional values.
Q.D. Leavis epitomises these attitudes, stating that 'suburban culture ... has failed to produce anything like as subtle a
medium ... it has no fine rhythms to draw upon, and is not
serious ... it is not only formed to convey merely crude states
of mind but it is destructive of any fineness'.[7] What these
approaches and assessments reveal are the limitations of the
'literary' in critical engagements with suburbia in all its
forms. Literary and literary-critical discourses tend to be geographically and ideologically polarised between country and
city, located in traditional cultural zones, which, though frequently in forms of oppositional or dialectical relationship,
rarely bestow on suburban culture an equivalent status.

However, the history of suburbia is more varied, subtle, and dialogical than such depictions might suggest. An early dissenting voice from the established cultural norms can be found in the novels of Arnold Bennett. His representations of suburbia are at times both innovative and ambivalent. Bennett's narrator makes the case for a suburban literary consciousness in *A Man from the North* (1898), suggesting a typical suburban street offers as much potential for the fictional canvas as any other traditional literary milieu:

> How many houses are there in Carteret Street? Say eighty. Eighty theatres of love, hate, greed, tyranny, endeavour; eighty dramas always unfolding, intertwining, ending, beginning … there is more character within a hundred yards of this chair than a hundred Balzacs could analyse in a hundred years.[8]

This is an early plea for, and anticipation of, a shift in perspective in portraying suburbia which has become increasingly apparent. In the latter decades of the nineteenth century and throughout the twentieth century the growth and ever-changing identity of suburbia have arguably made it the major consumer – and an increasingly significant producer – of culture. The privileging perspectives of country and city begin to erode when suburbia is perceived from within rather than from without. This is even true of writers such as John Betjeman who, despite being dismissive of suburbia in much of his poetry, produced a highly engaging portrayal of suburban life, characterised as much by idiosyncrasy, pastiche and the bizarre as by stereotypicality and convention, in his 1960s television documentary *Metroland*. His 'enthralled camp'[9] presentational style heightens the ambivalent and ironic mode, giving suburbia a treatment that anticipates more recent representations in both fiction and music. Hanif Kureishi and David Bowie are not far removed in time, space – or campness. It is noticeable too that when Betjeman utilises traditional cultural forms, as in the poem 'Slough' (1937), his detached aerial perspective on suburbia is entirely derogatory, but in the medium of television as engaged social and historical commentator his approach is more participatory and varied; fascinated, even if overindulgent and patronising at times.

If tension and contradiction are axiomatic conditions of modern existence, then they reside as much in suburbia as in the more traditional locations of urban and rural environments. Indeed, from its modern inception suburbia has been a

site of paradox and opposition. Idealism and exploitation
have enjoyed an alliance in the bourgeois exodus from the
city in the late nineteenth and early twentieth centuries. The
potential for reinforcing and normalising individual subjectivity and identity through various forms such as domestic
space and design, is epitomised in the signifiers and signifieds
associated with suburbia. From nineteenth-century stucco villas and the 'tudorbethan' semis of the 1930s and 1950s to the
shopping centres and malls of the 1990s – temples to commodification offering lifestyle and identity transformations
with the swipe of a credit card. As Joanna Price suggests in her
chapter, Baudrillard's conception of commodification and
consumption as being at the centre of western societies, their
potent signifying systems bringing hyper-reality into the market place of the everyday, is most manifest in suburbia. Suburbia as hyper-reality and liminality; an area of flux the
defining characteristic of which is redefinition, is a conception
far removed from the alleged unanimity of leafy avenues and
latticework windows.

This volume reveals that suburbia is a zone of contested
meanings; populated by visions both utopian and dystopian,
idyllic and ordinary, familiar and unfamiliar jostling across
space and time.

The essays are organised in a loosely chronological order,
but also develop from an emphasis on predominantly literary
material to music and film. Through the course of this development, the book traverses several major themes. Consumerism and commodification in their nineteenth- and
twentieth-century manifestations are consistent and pervasive
presences in representations of and discussions on suburbia.
The gendering of suburban space, from nineteenth-century
English to late twentieth-century America and Australia is
examined – revealing more complexity and ambiguity than
superficial domestic conventions and stereotyping would suggest. The general cultural hybridity combined with social het-
erogeneity (as opposed to the narrow conformity and
homogeneity normally attributed to suburbia) and beyond
this, immanent or repressed forms of desire, disruption and
violence are explored throughout the volume. In particular,
the setting of crime fiction in suburban locations pertinently
reveals the contradictions contained within suburbia, and
works as a potent defamiliarising device. The highly fragile
and often tenuous social and individual relations which lie
behind outward appearances – suburbia is a kind of wilder-

ness where masks have to be worn to protect its occupants from recognition – may not be so different from any other environment, but it is convenient to locate these tendencies in a defined, and therefore containable, territory. Suburbia as a frame of mind or psychological state, indeed as increasingly symptomatic of the universal condition, is a theme that becomes more pronounced as the book continues. Linked to this, the need to imprint the suburban vision as a form of individual assertion or local territorial or colonial hegemony reveals itself, the suburban form expressing itself in such displaced locations as Arsenal Football Club's pitch as lawn.

Simon Dentith's playfully entitled account of the antithetical issues surrounding the founding of what we might consider and recognise as modern suburbia reveals the tensions between the idealistic impulses behind the communitarian vision of the Garden City as opposed to the commercial and exploitative practicalities which drove the waves of commercial bricks-and-mortar suburban expansion. From the utopian vision of the garden suburb or city which informed every feature of its design – derived in particular from William Morris's Arts and Crafts movement and involving a regeneration of society itself – to the disappointing reality pointed to by contemporaneous commentators, these early manifestations were themselves sites of diversity and conflict. Recognition of the ideological implications of suburbia is not a recent phenomenon, and the competing structures of economy and class are extended into turn-of-the-century concerns over industrialisation and rural recidivism, imperialism, and even eugenics, all lurking behind half-timbered and stucco facades. The battle over suburbia, indeed what we may think of as modern consumerism, was arguably fought and lost a century ago.

Lynne Hapgood examines the construction of suburban values and the search for class identities within this new social terrain. As she illustrates, the term 'suburb' contains fluctuating and contested meanings, and writers were quick to recognise the dilemmas and tensions which suburban immigrants experienced in the formation of class-consciousness. 'Suburbs' and 'suburbanite' had not acquired the fixed connotations of monotony and bad taste at this stage, which only subsequently became more normative. Turn-of-the-century fictions map a range of responses on to suburban expansion – though crucially the missing voices are those of the suburbanites themselves. As Hapgood shows, along with Dentith, the range and differences in the design and quality of suburban housing were quite pronounced, replicating to a considerable extent those which suburbanites thought they were escaping from in the cities. The representation of the new suburbanites was also varied, from the satirical portrait of Mr Pooter in the Grossmith brothers' *Diary of a Nobody* (1891), to the much more positive depictions by William Morris and H.G. Wells. In an interesting link, Sidney Low's celebration of the dynamic suburbanite infused with the advantages of cleanliness and space, free from the debilitating effects of the city, his body tuned by football, becomes an ironic anticipation of Nick Hornby's central character in *Fever Pitch* (1993) a century later. As Hapgood argues, the impact of suburbia in England during the Victorian period was nothing short of an unspoken social revolution.

Gail Cunningham's discussion also considers the ambiguities and polyphony in depictions of suburbia of the same period, in particular of spatial dynamics in relation to gender. Significantly, external commentators belittle such features as the suburban garden and its products, but an internal perspective can offer quite antithetical responses. For Wells in *The New Machiavelli* (1911), the garden becomes at one level an outlet for existential anguish. Cunningham suggests that the subdivisions of suburbia in terms of gendered space, and the rise of the New Woman can be seen to inspire the feminist movement of the 1960s and 1970s. Suburbia in the early twentieth century can be viewed as a focal point for wider social anxieties, projected onto a confined space which contains their threat within the sphere of the culturally constructed.

Dominic Head's account of suburbia in a selection of post World War II fiction problematises definitions and locations of suburbia further in terms of the human, geographical and, increasingly, economic and material forces. These find their discursive nexus in a range of fictional texts from Alan Sillitoe and Stan Barstow to Julian Barnes and Hanif Kureishi. Head suggests that suburbia can 'absorb and distort' literary projects, a novel such as Angus Wilson's *Late Call* (1964) being colonised by the popular forms it seeks to parody – perhaps an inverted form of defamiliarisation. Nevertheless, he also argues that there are diverse and fracturing forms of culture beneath the surface uniformity; suburbia's continued centrality is founded on the paradoxes and contradictions that it promulgates and sustains. This, he asserts, accounts for the dimension of surprise, which continually appears in suburban narratives and makes suburbia exemplary of contemporary life. Head's discussion of a key text, Kureishi's *The Buddha of Suburbia*

(1990), points to the tension between the theme of escape and the need to recognise suburban roots and intrinsic cultural forms; suburbia can be a producer as well as consumer of cultural forms. In this novel, it is popular music – specifically punk rock – which is the agency that allows the formation of an identity both in contradistinction to, but also arising from, suburbia. Head points to the emergence of a new suburban figure, Karim, being the product of hybrid traditions; a character who can exist within the contradictions and multicultural forms of late twentieth-century suburbia and beyond.

Peter Childs expands this theme, considering the complications of race in a selection of texts which link suburban experience with colonial and postcolonial visions. As he demonstrates, there are important and revealing parallels between suburban and colonial identities. Viewing English suburbia through the eyes of visiting Indians provides an illuminating and unfamiliar perspective in place of the normal external/internal dialectic that has characterised most accounts. Such descriptions are less clouded by the pejorative or preconditioned responses to 'metroland' so inscribed in English attitudes. What these accounts reveal is the unexpected: not only poverty but also anti-establishment attitudes, which would ostensibly have no place in postwar suburban England. Childs also examines suburbia from within or more precisely from an 'inner–outer' position. That is, from the perspective of second-generation Indian writing located in postwar English suburbia. As he demonstrates, British Asian fiction addresses the double threat of, on the one hand, conformity, and on the other, the routine persecution of difference within a society based on sameness. The eruption of racism serves to excoriate suburban prejudice within a culture that is in fact based on difference and intolerance rather than homogeneity and community. However, there are possibilities for change and innovation, as Childs suggests; new identities can be forged as Karim in *The Buddha of Suburbia* discovers. The potential accommodation of difference, the rejection of the need to identify with one racial or class position and a shift to hybridity, indicate that suburbia may have a future.

Any future vision needs to address the contradictions and paradoxes contained within the repressed psyche of suburban consciousness, and as Linden Peach's reading of crime fiction set in suburbia reveals, forms of primeval immanence can be detected beneath a superficially ordered exterior. Serious crime is closely linked to the expansion of the suburbs, combined with their increased social complexity and lack of community. Peach suggests novels such as Suzanne Berne's *A Crime in the Neighbourhood* (1997) disclose that law and order have only a tenuous grasp on suburbia. Although middle-class mythology would locate and thus displace crime into either city or country, an internal event such as a child murder can undermine a central premise on which suburbia is constructed: that it is the ideal setting for a harmonious and safe family life. The slipping of the mask of suburban order and respectability also exposes the more widespread use of masks or disguise in everyday social interaction – so the revelations of crime fiction extend beyond the identification of an individual murderer. The artifices of suburbia make crime fiction a particularly suitable genre for investigating its plots and transgressions.

Joanna Price's chapter takes us potentially beyond suburbia, to the 'technoburb', all-containing and all-consuming social units, which dissolve the traditional boundaries between work and domesticity. Traversed by technological, commercial and communication infrastructures, the possibility of the global suburb emerges. Nonetheless, Price argues that the myths of suburbia will persist in order to assure identity at both subjective and communal levels. Suburbia also provides a convenient and powerful lens for viewing American everyday life. As in Peach's analysis, Price suggests that suburbia's fragile dependence on hybrid forms and its need to exclude 'otherness' makes it prone to self-subversion or defamiliarisation. It contains its own flaws and potential fractures and can thus serve as a model for wider social investigation. The endemic suburban culture of internal surveillance in its parochial and neighbourly forms can be extended to technical and global spheres as well as to the writer of fiction or social observer. Suburbia is the paradigmatic discursive form *nonpareil*. Price's examination of a selection of novels by writers of the American South – Bobbie Ann Mason and Richard Ford – reveals the radical instability of the everyday, of consumer culture. The illusions of transformation through the experience of the shopping mall or of friendship through the Divorced Men's Club illustrate the fabric of superficial and ephemeral suburban appearances.

The dream of suburban escape is central to Daniel Lea's discussion of Nick Hornby's novels, *Fever Pitch* (1992) and *High Fidelity* (1995). The theme of the all-pervasiveness of suburbia is examined; suburbia recolonising the urban landscape. The need felt by the protagonists of both novels to return to metropolitan centres of culture in order to discover their true identities results in ironic reversal. Suburbia is again revealed as a state of mind rather than a geographical location, Hornby's colonisation of space and culture in London, creating in effect a substitute mythical suburban lifestyle for the actuality of suburban Maidenhead from which he escapes, is one of dysfunction and dissonance – a significant inversion. The disintegration of Hornby's vision of community based around Arsenal Football Club supporters who have become largely dispersed across the Home Counties provides an illuminating parallel to views of suburban expansion. Instead of discovering a lost urban utopia, a conclusion to be drawn from the text is the realisation that the dissipation of community knows no boundaries. In *High Fidelity*, music provides an apparent means of escape in an urban context, but again it is at an imaginary level – the urban ideal is constructed from a suburban perspective. Ironically, the very music so strongly identified with the city owes as much to suburbia in both its production and consumption as it does to the city. Lea's contention that the suburban and urban can be seen as interdependent facets of consciousness in Hornby's fiction, providing imaginary points of identification for his protagonists as they are caught between these poles with no resolution, suggests an irreconcilable decentering of the suburban subject.

David Taylor discusses music's centrality to suburban experience. As with some other forms of cultural production and consciousness, the myth that English pop and rock music is rooted in the city can be questioned. The very titles of a number of key popular songs from the sixties onwards foreground suburbia in undisguised terms. Equally, there is no singular identifiable treatment of suburbia, but rather a multiplicity of styles and approaches both lyrically and musically. For all the satire, irony and rejection of suburbia in many of the songs which address suburban experience, Taylor shows that the spiritual home of much popular music resides in a suburban ambience if not location. Even David Bowie's experimental, groundbreaking and now global music involves the creation of a series of personae or masks which, undoubtedly, are at one level forms of suburban avoidance. As Taylor suggests, they can be read as concealing an underlying emptiness that may not be so far from Bromley.

David Bowie's emphasis on camp and stylistic excess links with Nicole Matthews' discussion of two Australian comedy films of the 1990s, *Strictly Ballroom* and *Muriel's Wedding*. Aus-

tralia has become the quintessential suburban setting through
television soaps, offering an idealised vision of family life and
especially youth culture. The normative reinforcement of gender roles, sexuality, ethnicity and nationhood in this context
combine to produce the screen version of suburban Australia
as an 'overdetermined setting'. Both films offer powerful critiques, significantly drawing on forms of artifice and ritual –
ballroom dancing and performances from wedding to karaoke
– to explore the not so latent hypocrisies and contradictions
embedded within and beyond suburbia. The emphasis on
camp style is, Matthews argues, a means of exposing the inauthenticity of homogeneous and heterosexual norms, permit-
ting a dialogic play of perspectives from within and without
suburbia. Nonetheless, Matthews concludes, it is still a privileged position.

These essays explore the increasingly significant and contested area of suburbia through a range of media: literature
from the popular to the canonical, music and film. The collection focuses largely on two central moments in the development of suburbia: the later nineteenth and early twentieth
centuries, and the postwar period. These witnessed unprecedented growth in the forms of suburbia – from geographical
and architectural to cultural and social. They are distinguished
not only by the shifting economic and class structures, which
were largely responsible for the production of suburbia as we
recognise it today, but also by a questioning of the identity – or
increasingly identities – of suburban life. The suburban dream,
or nightmare, oscillates between the poles of idealism and cyn-
icism, stasis and flux, tradition and experiment: a fabric of
space and time, which re-weaves itself in patterns familiar and
unfamiliar. As we move into the twenty-first century images of
suburbia permeate and saturate the media, its narratives are
unavoidable, its objects of desire ever present. Suburbia, home
of the ordinary and the extraordinary, has moved from the
margins to the centre of our experience.

Roger Webster

Notes

1. George Orwell, *Coming Up for Air*, Harmondsworth, 1971, 13–14.
2. See Kate Flint, 'Fictional Suburbia', *Literature and History*, vol. 8, no. 1
   (1982): 67–81.

3. Roger Silverstone, 'Introduction', in *Visions of Suburbia,* ed. Roger Silverstone London, 1997, 5.

4. See Raymond Williams, *The Country and the City,* London, 1985.

5. H.V. Morton, *In Search of England,* London, 1927, 2.

6. Bill Bryson, *Notes from a Small Island,* London, 1996, 41.

7. Q.D. Leavis, *Fiction and the Reading Public,* London, 1965, 210–11.

8. Arnold Bennett, *A Man from the North,* London, 1898, 102–103.

9. Andy Medhurst, 'Negotiating the Gnome Zone', in *Visions of Suburbia,* ed. Roger Silverstone London, 1997, 242.

≈ CHAPTER 1 ≈

FROM WILLIAM MORRIS TO THE MORRIS MINOR: AN ALTERNATIVE SUBURBAN HISTORY

Simon Dentith

Writing in 1913, a sympathetic critic of the Arts and Crafts movement, Holbrook Jackson, made a strong claim for the influence of its ideals upon the future shape of the country:

> By linking up art with the city and with common things the Arts and Crafts movement completed the sequence of its ideas, and if it has not yet succeeded in creating a new Jerusalem, it has indicated a way by pointing out the path for the Town Planning activities of a later date. Many craftsmen-visionaries saw afar off the Promised Land. William Morris set his own vision down in the magical prose of *News from Nowhere* (1891), and there is little doubt that his vision and their craftsmanship helped the ideas of Ebenezer Howard as expressed in *Garden Cities of Tomorrow* to come to such practical manifestations as they have received at Letchworth and Golders Green.[1]

By 'Golders Green' Jackson is referring to Hampstead Garden Suburb, then in the process of construction – a development that would be widely influential in the construction of suburbs throughout the century, as would Letchworth, the first 'Garden City'. This affiliation, of utopian idealism to suburban design, deserves to be further explored. What happened when utopian aspirations were translated into bricks and mortar? Did any of those aspirations survive in the suburbs they partially inspired? How did we travel from William Morris, socialist visionary, intellectual and design inspirer of the Arts and Crafts movement, to the Morris Minor, that quintessential vehicle of the English suburbs in the 1950s?

Since Jackson, the Arts and Crafts movement has routinely and correctly been cited as one of the influences on twentieth-century suburban design. If any one figure epitomised this influence, it would be Raymond Unwin. Architect and designer of the first Garden City at Letchworth, he went on to design Hampstead Garden Suburb, and to write the influential *Town Planning in Practice* (1909 and 1934), a crucially important handbook for town planners in the middle years of the twentieth century. As in the better-known case of Ebenezer Howard, Unwin's intellectual and political formation was in late nineteenth-century socialist utopianism. His first publication was in *Commonweal*, the journal of William Morris's Socialist League and the very journal in which Morris's utopian romance, *News from Nowhere*, was published. Here, then, is an extraordinary story – which leads, it seems, from the socialist utopianism of Nowhere, through Letchworth and the First Garden City Company, to Hampstead and its innumerable echoes and imitations in suburban estates across England. Is it a narrative of inevitable failure, of the hard compromises that ensue when idealism is confronted with practical realities? Or is it rather a story of the success of the dissemination of Morrisian Arts and Crafts ideals, in design terms at least, in remarkably extensive ways? Moreover, how were the various meanings that attached to the key moments in this narrative negotiated (Garden City, garden suburb, and suburb *tout court*)? Some of these meanings persisted well beyond the important first decade of the century, and we can find traces of that early utopian inspiration well beyond the scarcely-remembered past of Raymond Unwin, or, for that matter, of Ebenezer Howard.

The latter's antecedents in late nineteenth-century utopianism are certainly better known than Unwin's, and are anyway readily apparent in *Garden Cities of Tomorrow*.[2] Howard's plan, as laid out in this strikingly successful piece of utopian propaganda, is a frank amalgam of various preceding schemes and visions; it emerges directly from the milieu of socialist argument and debate that Howard inhabited in late nineteenth-century London. Jackson exaggerates the influence of Morris upon Howard in that comment in 1913, but there is no doubting the scale of his utopian ambition. As originally envisaged, the Garden City was far more than a plan for new towns based on low-density housing built on green field sites. It involved no less than the regeneration of society itself, via a solution to the complementary problems of urban overcrowding and rural depopulation. London, and other large cities, were to be transformed by the building of a ring of satellite cities which would draw off their vast overpopulation. These new cities would combine the attractions of rural and urban life, with the drawbacks of neither. Moreover, they were to be financed in a way that would mean that the landlords' 'unearned increment' – the profits gained by the simple increase in land values created by urban growth – would benefit the inhabitants of the town and not the owners of it. Within the garden cities, while there was to be no predisposition in favour of communal living or enterprise, there was to be ample space for such experimentation, and Howard himself, when a resident at Letchworth, would personally support one such communitarian experiment.

Howard had been responsible, in the late 1880s, for the publication of Edward Bellamy's *Looking Backward* in Britain, in a manner that is cognate with his eclectic assimilation of various utopian ideas and projects. Unwin's formation was more classically Arts and Crafts, by virtue of the stronger influence that William Morris had upon him, and his training as an architect. This meant that design was never to be understood by Unwin as a superficial or external matter; it had to emerge from profounder realities of social life. Thus, in *Town Planning in Practice*, the first chapter is entitled 'Of Civic Art as the Expression of Civic Life'. In it, Unwin makes the inevitable reference to Morris, and deprecates attempts to make the built environment 'artistic' by the use of superficial design features:

> William Morris said: 'Beauty, which is what is meant by Art, using the word in its widest sense, is, I contend, no mere accident of human life which people can take or leave as they choose, but a positive necessity of life, if we are to live as Nature meant us to – that is, unless we are to be content to be less than men'. The art which he meant works from within outward; the beauty which he regarded as necessary to life is not a quality which can be plastered on the outside. Rather it results when life and the joy of life, working outwards, express themselves in the beauty and perfection of all the forms which are created for the satisfaction of their needs.[3]

These are important principles, which take us to the heart of the narrative that I am telling. Is the influence of Arts and Crafts utopianism upon suburban design to be understood in superficial design terms, or do other, more utopian or radical meanings persist? It is certainly ironic that starting from these principles, it should be Raymond Unwin above all who was responsible for popularising Arts and Crafts design ideas in ways that do indeed open them to the charge of being 'plastered on'. I quote him here however to underline the utopian ambition that lay at the root of his thinking, and which persisted beyond his initial involvement with Letchworth.

If Unwin was prepared to countenance designing *suburbs*, Howard, by contrast, remained permanently hostile to them. The very idea of the Garden City was conceived in opposition to the suburban idea; its whole point was to combine working and living areas within easy reach of each other, and to provide independent and self-sufficient centres for a fulfilled life. The distinction between the Garden City and the suburb is one of the themes of C.B. Purdom's early history of Letchworth, *The Garden City: A Study in the Development of a Modern Town* (1913). Purdom was, he claimed, the 'first resident' of Letchworth, and a prolific writer on the themes of the Garden City and of town planning more generally. Howard contributed an Appendix to Purdom's book, on 'How far have the original Garden City Ideals been realized? He was already confronting a confusion that was permanently to dog the history of both the Garden City and the suburbs in general:

> one of the most disappointing experiences we of the Garden City have is that in the minds of the public and of writers in the press the idea of building new well-planned towns right away in the open ... is frequently confounded with a very different idea – that of building 'garden suburbs', that is, extensions, certainly often much-improved extensions, of existing towns; extensions sometimes of cities which it would be much better should not be extended. Indeed, the term 'Garden City' is often applied to a few well-planned or ill-planned streets and squares and garden-surrounded cottages, the dormitory of some other community.[4]

So from the very beginning, Howard resisted the assimilation of 'Garden City' to 'suburb', though in fact he was powerless to prevent it. Purdom himself emphasised a similar point: Letchworth did not resemble a suburb because it was 'balanced' by the industries (*The Garden City*,60).

One reason that Howard, and with him Purdom, so opposed this confusion, was that not to do so meant abandoning the far-reaching utopian hopes that were the very *raison d'être* of the Garden City. Their shared vision would be reduced to only the most visible and striking design aspects, such as the low-density housing, the innovative road lay-out and the inflections of vernacular building traditions that Unwin and his partner Barry Parker had encouraged at Letchworth (by no means to universal effect). Some utopian aspirations did survive into Letchworth, and later into Welwyn Garden City, although in some of his writing Purdom was keen to play down those counter-cultural or 'cranky' aspects of the new development.

Howard himself, after moving to Letchworth, encouraged an experiment in housekeeping, called Homesgarth. A group of flats was built without kitchens but with central catering and a dining room. The blueprint for this could have come from either *Looking Backwards* or *News from Nowhere* (despite the ideological and imaginative distance between the two texts). One of the most influential architectural innovations of Parker and Unwin at Letchworth, the group of four or six houses in a short terrace, was deliberately chosen over the semi-detached house as a model for cheap housing because of its communitarian appeal. Indeed, in *Town Planning in Practice*, Unwin anticipated a range of advantages which would spring from the diffusion of the cooperative principle among neighbours in groups of planned houses. For example, in place of the 'wasteful' Monday wash performed in hundreds of thousands of individual sculleries, there could be communal laundries:

> Where cottages are built in groups round a quadrangle, how simple it would be to provide one centre where a small, well-arranged laundry could be placed, with proper facilities for heating water, plenty of fixed tubs with taps to fill and empty them, and with properly heated drying-rooms. By two or three hours' use of such a laundry each housewife could carry out her weekly wash more expeditiously and more cheaply than she could do it at home. Perhaps some play-room would need to be attached.[5]

Further possible uses for the cooperative principle are suggested, including cloisters or covered play-places for the children, public rooms of reasonable size, reading-rooms and libraries, and common kitchens and dining-halls. It may seem a long way from *Nowhere* to detailed plans of laundry-rooms with careful attention to the appropriate positioning of the taps, nevertheless, in anticipations of this kind it is clear that Unwin's background in Arts and Crafts utopianism persists beyond the superficial design features that could be described as a 'style'. It should be added that Unwin's utopianism did not extend to any challenge to the entrenched sexual division of labour; women would still be doing the weekly wash, cooperatively or not.

Morrisian influence can also be seen in some of Unwin's ideas about suburban planning. The notion that towns should be organic, that is, that they should visibly express both their own history and their local character in terms of materials and vernacular style, was one that Unwin tried to act upon in planning both towns and suburbs – indeed, the individuality of a town was what led its residents to love it. He was hostile, therefore, to the anonymity of the typical late nineteenth-century suburb: 'Who has heard of the same feelings roused by the modern suburb? We may live there and be happy after a fashion, but we do not love the place, we can never begin to individualise or personify Kilburn'.[6]

In the planning of Hampstead Garden Suburb there was a very deliberate attempt to build a mixed-class community. Houses of different size and cost were placed close to each other, in order to do something to mitigate the social zoning so characteristic of late nineteenth-century towns:

> There is nothing whatever in the prejudices of people to justify the covering of large areas with houses of exactly the same size and type. The growing up of suburbs occupied solely by any individual class is bad, socially, economically and aesthetically ... in the English village we find all classes of houses mingled along the village street or around the green, from the smallest labourer's cottage to the large house of the wealthy farmer, doctor, or local manufacturer, and even at times there is included the mansion of the lord of the manor.[7]

Doubtless, Unwin is idealising the social integration of the English village here, and he is certainly accepting its unequal social relations in a manner that Morris never would have. Nevertheless, something of the Arts and Crafts ideal of social life is carried forward in Unwin's ideas about community planning for the suburb as a mixed-class area drawing its inspiration, in part, from an idealised view of the English village.

It is possible, then, to locate some of the most influential figures in suburban planning history in the milieu of late nineteenth-century utopian and Arts and Crafts communitarian thinking. It is also possible to trace the persistence of these ideals, (necessarily perhaps in modified forms) in some of the practical plans and suggestions in Unwin's *Town Planning in Practice* and in the plans for Letchworth and Welwyn, through which they have entered into English suburban design. However, it would not be surprising to find other ideals at work in the planning and building of both Garden Cities and suburbs; the prospectus for Letchworth, for example, includes the following:

> In the face of physical degeneration, the existence of which in our great towns is incontrovertible, imperialism abroad and progress at home seem alike an empty mockery. Sound physical condition is surely the foundation of all human development, and the directors submit to the public a scheme for securing it in a particular instance which they believe to contain all the elements of success, and which, if carried to a successful issue, will lead to that re-distribution of the people upon the land, in which, and in which alone, as they believe, is to be found a solution of the problem – How to maintain and increase industrial efficiency without impairing the national physique. [8]

The Garden City, in other words, could be construed as a solution to widespread turn-of-the-century anxieties about physical degeneration, closely connected to the requirements of an imperialist nation. At this point, the Garden City appears not so much as a manifestation of Morrisian ideals as a nexus where a range of ideological themes converges – back-to-the-land romanticism, imperialism, even eugenics. This is not an aberration or a mere catchpenny phrase for a prospectus; Purdom in 1913 could combine Morris and eugenics *in propria persona*:

> [Letchworth] was designed with the object of showing that the development of the towns of England need not be left to chance or to the mercy of speculators, and with the further object of making town life tolerable to people who have come to hate it not merely as William Morris hated it because of its ugliness and grime, but because it is a menace to the vitality of the race.[9]

This problematic was not special to the Garden City; one of the persistent selling points of the suburbs was to be the healthy environment they offered by contrast to the insalubrity of town life.

A number of potentially conflicting meanings thus gathered round the Garden City at the beginning of the twentieth century, and 'suburb' was one meaning that threatened it. However, more prosaic meanings threatened it also; there was a built-in conflict from the start between those who wished to build not merely Letchworth but the New Jerusalem, and those who were only interested in creating new factory towns. For example, the man who was appointed the estate agent for the First Garden City Limited in 1906, W.H. Gaunt, had previously worked in Trafford Park.

One way of writing the history of Letchworth would be as a conflict between these two parties; between the 'idealists' and the self-styled 'practical people'. Indeed, this was exactly the way that Purdom chose to write about the town in his autobiographical *Life Over Again* (1951). This was a departure from the earlier *The Garden City* (1913) and *The Building of Satellite Towns* (1925) in which he had chosen to downplay the utopian or cranky aspects of Letchworth's pioneer inhabitants, in the interests of boosting the new town's attractiveness to new residents and industrial investors.

There is no doubting the utopian expectations of many of the first-comers to Letchworth, as Purdom recalls in his memoir:

> Most of the new inhabitants had come to Utopia. This was the longed-for garden city, the first town in which exploitation by landlords and the ugliness and slums of the old towns were not to exist. There was excitement, a sense of brotherhood, and the conviction that a new order had been established. Raymond Unwin became the leader of these residents.[10]

These utopians were the ones who gave Letchworth its peculiar quality, and indeed established the manner in which it would be widely perceived. Although such people were distinctive in aiming to build a whole new town, they invite comparison with the many other communal experiments arising at the turn of the century, each also drawing inspiration from (among other sources) Morrisian Arts and Crafts, Edward Carpenter or Tolstoy.[11] Perhaps unsurprisingly these idealists were at once in conflict with the First Garden City Company itself which provided the capital and the management for the town, as Purdom again makes clear:

> Although Howard lived in the town, and another director, too, the lack of sympathy between the company and the inhabitants was marked. Indeed there was conflict. The inhabitants with the industrialists stood, they considered, for garden city ideals; the company, as its representatives declared, for the practical. The emphasis of the individuals on the new and untried, their independent and even socialistic and sometimes

anarchistic utterances and projects, were extremely distasteful to the company. Every member of the staff treated the middle-class Utopists with contempt. Through its agent the company set out to demonstrate that the town was intended to be all that could be expected in any town not called a garden city.[12]

In this narrative, the conflict is between the idealists and the 'practical' people. If we were to accept this account, then the descent from Nowhere would have to be thought of as a sad but necessary compromise with the real world. However, this is not the meaning that Purdom, in his old age, wished to attach to Letchworth; his sympathy is with the idealists, and against the narrow-minded practicality of the company and its agent. The quotation above continues thus:

> Especially were the characteristics of a Manchester suburb and the features of a Lancashire industrial town to be re-established there. The nonsense of the idealists was to be squashed. That was Gaunt's aim, who came from Trafford Park and had the Manchester mind and accent. His ideals were within the terms of business and common sense, and he said so in an unmistak-able way. He fell foul at once of Raymond Unwin, and would have none of his picturesque cottage building, declaring with no beating about the bush his intention of building square boxes with lids for workers, the kind of houses that William Morris had inveighed against. No doubt Unwin intended repeating at Letchworth something like Norman Shaw's village at Bedford Park, a William Morris scheme not far from the poet's Hammersmith. Gaunt wanted nothing of the kind. Any-how, the town was to be industrial, was it not? There was no one to contradict him, least of all the new industrialists, and everyone agreed that the idealists were too idealistic. So Unwin fighting a losing battle fled during 1906 to Hampstead Garden Suburb, and Letchworth hardly saw him again.[13]

This was published in 1951, so was written nearly fifty years after the events it describes; doubtless, the conflict appeared more pronounced in retrospect. It is nevertheless remarkable in indicating how the utopian and Arts and Crafts ideals of the Garden City were contested from within; how they always existed in conflict, in other words, with more 'practical' and profit-oriented conceptions.

Purdom's account here can be immediately compared with his earlier, more boosterish accounts in 1913 and 1925. Thus in *The Garden City* he wrote to deprecate the reputation for crankiness that Letchworth attained after its foundation:

The place came to mean, to the journalistic mind, a home of curious and comic people, and some such idea still seems, at times, to cling to the persons who write in the press. For a long time a reporter could not look at the roads of the town, or the sewers, without seeing something fantastic, and the most pro-saic thing he would enlarge into the grotesque. The plain truth is that the Letchworth people were in the past, as they are in the present, very ordinary people, the sort of English people you meet in every town. They were, as they are still, living on a new land; they hoped, as all wise men would have hoped, to see some new and more perfect thing arise on that land than it had been their lot to see elsewhere, and they did their best to make that new thing actual.[14]

Ten years later, in *The Building of Satellite Towns*, when Purdom was still keen to offer Letchworth as a practical and hard-headed model, he also played down its crankiness – although he could claim that some of what had been thought new and curious had subsequently become seen as commonplace by the 1920s, such as houses with 'red roofs and white rough-cast walls ... green paint and water-butts'.[15] In other words, Letch-worth no longer seemed so cranky in the 1920s because so much of the Arts and Crafts architecture that Parker and Unwin had popularised there (or at least established as a pos-sible manner of building for ordinary middle-class and even working-class housing) had spread widely to the suburbs.

Indeed, in Purdom's account it was just this effort at archi-tectural innovation, and the attempt to impose something of a uniform style to Letchworth, that smacked of eccentricity and utopianism to the Company managers. In a subdued ref-erence to the conflict that was to dominate his account twenty-five years later, Purdom indicated how Parker and Unwin's architectural ideals were thwarted in part by the very Com-pany that employed them:

> Indeed, the cultivation of architectural taste had, in the minds of the directors of the company and their officials, some associ-ation with the eccentricities of opinion and behaviour with regard to which there was already a determination that they should not be welcomed in the town. In the result the architects were forced to modify their attitude.[16]

Consequently, though Letchworth was widely visited, and highly influential on both town and suburban planning, it was not itself built to any uniform architectural conception and the results were indeed mixed.

We can summarise, then, by recognising that the Garden City movement was largely propelled by utopian and communitarian ideals, and that those who held these ideals most strongly, notably Ebenezer Howard himself, were strongly opposed to the dilution of his conception into a kind of superior suburb. By contrast, those charged with bringing Howard's ideal into fruition were strongly opposed to any association with eccentricity or utopianism. Their ideal, according to Purdom at least, was a suburban one, albeit that of a Manchester suburb. Meanwhile, those architectural ideas of Parker and Unwin deplored by the company managers as smacking of utopianism, were precisely the ideas that were to become influential in suburban design of the 1920s,1930s and 1940s.

Howard himself was disappointed by Letchworth, and eventually decamped to try again at Welwyn Garden City. Some of his dissatisfaction was perhaps inevitable, a predictable result of the translation of ideals into bricks and mortar. Although he deplored, as we have seen, the confusion of Garden City with garden suburb, it may be that some of his disappointment was created by the fact that Letchworth itself prompted confusion. It is certainly the case that many residents commuted to London from the outset.

One further complicating factor needs to be reckoned in to our assessment of the diverse ideological meanings that were invested in and gathered around the Garden City, from where they spread to the suburbs. This factor is the similarity of Letchworth to the paternalist company suburbs of Bournville and Port Sunlight. Cadbury and Lever were involved as Directors of the First Garden City Company, as was Harmsworth of the *Daily Mail*. (The town received such persistent attention from the paper that it was occasionally known as the '*Daily Mail* town'.) It was Harmsworth's interest in new housing schemes that led to his sponsorship of the Ideal Homes Exhibition, one of the principal media of suburban design in the 1930s. J. Saint Loe Strachey, the proprietor of the *Spectator* and *Country Life*, was another wealthy patron of the project. He jointly organised the 'Cheap Cottage Exhibition' at Letchworth in 1905, which attracted many visitors to the new town, and was a crucial event in its early history.[17] In short, despite the 'socialistic and even anarchistic' ideas of many of the early residents, and despite the novel way in which Letchworth was financed, it was still partly beholden to wealthy patrons and could be assimilated to the various model towns and villages that were influential in their own way on early twentieth-century suburban growth.

The reduction of the Garden City ideal to that of garden suburb, or the simple assimilation of Arts and Crafts and communitarian ideas into suburban design, took place, therefore, amid a range of conflicting notions about town planning and urban spread. No doubt the largest single factor in this reduction and assimilation were the straightforward pressures of commercial exploitation; in this respect what happened to Arts and Crafts ideas in building and town planning was cognate to what occurred in other areas also. Certainly, to return to the critic Holbrook Jackson, this is the meaning that he gave to the way that Arts and Crafts design ideals were diffused:

> The Arts and Crafts movement was thus checked in its most highly organised and enthusiastic period by the habit and necessity of cheapness. It was found possible to educate taste, for even modern commerce had not succeeded in killing the fundamental love of excellence in commodities, but as quickly as taste was improved by exhibitions of modern craftsmanship, commerce stepped in supplying those who could not afford the necessarily expensive results with cheap imitations. The ogre of shoddy stood across the path of quality, and many who were set upon the high trail of excellence by the Arts and Crafts movement ended as devotees of fumed oak furniture, and what began as a great movement was in danger of ending as an empty fashion with the word 'artistic' for shibboleth.[18]

Purdom's account of the commercial exploitation of the notion of the Garden City closely follows this pattern:

> a certain confusion grew up in the public mind, so that 'garden city', 'garden suburb' and 'garden village' came to be used indiscriminately. The worst result, however, was that 'garden city' was adopted in some instances by the promoters of private land speculation schemes with the apparent object of deceiving the public. In 1914 it was stated that 'many of the schemes that are called garden city schemes have nothing in common with the garden city movement but the name, which they have dishonestly appropriated. Schemes of the wildest speculation, land-sweating and jerry-building, have all been promoted in the hope that the good name would carry them through'.[19]

No doubt this last comment is overstated, but one way of telling the story of the diffusion of Garden City notions is certainly by appeal to the effects of straightforward commercial exploitation.

The more usual story is that many of the principles of the Garden City simply became widespread planning practice, not least through the influence of Unwin on the 1919 Housing Act.

Above all else, it was Unwin's insistence on low-density housing that informed the Act, which in turn contributed to the
massive growth of suburbs between the Wars – particularly
around London, which approximately doubled in area
between 1919 and 1939. However, true as this is, it is important
to recall that understanding the Garden City as merely a recipe
for low density housing, with perhaps some superficial cot-
tagey design features thrown in, is a massive reduction both of
Howard's original notion and of Unwin's development of those.

In considering the legacy of the Garden City movement –
and the Arts and Crafts and utopian aspirations which lay
behind it – for suburban planning and design, we are confronted with a not unfamiliar situation. Whereas the individuals who were most closely committed to the ideals informing
the Garden City movement, such as Howard and Purdom, felt
that only the most superficial aspects of their vision were
being adopted, those who took over the name 'garden city', or
who have written the cultural or design histories, have
emphasised the potency and success of those ideals. Before
attempting a judgement on this contentious history, however,
it is worth considering the afterlife of those Arts and Crafts
ideals in popular literary perceptions of the Garden City.

Two very different writers in the 1930s, John Betjeman and
George Orwell, both testify to the continuing presence of Arts
and Crafts and indeed counter-cultural meanings attaching to
the Garden City. Betjeman – the poet of the suburbs, perhaps
– presents the clearer case, since the inhabitants of Welwyn
provide him with easy opportunities for humorous condescen-
sion. The following poem, simply called 'The Garden City'
comes from the collection *Mount Zion* (1931); it was excluded
from the *Collected Poems*.

> O wot ye why in Orchard Way
>   The roofs be steep and shelving?
> Or wot ye what the dwellers say
>   In close and garden delving?
> 'Belike unlike my hearths to yours,
>   Yet seemly if unlike them.
> Deep green and stalwart be my doors
>   With bottle glass to fryke them.
>
> 'Hand-woven be my wefts, handmade
>   My pottery for pottage,
> And hoe and mattock, aye, and spade,
>   Hang up about my cottage'

> Men of Welwyn! Men of Worth!
> The Health Reform is growing,
> With Parsley girdled round the earth
> That recks not of its sowing.[20]

The object of Betjeman's mockery here is evident enough. This is just the Garden City of popular legend, committed to an Arts and Crafts lifestyle understood as a fake Morrisian medievalism and handmade craft objects. Even the green paint we have met before, singled out by Purdom in 1925 as one of the widely copied features of Letchworth-style design makes an appearance. In this particular corner of the Betjeman landscape, people can be mocked for seeking to abstain from commercialism and the commodity system; elsewhere in the suburbs, notably in Slough, they will be mocked for being in thrall to it.

Orwell's relation to Letchworth and its counter-cultural inheritance is not so visible, though it is very emphatic when it comes into view. His address in the late 1930s was 'The Stores, Wallington, near Baldock' – approximately eight miles from Letchworth, which by then had exceeded Baldock in size and was therefore the nearest big town. Orwell was travelling through Letchworth on the bus when he had that famous encounter with 'socialists' which followed his notorious diatribe against every 'fruit-juice drinker, nudist, sandal-wearer, sex-maniac, Quaker, "Nature Cure" quack, pacifist and feminist in England'.[21] This is how Orwell describes the encounter:

> One day this summer I was riding through Letchworth when the bus stopped and two dreadful-looking old men got onto it. They were both about sixty, both very short, pink, and chubby, and both hatless. One of them was obscenely bald, the other had long grey hair bobbed in the Lloyd George style. They were dressed in pistachio-coloured shirts and khaki shorts into which their huge bottoms were crammed so tightly that you could study every dimple. Their appearance created a mild stir of horror on top of the bus. The man next to me, a commercial traveller I should say, glanced at me, at them, and back again at me, and murmured 'Socialists', as who should say, 'Red Indians'. He was probably right – the I.L.P. were holding their summer school at Letchworth.[22]

If one asks what Orwell himself was doing in Letchworth in the summer of 1937, the answer is that he was attending the very Independent Labour Party (I.L.P.) summer school that he appears to mock here. In the mid-1930s the I.L.P. held their annual conference in Letchworth, and, in 1937, Orwell was invited to attend, the main topic that year being the Spanish Civil War – at the time, Orwell was still recovering from the wound he received while fighting in Spain. A visit to Letchworth precipitated an outburst of hostility to all the counter-cultural associations which attached themselves to 'Socialism' and which had their natural home in the first Garden City.

Orwell's sympathies in this anecdote are, it seems, with the man he presumes to be a commercial traveller rather than with those he takes to be socialists. His own brand of socialism thus seeks to accommodate the ordinary man on the Clapham (or Letchworth) omnibus, and the price of this accommodation is the ferocious repudiation of all the utopian and counter-cultural baggage that was symbolised by the Garden City. Orwell was also the novelist of the suburbs and of the little man who inhabited them, but to become so he had to dissociate them absolutely from the utopian ancestry that could be glimpsed in Letchworth.

Which takes us back to William Morris, unpleasantly referred to as one of the 'dull, empty windbags' of propagandist Socialism a few pages later in *The Road to Wigan Pier* (1937).[23] Earlier, I quoted Unwin quoting Morris to the effect that beauty cannot be 'plastered on', but has to emerge organically; from the inside out rather than from the outside in. It has to emerge, in other words, from the social relations that are at the root of all art forms and which underlie town planning and house design with particular visibility. I have suggested a range of reasons why the utopian ideals of the Garden City should have dwindled into designs for suburbs in which the Arts and Crafts inheritance should appear as one design option among many. However, the fundamental reason is surely that successful design has to express social relations, but social relations cannot be created by design. It is for this reason that *News from Nowhere*, which might make a wonderful propagandist text for those who wish to revolutionise work and class, can be a potentially disastrous handbook of design – for perhaps its weakest element is the occasional arbitrary connection between form and function. That is to say, Morris can at times describe a revolutionised function but match it with a medieval form. One sometimes experiences a similar sense of incongruity when contemplating the Arts and Crafts designs that permeate the suburbs created throughout the first fifty years of the twentieth century. The fundamental incongruity however is not a matter of design anachronism, but a reflection of the fact that these suburbs were built to house a population whose class character was untransformed, while the utopian inspiration that lay behind their designs had precisely been one of social transformation. It is for this reason that the 'suburb' was always going to eclipse the communitarian aspirations of the Garden City.

Notes

1. Holbrook Jackson, *The Eighteen Nineties; a Review of Art and Ideas at the Close of the Nineteenth Century*, London, 1913, 308.
2. Ebenezer Howard, *Garden Cities of Tomorrow*, Builth Wells, 1985. Originally published as *Tomorrow: A Peaceful Path to Real Reform* in 1898, it was reissued in a modified form and with its current title in 1902.
3. Raymond Unwin, *Town Planning in Practice; an Introduction to the Art of Designing Cities and Suburbs*, New York, 1971, 9.
4. Ebenezer Howard, 'How far have the original Garden City Ideals been realized?', in *The Garden City: A Study in the Development of a Modern Town*, ed. C.B. Purdom, London, 1913, 290.
5. Unwin, *Town Planning in Practice*, 38–3.
6. Ibid., 146.
7. Ibid., 294.
8. Quoted in C.B.Purdom, *The Building of Satellite Towns*, London, 1935, 60.
9. Purdom, *The Garden City*, v.
10. C.B.Purdom *Life Over Again*, London 1951, 48–9.
11. See, for example, Fiona MacCarthy, *The Simple Life; C.R. Ashbee in the Cotswolds*, London, 1981, and Joy Thacker, *Whiteway Colony; The Social history of Tolstoyan Community*, Stroud, 1993.
12. Purdom, *Life Over Again*, 52.
13. Ibid., 53.
14. Purdom, *The Garden City*, 52.
15. Purdom, *The Building of Satellite Towns*, 62.
16. Ibid., 96.
17. See Purdom, *Life Over Again*, 47.
18. Jackson, *The Eighteen Nineties*, 306.
19. Purdom, *The Building of Satellite Towns*, 31–2.
20. John Betjeman, *Mount Zion*, London, 1931.
21. George Orwell, *The Road to Wigan Pier*, Harmondsworth, 1984, 152.
22. Ibid., 152–3.
23. Ibid., 161.

CHAPTER 2

'THE NEW SUBURBANITES' AND CONTESTED CLASS IDENTITIES IN THE LONDON SUBURBS, 1880–1900

Lynne Hapgood

The new suburbanites were born in the expanding London suburbs of the 1880s, the progeny of a territorial and class war triggered by social conditions and urban developments.[1] The centrifugal impulse that had been gathering strength and drawing people away from the inner city into the suburbs in increasing numbers had long been noted. However, the late 1880s marked the dawning of a sudden and acute awareness of the dramatic changes which were taking place on the margins of London, and a shift of public interest away from its absorption in the dramas of the inner city which had previously dominated social commentary. The subsequent proliferation of writing about the suburbs, which responded to and further stimulated public concerns, began to engage with the suburbs as a qualitatively different kind of social terrain, creating a new kind of culture and consciousness. The perceived distinctiveness of the social identity of these migrants and the significance of their new habitats, which characterise these writings, are the focus of my discussion.

It is not easy to chart the emergence of these identities systematically. The suburbs inspired considerable comment but their fragmented development did not lend itself to the comprehensive survey or the profoundly engaged religious and political commentaries that inner city conditions did, nor did they generate urgent common focal points such as 'poverty' and 'unemployment' which, in the inner city, provided the measuring sticks of response for diverse viewpoints.[2] In addition, it is often difficult to disentangle the particular from the general. In many of the writings the actual world of the suburbs is a shadowy presence behind the critiques of society and civilisation for which it is a catalyst. The fluctuating meanings of the suburb word-family can further complicate understanding. Arthur Edwards's comment in relation to the word 'suburbia' – that it is 'both too precise and too general. It is precise in a geographical sense and general in the atmosphere which it describes' – is equally true of contemporary definitions.[3]

There were those who aimed for the big picture: sociological works such as Booth's survey and quasi-sociological works like Frederic Harrison's *The Meaning of History* (1884), H.G. Wells's *Anticipations* (1901) and C.F.G. Masterman's *The Condition of England* (1909) supply a crucial supporting framework in their broad consideration of urban and social issues. The visions of urban planners, whether preserved in the essays of social philosophers such as William Morris and John Ruskin; in the detailed records of the London County Council, or in the now famous works of Ebenezer Howard and Patrick Geddes, tell a fascinating story of the struggle between aesthetics and pragmatics; social engineering and social empowerment. Realistic novels – some of which are discussed elsewhere in this book – were increasingly located in the suburbs, and provided their own counterpointing debates. Juxtaposing William Morris's social reorganisation in *News from Nowhere* (1891), the suburban cultural debasement of George Gissing's *In the Year of Jubilee* (1896), the ambiguous suburbs of H.G. Wells's *Ann Veronica* (1909) and the suburban idylls of Conan Doyle and Keble Howard, gives some indication of public fascination with, but ambivalence about, this evolving world.

Although my discussion is contextualised by such works of social philosophy and fiction, I want to recover earlier and more immediate interventions in the new world of the suburbs. I shall do this by focusing on writings about the suburbs in the daily and periodical press of the late 1880s and early 1890s. The piecemeal and disparate nature of this literature reflects the diversity of public responses galvanised by what was seen as a new phenomenon. It also captures a moment of fluidity in public opinion before the terms 'suburbs' and 'suburbanite' had become unequivocally synonymous with monotony and bad taste. These polyphonic writings were produced in the heat of argument and counter argument; from the need to provide information and commentary on current issues, and to respond to the immediate concerns of an expanding and fickle readership. They map responses to the expansion of the suburbs, and make a significant contribution to reflecting and shaping contemporary opinion adrift on the hopes and anxieties of the age.

Despite the sheer bulk of these writings and the diversity of their orientation and audience, a clear, although often unformulated, underlying theme emerges, connecting the formation of the suburbs with the destiny of English nationhood and culture. Social commentators often invested the suburbs and suburban dwellers of this time with a significant power over the future of English society. This power was felt to be particularly influential in matters of class and related factors such as race, culture and morality. In this chapter I have chosen a range of illustrative writings to discuss, which offer clear insights into the contested and controversial constructions of suburban class identity.

The suburbs posed a challenge to notions of class and class relations, particularly to contemporary understandings of what it meant to be middle-class. W. Spencer Clarke's series of articles about the suburban homes of London, written for a property-owning, leisured middle class and published in *The Citizen* during 1880, provides a glimpse into the perceived nature of the pre-1880s suburban world which, by 1900, would have been usurped. The domestic world Clarke describes is a world made possible by the economic life of the city, but firmly insulated from it by distance and emphasis.[4] It is important that Clarke's articles are seen to predate the publication of Andrew Mearns's pamphlet, *The Bitter Cry of Outcast London* (1882), which helped to initiate fierce debates about political and social responsibility for urban conditions.[5] His confidence in the world he describes allowed him an honesty of appraisal that conveys a clear picture of suburban values and ideals of the time. He wrote from a basis of certainty about a world of choice, far removed from the imperatives of the inner city; a middle-class world for middle-class people who had not yet been made either guilty or afraid by the most recent exposures of working-class conditions, or their implications for the suburban environment.

Because of this, Clarke was able to record information that underlay the impending class battle without realising its sig-

nificance. For instance, he almost invariably introduces a systematic description of each suburb by an allusion to its railway station or its relationship with the various lines and
termini. The romance of the railway and its significance for
England as a world power is dominant, not its implications for
a suburban landscape, 'The access to Putney from anywhere is
easy because of the contiguity to Clapham Junction, whence
are lines that go to the end of the earth'.[6] In the same spirit he
records the growth of the populations of individual suburbs,
heaping up figures for descriptive emphasis and pointing out
the extent to which new building was beginning to change the
face of the landscape. None of this evidence struck him as
potentially ominous. On the contrary, he perceived growth as
a reflection of man's endeavour. Even the increasing appearance of working-class housing in particular suburbs such as
Camden Town and its relationship to the housing difficulties
of the inner city is noted without concern, as those developments, too, revealed 'The energy of the English character'.[7]
The fact that Clarke lamented the loss of attractive woodland
and pasture, and commented, although briefly, on the overspill of the working classes, indicates that his perception of the
suburban world was not a deliberately blinkered one. It was
not that he ignored what he did not want to see, but that, in
1880, the evidence did not suggest that the world of the suburbs as he knew it could ever be fundamentally changed.

By the late 1880s, however, many of the inhabitants of the
suburbs were on the defensive. Their anxieties centred most
obviously on the loss of what they had always considered
theirs – the space, beauty and remoteness of the rural suburbs.
They also feared the threat that developments posed to their
class identity. Their concern about the encroachment of 'a
large and distinctive class of people who ... descended daily
upon the city and then returned every evening to their curious,
and unknown, tribal rites and customs' (as C.F.G. Masterman
was later to describe suburban dwellers) – was immediate and
concrete.[8] Another, more insidious threat, was their sense of
having been betrayed by members of their own class. Some
were campaigning on behalf of the poor and the homeless in
the inner city and had exerted considerable pressure to find
political answers to the housing crisis. Wealthier landowners
were taking advantage of the situation to sell off small estates
at a profit and to move further out.

Although the fight appeared to be a defensive action
against territorial encroachment, it was in fact a struggle to

retain class status. The suburbs became an arena for a many layered class war, with boundaries blurring and nuances of class definition rapidly increasing as the middle classes fractured. Those who were left watched those wealthier than themselves move away from the building developments and then tried to preserve their way of life against the aspirations of the immigrants. In their turn, the new suburbanites struggled to put the grimness of the inner city behind them and to adopt the middle-class models which appeared to promise comfort and prosperity. Many members of the middle classes perceived themselves as effectively trapped between the self-interest of the landed and upper middle classes and the increasing power of the working classes, just as, topographically, they were trapped between superior residential housing being built on the outskirts of the suburbs on old suburban estates and the houses and railways moving relentlessly out from the city to serve the masses.[9]

An insight into the mood of the middle classes just a few years after Clarke's articles is offered by Frederick Greenwood in, 'What has become of the Middle Classes?' published in *Blackwood's Magazine* in 1885.[10] Greenwood, who had a considerable reputation as a fearless social commentator, records just how deeply shaken the middle classes had been by the accusations aimed against their values and social system following the revelations about the poverty and housing conditions of the working classes. Greenwood's article reads like a rallying call to a retreating army, reminding the middle classes of their former triumphs, summoning up their determination to reassert their moral superiority and to take pride in their related economic deserts. He clearly demonstrates the link between the working classes' search for a public voice and the middle classes' increasing unease with their own, pointing out that an intimation of their diminished confidence was confirmed by their growing silence in the face of the vociferousness of the working classes.[11] One of the ways Greenwood attempted to reassert the class lines was by rejecting the new names given to the classes in the public debate – names suggested by a Socialist ideology – and to reinstate the traditional social hierarchy inscribed in the old terminology:

> Of classes we hear very much, no doubt, but of the great middle classes, as they used to be called, nothing ... those classes are effaced, and only two remain for the politician to deal with – landlords, and the most indigent and ignorant poor.[12]

His solution upholds the status quo. Economic success as a criterion for personal worth would, he feels, rationalise the problem by ensuring that what a man owned was a measure of his value. He decries the Tory government's ambiguous philosophy which appeared to haver between humanitarian concerns and profit motives. Such ambivalence had helped to engender and foster guilt among the middle classes about ownership and indirectly to teach the working classes the lesson that 'it is lawful, and even a duty, to knock property on the head and take its goods'.[13]

That such defensiveness characterised the suburban middle classes in particular during this period was acknowledged by a leader in *The Times*, 1892, which drew to a conclusion correspondence concerning the fate of St John's Wood should a Private Members' Bill sanction the extension of the Sheffield, Manchester and Lincolnshire Railway through it. This correspondence confirmed the sense that the fight for the suburbs was becoming the responsibility of an increasingly isolated section of the middle classes. *The Times* notes the domino effect of centrifugal migration as 'panic seizes all' and those who can, move on.[14] Those members of the middle class who were unable to exploit the housing boom were engaged in a last ditch defence against the invasion of a lower middle class and a rising artisan class. That this two-pronged anger against the landed classes and the working classes was a prevalent reaction is confirmed by a ditty appearing in *Punch* a month later:

> These hapless homes of middle class,
>   Can they escape annihilation
> When come, in place of trees and grass,
>   A filthy goods-yard and a station?

> If such seclusion sheltered Peers,
>   Their wealth and influence might save it;
> No speculator ever fears
>   Artists and writers such as crave it.

> Or if it housed the WORKING MAN
>   Would Lords or Commons dare eject him?
> Picture the clamour if you can!
>   His vote, his demagogues, protect him.

> But you, who only use your brains –
>   The peoples' voice, the noble's money,
> Not yours – why save you from the trains?
>   For quiet so you say? – How funny![15]

As this parody suggests, *Punch* was also rallying the middle classes. The magazine defended their position by launching an energetic debunking campaign against the enemy – the new immigrants to the suburbs. Its extensive coverage in numerous snippets, jokes, cartoons, illustrations and articles pitched at a middle-class audience suggests that this issue of class boundaries was one of the obsessions of the day, while its light-hearted satire set a reassuring distance between the beleaguered middle classes and the encroaching migrants. Suburbs and aspiring suburban dwellers filled the pages of *Punch* during the years 1889 to 1892. Thereafter, about 1894, interest began to fade. By then, however, *Punch* had done much to suggest changing modes of class relations and, in doing so, to establish, or even to create, the identity of a new consciousness and a new class. It is probably true to say that the various suburban stereotypes that are still around today were derived from the mass-produced man and woman in the pages of *Punch*.

Punch created out of the class conflict a new suburban type, a mutation from the suburban melting pot of working, artisan, blue collar classes and the lower echelons of the middle classes. The medley of material out of which *Punch's* new suburbanite was constructed literally and figuratively belittles the pretenders to the suburbs. The class pretensions of those who hung precariously on the edges of a culture whose models of comfort, security and power they desire, are shown to be ineffective and ridiculous rather than threatening. Dabchick is one of *Punch's* fictional examples of the aspiring working class. His path to success is charted in a series of 'letters' during the early 1890s. One example is the 'Letter to Social Ambition' from the sorrowing, moralising Diogenes Robinson in July, 1891. Dabchick is apparently driven by that demonic force which 'impelled grocers to ludicrous pitches of absurdity' and drove 'the wife of a working man to distraction because her neighbour's front room possesses a more expensive carpet'. More significantly, *Punch* makes clear that Dabchick's rise from Balham to South Kensington marks his spiritual change from happiness and serenity to being a 'profoundly miserable man'. This so-called 'moral' point surfaces consistently, implying that those who do not keep to their place will suffer for it. Dabchick's unexpected success in financial speculation is shown to be inappropriate. Praise for playing the economic market successfully – the keynote of middle-class power – is conspicuous by its absence. Dabchick is punished with unhappiness and social isolation for the confusion of class identity he has produced.

Punch's master-stroke in this class offensive was the creation of Mr Pooter in a bimonthly feature that ran with enormous popularity from May 1889 to March 1890, called *The Diary of a Nobody*, which successfully created a ruthless and enduring joke at the expense of those who lived in the suburbs.[16] Pooter, a City clerk, is the unhappy victim of late nineteenth-century transitional class definitions. He inhabits the uncomfortable no man's land between the respectable working class and the lower middle class and is ridiculed for his attempts to establish middle-class status, not least by tradesmen who recognise one of themselves in disguise. So inept is his claim to a superior class identity that they treat him with contempt. They trample in his hall, thrust cabbages in his hands, and protest abusively when he complains of the quality of their goods. His only strategy for retaining his own sense of distance is through an internalised class-based judgement, meaningful only to himself, that they 'are getting above themselves'. As Pooter helped the middle classes to discover, adopting an attitude of class relativity always ensured the existence of a subclass and, therefore, the means of retaining and asserting class status.

Pooter's beloved home, 'The Laurels', is haunted by what *Punch* perceives as the same weaknesses that haunt Pooter's life philosophy. Its name hankers after the remote garden estates of the moneyed classes, yet its road, Brickfield Terrace, places it as one of the 'thousands of grey streets' noted by town planners and many others. There is a garden, but so close to the railway line that the wall is cracked by the continual vibration of passing trains. Its railway location clearly identifies the house as part of one of the least desirable sections of a new development dependent on quick and easy access to the City. It also identifies Pooter as a user of the Great Northern Railway that by 1898 'carried 28 million in the suburban service... [in] the pressure that took place between 8 and 10 o'clock in the morning, and 5 and 8 o'clock in the evening'.[17] His 'simple domesticity' is ridiculed as thoroughly as his pretensions, despite his obeisance to the tradition – claimed to be essentially English – that, 'The Englishman sees the whole of life embodied in his house. Here ... he finds his happiness and his real spiritual comfort'.[18]

The Grossmith brothers, who created Pooter, do not portray him as totally devoid of positive characteristics. Yet the 'virtues' for which he is praised are seen to be merely a means of control over those such as himself who aspire to the middle classes. His love for his wife, Carrie (despite their occasional tiffs, he is lonely without her, appreciative of her good nature and always glad to please her) is only further evidence of the smallness of his world. He is satisfactorily defined by the insularity of marriage and the domestic sentiment of marital love. Carrie, who is the essence of good sense, affection and thrifty house management, is equally delimited by her love for and loyalty to Pooter. Similarly, he only earns his place among the home owning middle classes when Mr Perkupp, Pooter's boss, in his role of administering rewards and punishments like a god, sanctions Pooter's elevation by giving him the freehold on his house for his hard work. The deeds are only handed over after Pooter has passionately declared his acceptance of his lot: 'I love my house and I love the neighbourhood, and could not bear to leave it'.

The characterisation of Mr Pooter and Carrie served a serious integrative purpose for *Punch's* readers. It deliberately marked out the new suburbanite as different from those barbaric hordes who were supposedly issuing from the city and whose life style was threatening the suburbs. Mr Pooter is constructed to satisfy what the middle classes wanted suburban man to be. With considerable skill, the Grossmiths created a silly, inoffensive, harmless and well meaning representative of the anonymous masses to amuse and placate the middle classes. The reassuring message was that the most private and cherished thoughts of the new suburbanites were not dreams of the class struggle envisaged by Socialism and labour politics, but dreams of acceptance into the middle classes – their only desire, not revolution but endless imitation.

The appropriateness of the world of domestic space and domestic sentiment for suburbanites is an important target of *Punch's* satire which, although it cannot stop suburban migration, can diffuse the sense of danger it threatens. In the world of love, 'peaceful domesticity' and 'simple happiness' suburban families can safely be allowed to revel. The fact that suburban life is underpinned by the economics of the city and the realities of commuting is ignored; suburban life is domesticated and feminised, its values those of the family and the emotions. In a pale imitation of his betters, *Punch* suggests, suburban man conquers domestic space but in doing so becomes domesticated and therefore unfit for the public sphere – just as suburban woman's domestic goodwill is a much diminished version of the mid-century Ruskinan spiritual ideal. The implication is that, while the middle classes have the good sense and the good taste to distance themselves both geographically and aesthetically from the building developments, new suburban man and woman deserved the 'stucco-faced Sahara such as spreads, and spreads, and spreads', demonstrating their tastelessness by living in such developments, and their stupidity by being fair game for exploitation by unscrupulous builders:

> 'A fair return,' the Builder said,
> 'Two hundred, say, per cent.,
> Is all the profit that I want
> On anything I've spent.
> Now, if you're ready, tenants dear,
> I'll take the quarter's rent'.[19]

This version of suburban man and woman affirmed and consolidated the class they sought to emulate. Their geographical distance from the heart of London now appeared to serve as a safety valve, severing their potential engagement with inner city collectivism. Once removed from the conditions that were creating a catalyst for change, inner city 'barbarians' were rendered harmless in a traditional framework of values built on hard work, respectability and domestic harmony. They could be exploited for profit by pretending capitalist investment in tiny houses dressed up in 'stucco', where they then perpetuated the values of marriage and family in their 'mournful and monotonous, though moral existence', and where they could pursue 'crazes' instead of ideas. Territorial rights had to be acceded, as they finally were to Pooter, but moral and class rights could be reasserted over them, reordering the confusion that had been so terrifyingly created by the problems of the inner city and rapid suburban expansion.

I don't think it is too extreme to claim that the *Punch* onslaught against migrants to the suburbs focused and gave substance to a change of class consciousness. It popularised the words 'suburbanite' and 'suburbia' which, by 1896, had become common currency. Other phrases like 'a Claphamite order of mind' abounded, indicating more than the pretentiousness and lack of taste with which we are familiar today. The intended sneer was very specific. It was directed at those who worked hard to improve their economic and domestic security and who claimed the right to a personal meaning for their lives. If, today, we laugh at *The Diary of a Nobody* (or, indeed, any of *Punch's* suburban spoofs), we have probably failed to understand the source of the joke.

By no means all commentators envisaged the suburban migrants in such demeaning terms. H.G. Wells and William Morris, for instance, welcomed a vision of England as a series of suburbs.[20] A rather different commentator, Sidney Low, in 'The Rise of the Suburbs', written in 1891 for the *Contemporary Review*, celebrates the dynamism that suburban development exemplifies, and argues that the suburban environment was evolving a new 'suburban type'.[21] Writing in the spirit of social prophecy, Low does not couch his argument in existing class terms. Rather, he argues that the merging of rural and urban, of nature and civilisation, suggested the possibility of an Anglo super-type, which would evolve beyond the current limitations of national class identities and classifications into a more highly developed human grouping which would assert racial superiority on the world stage.

Low's article is framed by several contemporary debates which gathered in intensity as the century drew to an end, notably those concerned with the degeneration of the race.[22] Low bases his argument on the familiar – but yet to be generally accepted premise – that inner city conditions stunted physical and moral health, and that London (the 'Circe of Cities' as Charles Booth called her in 1888), was a place where 'muscular strength and energy get gradually used up'.[23] However, he rejected its corollary that 'the feeble anaemic urban population' had to be replenished from rural stock, arguing, as Lord Rosebery was later to do, the need 'to make the best of our admirable raw material'.[24] Low claimed that the modern suburbanite, who now benefited from the fusion of a physical environment of rural cleanliness and space with an enhanced mental environment made possible by the educational and social resources of the city, would be free from the destructive forces of urbanisation. Physically tuned by 'football, cricket and tennis' and mentally tuned by their link with London, suburbanites had a 'higher nervous organisation and better intelligence' than either urban or rural dweller.

This vision of the suburbs was partly a domestic version of England's imperialist project. Just as suburban development was taking place on the outskirts of London, England's 'Frontier expansion' was taking place 'on the outskirts of the Empire', and, Lord Curzon claimed, was providing 'an ennobling and invigorating stimulus for our youth, saving them alike from the corroding ease and the morbid excitements of Western civilization'.[25] It also had a specific role to play in that project. Ten years before the Boer War drew widescale attention to the inadequate physical condition of large numbers of young men, and triggered a widespread anxiety about the health of the nation, Low had envisaged the new breed of suburbanites as a national resource, whose mental and physical vigour could swell the ranks of the army. Low's enthusiasm for this new suburban type as the saviour of the nation, and the unequivocal pleasure with which he notes that, 'The life-blood is pouring into the long arms of brick and mortar and cheap stucco that are feeling their way out to the Surrey moors, and the Essex flats and the Hertfordshire copses', resonates with a colonial discourse which finds an echo in later popular novels located in the suburbs.[26]

The belief that organised physical activity, moral character and social usefulness were linked (a notion inherited from a public school ideology), was widely popular. Low applied to the suburbs the same rationale for national development which later informed the spirit of the Boy Scout movement, an international youth movement founded by Major-General Baden-Powell in 1908. This kind of focused energy as a national ideal was pitted against less disciplined activities – those 'aimless activities' which Masterman also feared would dissipate the 'storehouse of the nation's energies' which the suburbs represented.[27] For Low, the suburbs and their inhabitants did not threaten the spirit of England, but nurtured, reproduced and refined the essence of middle-class life on which England's future was founded. Low indicated the apotheosis of the suburbanite to a figure of national importance. He was 'the evolution of the age', embodying the old values of patriotism and class identity with a fresh physical and moral fitness created by the new suburban life style.

Richard Jefferies had a darker vision of the long term impact of suburban life on the 'higher nervous organisation' of suburban dwellers, particularly on those members of the new successful business class who commuted between the City and the more desirable suburbs and whose move to the suburbs was merely a quest for class status disguised as a love of the countryside. He criticised 'semi-country seats, as the modern houses surrounded with their own grounds assume to be', and attempts of suburban gardens to 'mimic the isolation and retirement of country houses'.[28] In his series of articles for *The Standard* on 'Nature Near London', written between 1888–1889, Jefferies argues that this kind of social climbing is a breeding ground for a new consciousness generated by the confusion of rural and urban lifestyles.[29]

However, the crux of Jefferies' argument goes beyond mere status seeking, claiming that the falsity of suburban man's relationship with the natural world is symptomatic of a deeper cultural unease. He argues that such manifestation of social and class mobility is an expression of a modern psychological restlessness. To attempt to divide life, working in the city and seeking rural peace in the suburbs, is presented as impossible. Each world, he argues, has a coherence of its own but the power of each of them is unequal, destroying the integrity of the countryside and the stability of individuals. Jefferies' notion that a psychological restlessness was being engendered by modern living was widely shared by contemporary writers, finding particularly powerful expression in fiction.

Echoing an experience described in George Gissing's *The Nether World* (1889) and even more poignantly at the end of Mark Rutherford's *Autobiography and Deliverance* (1882), Jefferies observes that once the 'unseen influence of mighty London' has been experienced it will always colour the suburban dweller's perception of his world. Thomas Hardy extended the suburban/urban terms of reference in his exploration of 'the modern vice of unrest', which reflects the breakdown of the rural community in *Jude the Obscure* (1896) as people move into the cities. This conflict, which suburban social climbers failed to recognise, was internalised as what Jefferies saw as a kind of false consciousness. People were withdrawing from the dynamic universe of the city where living and working were bound together, in search of an ill-defined, ill-founded ideal. This ideal seemed to him as little more than conformity to a new version of depoliticised conservatism. This new kind of middle class did not understand the old aristocratic way of life, nor the essentials of natural processes, and yet were turning away from their responsibility to the city from which their economic and class power was derived.

All the commentaries I have discussed so far have based their arguments on the tacit assumption of the co-identity of suburban house and suburban dweller, and indeed, the semiotics of housing were crucial inscribers of class status. Architects and planners who contributed to debates about the housing of the working classes and suburban development during this period were conscious that 'In every age and in every country the spirit of the time is shown in the homes of the people' and that the houses that were being built would be 'read' as a cultural and moral comment by future generations.[30] In fact, the enormous demand for reasonably priced housing outstripped many of their best efforts. It was the speculative builders whose relentless activity from the 1870s was largely responsible for 'writing' suburban housing and exploiting its class identity for profit. The professional journal, *The Builder*, provides a fascinating record of this ideological battle and its bearing on class perspectives in the suburbs during the 1890s.

The Builder frequently, and often anxiously, records how house building and selling have become part of a class game. An anecdote, told in a lecture on 'London House Planning' in 1894, assumed a shared knowledge of the builder's part in this game:

> A speculative builder, whose name I daresay many of you would know if I mentioned it, who had made his pile on rather small class houses, was once asked how he had been so successful, and his reply was: 'Well, yer see, I always put a Corinthian cornice in the front porterco'. [31]

The game was pervasive; the rules consistent. The building structure was made as cheap as possible. Its shoddiness was then disguised with symbols taken from the language of classical architecture. A building would be described with a vocabulary appropriated from middle-class expectations of a world of spaciousness, solitude and elegance, as Jefferies also notes, and Mr Pooter's home, 'The Laurels', demonstrates. The fact that the strategy and its class implications continue to be applicable today should not obscure its newness and effectiveness in the 1890s for creating models of middle-class life. 'The jerry-builder has absolutely invented a new language to describe his operations in these parts', declared the editorial leader of *The Builder* in 1897, in an attack on the aesthetics of the London suburbs.[32] In one sense it was not a 'new' language since the signifier remained the same, but what was signified had changed. This created a strangely absurd verbal territory for suburban immigrants to inhabit, where the concept held more weight than the reality. That is, speculative builders acted on the assumption that commitment to joining a class hierarchy was more important to the buyer than the possibility of exploitation. The editor of *The Builder* continued:

> It is quite evident that we must reform our language, and we suggest the following corrections to our future dictionary compilers:-
>
> "Park" – A district covered closely with houses but without either grass or trees.
>
> "Grove" – A street of shops with plenty of flaring gaslights.
>
> "Garden" – A collection of houses without a patch of ground attached to them.

"Avenue" – Two rows of houses opposite each other with lamp-posts planted at intervals.

This comment is, of course, meant to be humorous, but the seriousness of its implications cannot be dismissed. It reveals a process, identified in *The Diary of a Nobody*, by which the desire of the working classes to move to decent housing was exploited for profit and culturally branded to satisfy their aspirations and encode their inferiority. Property owning opportunities were on offer, but the actual benefits and power they denote are withheld. Those wishing to leave the congestion and poverty of the inner city behind them were tempted to buy under the illusion that they would be entering a middle-class world of space and choice. In fact, these people had little choice. Housing was desperately needed, and cheap housing was being provided by the jerry-builder who, in the face of governmental slowness, became 'the necessity of the age'. In other words, the new suburbanites, whether they wished it or not, were co-opted into capitalism.

The speculative builder who offered those who inhabited the working-class/lower middle-class borderline the opportunity to move into the suburbs ensured their commitment to regular employment, hard work and social/political conformity. *Punch* lampooned such people mercilessly as we have seen. The tragic aspect is described in 'The Transformation of John Loxley', a short story by W.J. Dawson, in which he tells how a newly married wife dies in a jerry-built house constructed on marshland with inadequate drainage, leaving her young husband to continue to pay the crippling mortgage.[33] The exigencies of cheap housing created ugliness and a new kind of suburban desolation; the imperatives of a regular income demanded conformity, but for those trying to leave appalling inner city conditions behind them, buying a suburban house seemed to promise an escape into a middle-class world of space and time. The general (and class positioned) cry, exemplified by J.T. Emmett in the *Quarterly Review* in 1895, was that Londoners, 'habitually substitute pretentiousness for dignity, and vanity for happiness'. Such a statement may well be voiced today in debates about consumerism and lifestyle.[34]

For a working-class family to buy a house may (or may not) have implied the endorsement of the middle-class property owning system. The middle classes certainly believed that such a purchase was inextricably linked with their view of an appropriate morality. *The Builder* reflects and participates in the con-

temporary debate whose premise was that, 'all who are con-
versant with the working class [know] that until their domicil-
iary conditions were Christianised ... all hope of moral or
social improvement was utterly vain'.[35] While the conditions
and temptations of the inner city were seen as directly inimical
to the maintenance of stable family life, the suburbs offered a
possible utopia of domestic strength and harmony. The broad
evolution of the notion of the desirability of suburban housing
owed equal debt to radical, philanthropic, christian and socialist thinking. Yet the outcome – to rehouse the urban masses in
small individual houses, safe from the problems of the inner
city, and protected by inward turning family interests – had the
effect of reinforcing domestic insularity and enhancing the
power of the Pooter myth. This late nineteenth-century domestic ideal became persistent and influential, consistently surfac-
ing in the housing discussions of the 1890s. Family life was
seen as a religion in its own right. At a time when religious traditions and practice were being questioned, the home offered a
kind of secular religion where individual interest and Christian
ethics could be merged. In the words of the architect, Ernest
Newton, in his plea for 'Home-Like Houses' in 1891:

> Nowadays, when all religion is assailed, and we believe in
> nothing very strongly, it is almost impossible to make our
> Church express anything more than a sort of galvanised enthu-
> siasm ... Belief in the sacredness of home-life, however, is still
> left to us, and is itself a religion, pure and easy to believe.[36]

He goes on to say that: 'Love of home ... is perhaps the only
sentiment which a reticent Englishman is not ashamed to con-
fess to; indeed, it is his boast that the English language alone
possesses the word 'home' in its fullest sense'.

Despite the diversity of perspective which I claimed to reveal
at the beginning of this chapter, a dominant narrative begins
to emerge from the material I have discussed. It tells the story
of the migration of the new suburbanites at the end of the
nineteenth century, and, in speculating about their social significance, reveals a consensus that they represented some new
stage (of whatever kind) of social evolution. It also tells the
story of a middle class which proved to have a greater ability
to adapt than they themselves were aware of. At the turn of
the century, although Walter Besant's 'aristocrats of the suburbs' had vanished forever, the middle classes had reinvented
themselves.[37] Threatened by 'barbarous masses', undermined

by cultural mediocrity, attacked by men and women of their own class and embattled by the invasion of their domestic territory, the literature of the suburbs shows that within twelve years they had laid out the suburbs for their own profit, designated class areas for their own convenience, and absorbed the social climber into their domestic and hierarchical morality. The values of individualism, free enterprise and family not only survived the crisis but still reigned supreme.

The apparent coherence of such a narrative though is surely a consequence of the shared class orientation of late Victorian social commentators, which overlays and obscures fundamental differences of political and moral positioning. It slips out of touch with history by being concerned only with what the middle classes wanted to tell and to hear. The missing voices in my discussion are, of course, those of the suburbanites themselves, who, like the working classes of the slums in the 1880s, remained profoundly silent. Because of this silence, reading the literature of the suburbs can be a surreal experience, as it creates the impression of a parallel universe, apparently unrelated to the daily realities of men's and women's lives. In the 'real' world, decent housing, a regular job and education were known to hold the threat of slumdom at bay at the very least, and at best, generated new communities, increased incomes and leisure, and held out the promise of fulfilling futures.

For this reason, I think we can remain sceptical of the answer Masterman gives, on the suburbanites' behalf, to his own question in 1901, 'Is this the type of all civilisations, when the whole Western world is to become comfortable and tranquil, and progress find its grave in a universal suburb?'[38] His answer – 'Why not?' – betrays his paternalistic, class-based acceptance of what he perceives as an inadequate compromise. I would suggest with hindsight, that those suburbanites who constructed their own version of civilisation, tranquillity and comfort in the suburbs, effected a profound and far reaching social change which transformed and redefined what it meant to be middle-class in late Victorian England.

Perhaps Charles Booth was the closest to recognising the dramatic class mutation which had taken place when, in the final volume of his great survey, he looked back on the development of the new suburban communities which by 1900 had surrounded London. In a concluding flourish, he provided a convincing grand narrative for the new suburbanites dubbing them 'A new middle class ... which will, perhaps, hold the future in its grasp'. He continued:

Its advent seems to me the great social fact of today. Those who
constitute this class are the especial product of the push of
industry; within their circle religion and education find their
greatest response; amongst them all popular movements take
their rise, and from them draw their leaders. [39]

The process that Booth described was in some ways analogous
to the boom in jerry building which happened even as the
town planners, the architects and the sociologists dreamed of
a better future. The new suburbanites were a catalyst for what
Donald Olsen rightly calls a 'social revolution'.[40] Engaged in
their own version of the class struggle and regardless of the
cacophony of middle-class comment and intervention, they
successfully transformed themselves into the very class which
had sought to confine or prescribe their identity.

Notes

1. The term 'suburbanite' did not become generally used until the 1890s. The
   1890s were plagued by all forms of the 'new': the New Woman (Sarah
   Grand, 1894): the New Journalism (W.T. Stead, 1888); the New Humour
   (*The Idler*, 1891), arguably reflecting a pervasive sense that society was
   radically changing.
2. Charles Booth was the exception. His survey, *Life and Labour of the People of
   London* (1902), which began as a survey of poverty in the East End during
   the 1880s, developed into a full-scale survey of London life covering each
   of the suburbs and describing suburban patterns of employment, leisure
   and religion. While it is arguably the most accurate and objective account
   we have of suburban life in the 1890s, it is necessarily expressed in very
   general terms and appears to have had little, if any, influence on general
   perceptions of the value of suburban existence which Booth rated highly.
3. Arthur M. Edwards, *The Design of Suburbia: a Critical Study in Environmental
   History*, London, 1981, 1.
4. W. Spencer Clarke, articles from the *Citizen* collected in *The Suburban
   Homes of London*, London, 1881.
5. Andrew Mearns, *The Bitter Cry of Outcast London*, Leicester, 1986. The
   excellent introduction gives an account of the impact of this pamphlet on
   urban debates.
6. Clarke, *The Suburban Homes of London*, 413.
7. Ibid., 49.
8. Cited in P.J. Keating, *The Haunted Study: A Social History of the English Novel
   1875–1914*, London, 321.
9. H.J. Dyos's classic study, *Victorian Suburb: A Study of the Growth of Camberwell*, Leicester, 1961, demonstrates how piecemeal building led to suburban slums and 'geographical insularity' (103–113). Alan A.Jackson,
   Semi-Detached London: Suburban Development, Life and Transport, 1900–39,
   London, 1973, 21, notes class divisions based on nearness to the station.
10. Frederick Greenwood, 'What has become of the Middle Classes?', *Black-
    wood's Magazine* 138 (1885): 175–80.

11. Commentators on the inner city offer a profoundly different perception of the situation. Social commentators, churchmen and novelists frequently comment on the 'silence' of the working classes. As early as 1848, Elisabeth Gaskell in the Preface to *Mary Barton* claims to speak for 'those dumb people'.
12. Greenwood, 'What has become of the Middle Classes?', 175.
13. Ibid., 179.
14. *The Times*, 'The Debasement of the London Suburbs', 21 April, 1982, 14.
15. 'St John's Wood', *Punch* (28 May 1892), 262.
16. 'The Diary of a Nobody', *Punch*, May 1888 to March 1890. Articles were later collected and published in book form in 1891.
17. *The Times*, 'Suburban Railway Traffic', 21 January 1899, 10.
18. Hermann Muthesius, *The English House*, London,1979, 7. First published in Berlin 1904.
19. 'The Builder and the Architect', *Punch* (27 August 1892): 96.
20. For instance, see H.G. Wells, *Anticipations of the Reaction of Mechanical and Scientific Progress upon Human Life and Thought*, London, 1902, 46, and *Political Writings of William Morris*, ed. A.L. Morton, London,1979, 58.
21. Sidney Low, 'The Rise of the Suburbs', *Contemporary Review*, vol. LX (1891): 545–58.
22. The fear of the degeneration of the race was endemic at the time. See W. Greenslade, *Degeneration, Culture and the Novel*, Cambridge, 1994, particularly Chapter 9, 'Race-regeneration'.
23. Charles Booth, vol.1, 553.
24. Cited in Greenslade, *Degeneration, Culture and the Novel*, 184.
25. Lord Curzon, *Frontiers*, 1907, 55–8. Cited in David Trotter, *The English Novel in History, 1895–1920*, London, 1993, 146.
26. See *Architect* 30 (1883): 169, and for a fictional example, the early chapters of Arthur Conan Doyle, *Beyond the City*, London,1899. See also my discussion of Galsworthy's use of the suburban pioneer in 'The Unwritten Suburb' in *Outside Modernism: in Pursuit of the English Novel*, Basingstoke, 2000.
27. C.F.G. Masterman, *Condition of England*, 1909, London, 1960, 65.
28. Richard Jefferies' articles for the *Standard*, published during 1888, were collected and published in book form, *Nature Near London*, London, 1889.
29. Jefferies, *Nature Near London*, 197-9.
30. Ernest Newton, *Architect*, 45 (1891): 330.
31. 'London House Planning', *Builder* (5 May 1894): 344.
32. 'The "Uglification" of London', *Builder* (27 March 1897): 288.
33. W.J. Dawson, 'The Transformation of John Loxley' in *London Idylls*, London,1895, 145–78.
34. J.T. Emmett, 'Londoners at Home', *Quarterly Review* , vol.185 (1895): 59–82.
35. Cited in W.G.S.S. Compton, 'The Homes of the People', *New Review*, vol.1 (1889): 51.
36. Ernest Newton, 'Home-Like Houses', *Builder* (10 May 1891): 60.
37. Walter Besant, *South London*, London, 316.
38. Masterman, *Condition of England*, 74.
39. Charles Booth, *Life and Labour in London*, Final Volume, London, 1902, 204.
40. Donald J. Olsen, *The Growth of Victorian London*, London, 1976, 201.

CHAPTER 3

THE RIDDLE OF SUBURBIA: SUBURBAN FICTIONS AT THE VICTORIAN *FIN DE SIÈCLE*

Gail Cunningham

Although the term 'suburb' was used from Shakespeare and Milton onwards as a geographical designation in very much its modern sense, it was not until the final decades of the nineteenth century that writers turned to suburban life as a subject of imaginative investigation. This may be due to what was recognised, even then, as the spectacular expansion in suburban building, particularly around London, from the mid-nineteenth century to the end of the Victorian period. Between 1851 and 1901 the population of England and Wales grew from 18 million to over 32 million, and in the decade 1881–91, the four areas which recorded most rapid growth were all suburbs of London. Contemporary commentators such as Walter Besant noted these demographic changes (claiming a tenfold population increase in the London suburbs over the nineteenth century, compared with only fivefold in central London) and mourned the destruction of the rural loveliness they had known, 'All this beauty is gone; we have destroyed it; all this beauty has gone for ever; it cannot be replaced'.[1] From the first, these cataclysmal social and structural changes were linked to moral, aesthetic and value judgements; and novelists of the late Victorian and Edwardian periods both responded to, and were instrumental in, constructing the new imaginative category 'suburban' to which these judgements adhered.

Words derived from 'suburb' carried pejorative connotations in this period just as they did in the eighteenth century and continue to do today – interestingly, on grounds which appear to have changed remarkably little. Cowper, writing in 1782, describes how,

> Suburban villas, highway side retreats,
> That dread encroachment of our growing streets,
> Tight boxes, neatly sashed and in a blaze
> With all the July sun's collected rays,
> Delight the citizen, who, gasping there,
> Breathes clouds of dust, and calls it country air.[2]

In *The Rise of Suburbia*, F.M.L. Thompson characterises the undesirable features of suburbia in terms that would be as familiar to Cowper as to modern lifestyle commentators:

> The suburbs appeared monotonous, featureless, without character, indistinguishable from one another, infinitely boring to behold, wastelands of housing as settings for dreary, petty, lives without social, cultural, or intellectual interests, settings which fostered a pretentious preoccupation with outward appearance, a fussy attention to the trifling details of genteel living, and absurd attempts to conjure rusticity out of minute garden plots.[3]

The features noted by both writers – the dreary homogeneity of 'tight boxes' as domestic dwellings for limited and pretentious living, the self-delusion of *rus in urbe* pastoralism – were also strongly associated in the minds of *fin-de-siècle* commentators with a wholly undesirable rise in middle-class democratisation. T.W.H. Crosland, whose vigorously splenetic anatomy, *The Suburbans*, was published in 1905, levels at suburban living not merely the familiar accusation that it is 'humdrum, platitudinous', but also that it exemplifies all that is 'inconveniently democratic'.[4] As evidence of this he cites factors of suburban living which – though to unprejudiced eyes models of convenience – clearly contribute to the inclusion of the newly massed middle classes into activities previously reserved for a more affluent and select elite, 'free public libraries ... police and county courts ... public museums, public baths, indifferent academies for young ladies'.[5]

This association of the rise of suburbia with a new mass culture, and the consequent fear and disdain with which it was received by intellectuals, is a prime factor in the rise of modernism. John Carey makes this case powerfully in *The Intellectuals and the Masses*, arguing that modernist art and literature derive largely from 'the response of the English literary intelligentsia to the new phenomenon of mass culture'.[6] The new suburbia, which provided the most visible location and outward symptom of mass culture, was a provocation to the intelligentsia's contempt. This is, as Carey says, 'distinctive in combining topographical with intellectual disdain. It relates human worth to habitat'.[7] Crosland's identification of the suburbs with a democratic tendency which is 'inconvenient' to those concerned to preserve clear social and cultural distinctions, and to differentiate values accordingly, is an early example of this thinking.

The features of suburbia, which developed most rapidly from the 1880s onwards, combine elements that could understandably engender dismay at the creation of undifferentiated mass culture with others which are not in fact indicative of crass homogeneity. Besant's perception of ecological and aesthetic catastrophe was shared, perhaps unsurprisingly, by many writers who witnessed the replacement of familiar countryside by the ugly products of the speculative builder. H.G. Wells's lyrical elegy to 'Bromstead' (the Bromley of his own childhood) in *The New Machiavelli* includes the perception that resonates through much contemporary literature of the suburbs, 'I realised that building was the enemy'.[8] Similarly, in 1899, the sheer volume of humanity concentrated into the suburbs – and made visible daily as commuter trains shifted them to and from the workplace – impressed and dismayed Walter Besant at Cannon Street station in ways which prefigure T.S. Eliot's London Bridge in *The Wasteland*:

> See them pass out – by the hundred – by the thousand – by the fifty thousand. The brain reels at the mere contemplation of this mighty multitude which comes in every morning and goes out every afternoon.[9]

However, the proliferation of buildings, and the hugely inflated numbers of the suburban classes that inhabited them, were outward and quantifiable signs of new mass living patterns whose most significant characteristics were inward and individualistic.

The configuration of suburban building plots, and the dwellings erected on them, were conceived to satisfy a demand for privacy, for retreat and seclusion within a clearly delineated private space. The detached and semi-detached villas which spread across the outskirts of London were designed specifically for single-family occupancy, emphasising the family as the defining social group and arranging discrete housing units in roads and avenues rather than the metropolitan squares and terraces. Their much-derided gardens served not merely to reinforce the notion that the suburbs provided purer living conditions and rural illusions, but also created psychologically significant separation; separation from neighbours, and, importantly, from the street. Working patterns, which took the male breadwinner on a daily journey into the city, created a suburban space which for six days a week was predominantly female-orientated, leaving women to define the interior and exterior aesthetic which was to become associated with suburban taste.

All these features, embedded in the structural, geographical and cultural characteristics of suburbia, contain the potential for the kind of individual and social conflict which could be exploited by novelists. Social patterning, which confined women within an isolating domestic routine while men centred their lives on the metropolis, split home and work across divides that exacerbated gender conflict. The vastly expanded section of the middle class, based on city clerks and the lower ranks of the professionals that formed the bulk of suburban dwellers, inserted a new element into the clashes of class values that informed much Victorian fiction. The beginnings of cultural polarisation between a decadent, 'high' aesthetic and the demotic, popular and accessible literature (of which the new suburbanites were frequently both subject and consumer) fostered the snobbery and exclusiveness of the intelligentsia noted by Carey. The tension between continuity and tradition on the one hand, and change and challenge on the other, which informed much *fin-de-siècle* debate, was visible in the 'long, unlovely rows of semi-detached villas' between country and city.

Carey exposes the degree of disdainful snobbery which pervades much fictional writing on Victorian and Edwardian suburbia, even – perhaps particularly – by novelists such as Wells and Gissing whose backgrounds and beliefs might be expected to foster more sympathetic treatment. His argument that the intellectuals' contempt for the suburban 'relates human worth to habitat' finds surprising confirmation in novelists' treatment of two apparently innocent suburban pastimes, gardening and home improvement. Crosland devotes an entire chapter to gardens, mockingly equating horticulture with social aspiration ('a love of flowers is a true sign of gentle birth and reasonable breeding'[10]) and defines the suburban aesthetic as 'an appreciation of red-brick villas, seven-guinea saddle-bag suites, ceraceous fruit in glass shades, pampas grass ... and kindred horrors'.[11] A liking for the red-brick villas of suburbia, he implies, inevitably signals a debased aesthetic judgement both inside and outside the house itself.

Crosland's link of the architectural qualities of suburban houses with the tastes of their inhabitants is symptomatic of a common elision between the values of suburban developers and those of the inhabitants of their developments. By the 1890s, speculative building was genuinely a trade of mass production. Credit was readily available, and no particular skills or qualifications were required to set up as a builder. A rapidly growing body of technical literature – builders' manuals and pattern books – and the sub-contraction of labour made it relatively easy for a bricklayer or carpenter to set up as a suburban builder, and many did. By 1880, for example, in Camberwell alone there were 416 firms or individuals engaged in building houses.[12] It was these builders, intent on quick profit and largely indifferent to the visual qualities or structural soundness of their houses, who were the real 'enemy' identified by Wells in their mass production of an ill-designed, homogeneous, and stylistically incoherent environment. Engulfing older village settlements in their tentacular grasp, and destroying the intervening countryside, these developments appeared to encapsulate the full range of contemptible qualities, from the vandalism of an English tradition going back to the medieval to ignorant rejection of the new aesthetics in the clean lines of art nouveau or the individual workmanship of the Arts and Crafts movement. As the Victorian period associated all these elements with political and social issues – the past (particularly medieval) with systems of social cohesion and a regenerative work ethic, the new art with social revolt and decadence, arts and crafts with Fabian socialism – the rise of suburbia could readily be linked to a crassly ignorant or reactionary set of values.

It is by no means obvious that tenants should reflect the assumed tastes or beliefs of their builders. However, novelists of the period habitually made use of suburban dwellers' household activities to figure a wider triviality – to indicate petty-minded conformity or limitation of the kind embodied by their houses. The suburban garden – perhaps partly in revenge for its grotesque parody of the rural spaces it has usurped – was, for novelists, a favoured signifier of stifling convention. In Wells's *Tono-Bungay* George Ponderevo secures his fatally unsuitable suburban wife by dangling before her the prospect of 'a double-fronted detached house – at Ealing, say – with a square patch of lawn in front and a garden behind', a bribe which instantly elicits (as Crosland would have predicted) effusions on 'Pampas Grass ... I love Pampas Grass'.[13] With marriage he acquires a father-in-law who tiresomely exhorts him to gardening as a panacea for his discontents, and gives maddeningly inappropriate displays of his own prowess:

> ... in the summer time he never came in without performing a sort of conjuring trick in the hall, and taking cucumbers and tomatoes from unexpected points of his person. 'All out o' my little bit,' he'd say in exemplary tones. He left a trail of vegetable produce in the most unusual places, on mantelboards, side-boards, the tops of pictures. Heavens! How the sudden unexpected tomato could annoy me![14]

Wells prefigures the collapse of George's marriage with the comically prosaic implications of the unexpected tomato, indicating as it does that 'all our conceptions of life differed', that the suburban values of his wife and her family are 'a narrow deep groove in the broad expanse of interests in which I was living'.[15]

Wells uses the suburban garden as symbolic defence against modern ideals and values again in *Ann Veronica*, as aunt and father conspire over the dinner table to prevent the rebellious young heroine from raising the subject of a daring expedition to a fancy-dress ball by talking resolutely of, 'the alarming spread of marigolds that summer at the end of the garden, a sort of Yellow Peril to all the smaller hardy annuals'.[16] Later, Ann Veronica, adopting the role of conventional innocent, repeats their technique, fending off the amorous attentions of Mr Manning by prattling about her hostess's Michaelmas daisies. On the brink of her final flight from suburbia to illicit passion with her lover, her elegiac farewell to the garden is linked to her rejection of suburban values in favour of fully lived womanhood: 'She walked about the garden in the dewy June sunshine... She was going out into the great, multitudinous world... She was ... on the eve of a woman's crowning experience'.[17] More seriously, in *The New Machiavelli* the protagonist's father, unwillingly yoked to suburban Bromstead through the inheritance of 'three palatial but structurally unsound stucco houses',[18] interprets his monumental incompetence at gardening as a symptom of existential anguish:

> 'I'm no gardener,' he said, 'I'm no anything. Why the devil did I start gardening?
> 'I suppose man was created to mind a garden .... But the Fall let us out of that! What was *I* created for? God! What was *I* created for?'[19]

He is justified, as it turns out, in this gloomy association of ideas, since in the end gardening is literally the death of him – he is killed falling from a ladder as he tries to prune the vine. For the unwilling inhabitant, Wells implies, suburban values can prove fatal.

While the suburban garden can signify triviality and convention, it also carries inherent ambiguity; it may be nature tamed and marshalled, but it retains its potential for natural beauty, and a tomato, no matter how irritating, is at least a useful object. At various points, both Wells and Gissing celebrate and satirise this suburban space. The garden, moreover, is generally represented as male space, a locus for physical activity and an escape from nursery or drawing room. The suburban interior, by contrast, is habitually conceived of as woman-dominated and as indicative of the useless and destructive. Its prime quality, noted consistently by the full range of writers on suburbia, is pointless elaboration. Ella D'Arcy's suburban sisters in 'At Twickenham' are typical as they

> dressed the windows ... with frilled Madras muslin, draped the mantel-pieces with plush, hung the walls with coloured photographs, Chinese crockery, and Japanese fans. They made expeditions into town in search of pampas grass and bulrushes, with which in summer-time they decorated the fireplaces, and in winter the painted drain-pipes which stood in the corners of the drawing-room.[20]

Carrie Pooter, wife of the eponymous Nobody whose diary provides an invaluable index of suburban taste, shares this penchant for drapery and knick-knacks. She 'hung muslin curtains over the folding-doors' and 'arranged some Liberty silk bows' on the 'tinted photographs'.[21] Later, in deference to what she is told is 'fashion', she 'draped the mantelpiece in the drawing room, and put little tiny spiders, frogs and beetles all over it'.[22] The Grossmiths' readers are of course, as persons assumed to be of superior taste, invited to laugh at such examples of harmless vulgarity, but other writers unearth more sinister undertones.

In Gissing's *The Paying Guest*, an uncharacteristically light-hearted and affectionate portrayal of suburban life in the main, interior décor is directly to blame for the fire that ultimately destroys the Sutton sitting room. When the paying guest, Louise, quarrels with her lover the unsuitability of suburban space for physical tussling becomes catastrophically apparent:

> Louise sprang away from him; but immediately behind her lay the foolish little chair which he had kicked over, and just beyond *that* stood the scarcely less foolish little table which supported the heavy lamp, with its bowl of coloured glass and its spreading yellow shade. She tottered back, fell with all her weight against the table, and brought the lamp crashing to the floor .... A great flame shot up half way to the ceiling.[23]

The feminine foolishness, which clutters an interior with fabrics and bric-a-brac, here appropriately causes the destruction of its own bad taste. However, such propensities can be even more profoundly destructive to cultural and spiritual aspiration, as novelists repeatedly claimed. George Ponderevo's marital home in *Tono-Bungay* displays the usual overdraped suburban interior to the extent that 'there wasn't a place where one could sit down and read in the whole house'.[24] This conflict between the home as display case or as seedbed for personal and intellectual development is specifically associated with the limitations of women. George's wife Marion:

> had no faculty of growth or change; she had taken her mould, she had set in the limited ideas of her peculiar class. She preserved her conception of what was right in the drawing room chairs and in the marriage ceremonial and in every relation of life with a simple and luminous honesty and conviction, with an immense unimaginative inflexibility – as a tailor-bird builds its nest or a beaver makes its dam.[25]

Thus Marion's limitations, displayed in the suburban taste that informs her home, are the innate, instinctive manifestations of her class and sex, and as immutable as the behavioural traits in nature to which they are compared.

This gendering of suburban characteristics is one of the most interesting features of turn of the century texts. Coinciding exactly with the rise of the New Woman and the radical feminism with which she was associated, the writing of suburbia could be expected to draw the sort of connections between female suppression and the common conditions of living which were a prime feature of second-wave feminism. It was the plight of the suburban housewife as anatomised in Betty Friedan's *The Feminine Mystique*, which could be said to have inspired the feminist movement of the 1960s and 70s. What is surprising about these *fin-de-siècle* texts, by contrast, is the extent to which feminist writers ignored, and others condemned, suburban womanhood. It was not simply that the link between suburban conformity and the repression of women went unnoticed. Amy Levy, for example, writing to Vernon Lee in the late 1880s, draws exactly the sort of connections that we would expect of a Victorian feminist observer:

> I dined with Miss Blomfeld on Tuesday & went down with her to a working girls club at Westminster. Somehow those girls fr. the streets, with short and merry lives, don't excite my compassion half as much as small bourgeoisie shut up in stucco villas at Brondesbury or Islington. Their enforced 'respectability' seems to me really tragic.[26]

Yet, fictional New Women are almost invariably either metropolitan or rural, upper-middle-class or interestingly bohemian. There is little sign of sympathy for the plight of the Carrie Pooters, condemned to lives of stultifying respectability and confinement in suburbia.

It was not that commentators of the time ignored the gender tensions inherent in suburban living conditions. Rather, it is that writers – with remarkable consistency – construct women not as victims of these conditions but as perpetrators of all their worst features. Crosland, for example, levels two serious – and on the face of it contradictory – charges against women. The conformity and respectability which make suburban life so dreary are, firstly, predominantly female qualities, 'It is eminently suburban and eminently feminine to think as majorities think'.[27] Secondly, and more surprisingly, it is the female suburbanite who is responsible for the contemporary demands for women's rights, where the 'question of daughters' used to be a simple matter of securing husband, house and children,

> nowadays all that is changed, and it is the suburban female who has been the principle agent in changing it. The grand principle of female independence had its rise in Suburbia as surely as Providence made little apples.[28]

Crosland reconciles these apparently conflicting positions by interpreting the quest for female independence not as a move towards personal autonomy but simply as a means of acquiring the objects of materialistic display that he associates with suburban living. The suburban woman, he suggests, is motivated entirely by selfish acquisitiveness:

> Marriage is a poor look-out from downtrodden woman's point of view. Shorthand, typewriting, the instructions of the small children of the wealthy – nay, even ribbon-measuring in drapers' shops or a position in the third row of a ballet – are greatly to be preferred. Always be independent, dear girls, and then, if a man asks you to marry him, you can inquire with a good heart how much money he has got.[29]

In a striking inversion of the New Woman's position, he reinterprets her opposition to marriage and aspiration for financial independence as manipulative steps in a move towards ensnaring the male provider of suburban goods. The outcome is, Crosland claims, that 'the male suburban is a hen-pecked, shrew-driven, neglected, heart-sick man'.[30]

In much of the discourse of suburbia, then, it is women whose limited horizons and facile materialistic ambitions are responsible for the pettiness and trivialities symbolised in suburban domestic interiors, of which men are the hapless victims. A pattern repeatedly played out in fiction is of women quietly but relentlessly ensnaring men into suburban domesticity. Images of dark and dreary redbrick villas, with a woman waiting spider-like behind door or window to entrap the passing male, recur with telling frequency. As men pass from the free, masculine space of town and street, through the transitional front garden and into the domestic interior they enter a world alien to their nature. The sinister undertones of such transitions are often signalled through images of darkness and constraint, of gloomy interiors revealing small but potentially malignant female figures. For several writers, suburbia comes interestingly close to a perilous fairyland. In Ella D'Arcy's 'A Marriage', the naïve young Catterson who is ultimately to be destroyed by marriage to his lover, takes a city friend out to Teddington in the hopes that he will admire his suburban love nest and its chatelaine. The house:

> stood separated from the road by a piece of front garden, in which the uncut grass waved fairy spear-heads, and the

unpruned bushes matted out so wide and thick as to screen the sitting-room completely from the passers-by…

Catterson rang that he might give notice of [their] arrival, and a thin bell responded to his pull from the interior of the house. It was succeeded by the tapping of high heels along the oilcloth, the door opened, and a very little woman, in a dark woollen gown, stood within the threshold.[31]

Bennett uses similar images of symbolic threshold-crossing and incorporation of the male into a dark female interior when his 'Man from the North' first enters the Fulham home of the woman he is later tempted to marry:

The slender, badly hung gate closed of itself behind him with a resounding clang, communicating a little thrill to the ground.

In answer to his ring a girl came to the door. She was rather short, thin, and dressed in black …. In the half light of the narrow lobby he made out a mahogany hat-rack of conventional shape, and on a wooden bracket a small lamp with a tarnished reflector.[32]

Both passages stress the sinister and destructive sexuality that lurks behind suburban frontages, and thus link the conventions of suburban domestic space to the dominance of female concerns and the overthrow of male ambitions. The restrictions which suburban living imposed on men, and the superficial, meretricious values of the women who lure them into domesticity, provided a major theme for Gissing's novels of the 1890s. At the beginning of *The Whirlpool* (1897) Harvey Rolfe habitually rejoices in his bachelor state, but, 'sometimes, by a freak of imagination … pictured himself a married man, imprisoned with wife and children amid … leagues of dreary, inhospitable brickwork, and a great horror fell upon him'.[33] Subsequently becoming engaged – almost accidentally – to the spoilt but impoverished society woman Alma Frothingham, Rolfe becomes sucked into the vortex of a domestic life which progressively erodes his habits and values. Gissing himself defined the theme of his novel as 'the decay of domestic life among certain classes of people,'[34] and these classes are those which, from various parts of the social scale, cluster in suburbia.

Rolfe and Alma begin married life with a conscious decision to reject the aspirational acquisitiveness of urban life in favour of plain living in Wales. The choice, as Alma explicitly defines it, is 'between vulgar display … and a simple, refined life,'[35] and Gissing implicitly but approvingly contrasts their domestic interior with the customary clutter which denotes vulgarity, 'only the absence of conventional superfluities called for remark; each article of furniture was in simple taste; the result, an impression of plain elegance'.[36] Nevertheless, in a novel about the 'decay of domestic life' this secluded marital idyll must be revealed as nothing more than a temporary freak of Alma's imagination, and as her health begins to suffer, Rolfe allows himself to be persuaded that a return to London is in their mutual interest.

Throughout *The Whirlpool* Gissing represents his characters' living conditions as products of their own deliberate choice, a mark of the disintegration of settled patterns that characterises modernity. Again, as an indication of social fracture, it is women who force men into the moulds that appear appropriate to their growing enfranchisement, but which run directly counter to domesticity. The London suburbs, ostensibly structured entirely to house and support secure family units, are portrayed by Gissing as directly threatening to them. Alma's choice of Pinner for their first suburban home suits her purposes not for creating family comfort but because it is 'so convenient for the concerts'.[37] Her neglect of her child to pursue a career as a professional violinist is indicative of the tensions between male desire for conventional living patterns and female demands for personal recognition. For Gissing, Alma's desire to display herself before a paying audience as a violinist is merely a public form of the debased and vulgar female taste that drapes and decorates private suburban interiors. In the outer London suburbs – Pinner, Gunnersbury, Putney, Wimbledon, 'on the outer edge of the whirlpool'[38] – women are drawn into the most trivial and sordid forms of social exhibitionism.

The fracturing of marital and domestic lifestyles under the pressure of women's demands is also signalled through the absence of male integration into suburban space. The Leach family, friends and neighbours of the Rolfes, exemplify for Gissing the living patterns indicative of domestic decay in modern conditions. Mrs Leach, imagining herself an invalid, 'could do nothing but collapse in chairs and loll on sofas'; her daughters 'had never dreamt of undertaking household management'; and Mr Leach 'had no function in life but to toil without pause for the support of his family in genteel leisure'.[39] So extreme are the demands of this toil, that he sleeps at his office throughout the week, returning to Kingsbury-Neasden only on Saturdays. Even when men technically share the suburban living spaces of the families for whom they work, they are emotionally displaced. For the new commuting classes, Gissing suggests, suburbia fails entirely to provide the promised rootedness and solace:

> Thousands of men, who sleep on the circumferences of London, and go each day to business, are practically strangers to the district nominally their home; ever ready to strike tent, as convenience bids, they can feel no interest in a vicinage which merely happens to house them for the time being, and as often as not they remain ignorant of the names of streets or roads through which they pass in going to the railway station .... In returning to Gunnersbury ... [Rolfe] felt hardly more sense of vital connection with this suburb than with the murky and roaring street in which he sat at business.[40]

At the end of *The Whirlpool* Alma dies from an overdose of the sleeping draft to which she has become addicted, a further symptom of the irresponsibilities inherent in her lifestyle, and a blessed release, Gissing implies, for husband and child. This is a brutal punishment for her attempts to forge independence within the domestic sphere.

In his earlier novel, *In the Year of Jubilee* (1894), Gissing evokes an even more striking picture of the separation of gender spheres in a suburban setting. The novel was originally to be called 'Miss Lord of Camberwell', a title combining a gendered aristocratic name with a drearily mundane location, thus signalling the novel's concern with tensions between female aspiration and constrained setting. In his treatment of Camberwell in the late 1880s, Gissing anatomises a suburb that is actively destructive of domestic life, where women's discontents with traditional roles impel them to invade alternative – and in his view fatally inappropriate – spheres.

All the main female characters of the novel are products of a modern culture that finds its typical outlets in suburbia. Nancy Lord, the eponymous heroine of the original title, has taken an exaggerated sense of her educational and cultural status from her time at a local day-school for girls and, 'an uneasy doubtfulness as to her social position'.[41] Both are responsible in some measure for her seduction by, and secret marriage to, the urbane metropolitan Lionel Tarrant, who leaves her pregnant in Camberwell while he unsuccessfully seeks his fortune in America. Nancy's friend, Jessica Morgan, 'a dolorous image of frustrate sex,'[42] sublimates her feminine inadequacies by cramming hysterically for London University examinations which she is doomed to fail. Also, the French sisters, whose home combines 'slovenly housekeeping' with 'pretentious ornaments,'[43] display features which for Gissing typify suburban womanhood: Ada, slatternly and incompetent in domestic management and a neglectful mother; Beatrice, cunning, manipulative and ambitious; and Fanny, weak-willed, flirtatious and empty-headed.

When Nancy's brother expresses a desire to marry Fanny French, Gissing allows their father a violent outburst directly blaming female pretension for the decay of domesticity:

> Wherever you look now-a-days there's sham and rottenness; but the most worthless creature living is one of these trashy, flashy girls ... thinking themselves too good for any honest, womanly work .... They're educated; oh yes, they're educated! What sort of wives do they make, with their education? What sort of mothers are they? Before long, there'll be no such thing as a home.[44]

Although Mr Lord's wild generalisations are often taken to be the author's own, Gissing in fact draws distinctions among his female characters that are mirrored in a very precise demarcation of different suburban social layers. Camberwell is not an undifferentiated, homogeneous mass; its developmental phases create differences in domestic spaces which are lived out in the characteristics of the women who inhabit them.

Perhaps because much of the novel was written in Camberwell itself, in a room Gissing had rented to escape family pressures, the locations (most of them actual and surviving streets) have a precision that informs meaning. Nancy Lord's home in Grove Lane is 'old Camberwell'. Although 'architectural grace can nowhere be discovered', the varied styles and dates of the houses give it 'a certain picturesqueness'.[45] Mr. Lord is not a commuter, as his local piano-dealing business is within easy walking distance of home, and when Tarrant first visits the Lord household he is surprised and gratified to note that even 'in so small a house the drawing-room should be correctly situated on the upper floor'.[46] This family rootedness in the district, and the innate good taste which informs Nancy's domestic arrangements, signal the values in Nancy which ultimately separate her from 'trashy, flashy' modern suburban womanhood. The French sisters, by contrast, are irredeemably products of modern suburbia. Living, significantly, in De Crespigny Park, an address whose pretension is symptomatic of their *arriviste* vulgarity, they are, for Gissing, definitively suburban; not merely are they located in and characteristic of suburbia, they draw the income which permits their meretricious lifestyle from it. Their father made his money out of speculative building, and his legacy of house-property provides their regular income, 'sham and rottenness' infuses their gentility, just as it does the buildings on which it is based. Jessica Morgan's family, who have elected to live in the very newest products of the speculative builder, are direct victims of this very literal rottenness:

> with the coming on of winter, they found themselves exposed to miseries barely endurable. At the first slight frost, cistern and water-pipes went to ruin; already so damp that unlovely vegetation had cropped up on cellar walls, the edifice was now drenched with torrents of water. Plaster fell from the ceilings; paper peeled away down the staircase; stuccoed portions of the front began to crack and moulder.[47]

Mr Morgan, like so many suburban husbands, is a mild and bemused man, forced into uncongenial toil in order to support idle or incompetent women.

A highly gendered distinction between metropolitan and suburban space informs the novel's central tensions and contributes to a resolution that is extraordinary in its masculinist wish-fulfilment. While Nancy yearns to live in the conventional family unit of father, mother and child, Tarrant has decided that it is precisely these conditions which are responsible for the domestic misery observable in modern life:

> The ordinary eight or ten-roomed house, inhabited by decent middle-class folk, is a gruesome sight. What a huddlement of male and female! They are factories of quarrel and hate – those respectable, brass-curtain-rodded sties – they are full of things that won't bear mentioning.[48]

Thus while Nancy is consigned to a reclusive life with their child in Harrow, Tarrant occupies lodgings in London and frequents society gatherings. Even when an inheritance frees Nancy of financial worries, Tarrant refuses her plea that they should now live together. He will continue his semi-bachelor existence while advising her to 'take a house somewhere in the western suburbs' where 'one or two men I know have decent wives'.[49] For Gissing, if not for Nancy, this is a highly satisfactory resolution.

Here, then, the conditions of suburban living are determined by and for women; men who become entangled in

them, as husbands and breadwinners, are generally represented as miserable, inadequate and emasculated. Tarrant's
choice of metropolitan over suburban space for himself but
not for his wife and child signals with brutal clarity the gender
lines along which living conditions and values divide. However, although Gissing appears to endorse Tarrant's solution as
groundbreakingly modern, the general tone of the novel's concluding chapters is retrogressive, even elegiac. In the final
book, 'A Virtue of Necessity', both Nancy's hopes – independence through novel-writing on the one hand, and living with
Tarrant in conventional harmony on the other – are disappointed; Horace Lord dies, Jessica Morgan descends into religious fanaticism. The one truly modern and forward-looking
alternative living pattern is shown in Beatrice French. Though
Gissing everywhere deplores the superficial, meretricious
entrepreneurialism of modern society, he nevertheless
responds imaginatively to its sheer vigour and energy. Beatrice
displays in the end a racy alternative to common suburban
womanhood, not merely escaping its dreary conformity but
preying profitably upon it. Her business enterprise, the South
London Fashionable Dress Supply Association, brilliantly
identifies and exploits the ignorant aspirations of the suburban middle-class female. Its financial success purchases her a
flat in a modern block in Brixton, where a 'natty parlour-
maid' serves 'a very satisfying meal' which includes 'sound
Stilton' and two wines.[50] She smokes cigarettes, bandies sexual
innuendoes and ruthlessly pursues self-interest in both private
and business affairs. She displays, in fact, all the qualities of
successful survival and fulfilment that the novel's male characters so conspicuously lack; in colonising a new kind of suburban living space, she also appropriates masculine values.

Gissing's anatomy of suburbia condemns not the mass but
the individual; modern suburban living is conducive to much
that he deplores, but within it, there are choices, alternatives,
and individual characters. Other writers also penetrated the
ostensible homogeneity of the suburbs to see the individualised
components, and with greater imaginative sympathy for the
parts. Though some, like Chesterton, claimed to find a bizarre
exoticism in suburbia,[51] more usually the pro-suburbia writer
was concerned to champion the autonomous individual within
the mass structures of suburbia. In Bennett's *A Man from the
North*, the country-bred Adeline expresses the commonplace
view of suburbia: 'I think these suburbs are horrid... And the
people! They seem so uninteresting, to have no character!'[52]

This provokes from her uncle, Mr Aked, an impassioned defence which, as the novel confirms it, is also Bennett's own:

> Child! ... the suburbs ... are full of interest, for those who can see it. Walk along this very street on such a Sunday afternoon as today. The roofs form two horrible, converging straight lines I know, but beneath there is character, individuality, enough to make the greatest book ever written. Note the varying indications supplied by bad furniture seen through curtained windows, ... listen to the melodies issuing lamely from ill-tuned pianos; examine the enervated figures of women reclining amidst flower-pots on narrow balconies. Even in the thin smoke ascending unwillingly from invisible chimney-pots, the flutter of a blind, the bang of a door, the winking of a fox terrier perched on a window-sill, the colour of paint, the lettering of a name, – in all these things there is character and matter of interest, – truth waiting to be expounded.[53]

So convinced is Mr Aked by his own rhetoric that he invites the novel's protagonist, Richard, to collaborate with him on a volume to be called 'The Psychology of the Suburbs', a project which he enthusiastically embraces. Setting forth instantly to do some primary research in the streets of Fulham, his earlier perceptions are wholly altered, 'It seemed to him that the latent poetry of the suburbs arose like a beautiful vapour and filled these monotonous and squalid vistas with the scent and the colour of violets, leaving nothing common, nothing ignoble'.[54]

Richard's response, however, is the misplaced fervour of youth; Mr Aked has neither the talent nor the application for the job, and is in any case dying. More significantly, Richard has fundamentally misinterpreted the enterprise; Aked's claim is not for 'latent poetry' in suburbia, for finding violets amidst monotony and squalor. His vision of suburbia is in fact of the prosaic and the mundane – the furniture is bad, the melodies are lame, the women enervated, the smoke thin. Yet, it is precisely within the common and ignoble that truth is to be found, and the truths of Richard's life are finally neither comfortable nor exceptional. His love for Adeline is revealed as misplaced, his attempts at writing show neither talent nor inspiration, and his ultimate marriage to Laura is at best affectionate. He settles for life in a 'suburban doll's house' and a future as 'simply the suburban husband'. Yet here perhaps Bennett does find a sort of poetry in the very ordinariness and triviality of common life, as his incantatory list of Richard's unexceptionable desires suggests:

He wanted to have Laura's kiss when he went out of a morning
to earn the bread-and-cheese. He wanted to see her figure at the
door when he returned at night. He wanted to share with her
the placid, domestic evening.[55]

Although Richard's capture by the commonplace is a sort of
failure, it is, Bennett suggests, a failure appropriate to his
qualities and one which, in its vision of 'the placid, domestic
evening', promises a quiet contentment.

If Bennett's concluding cameo is, in view of Richard's earlier
aspirations, somewhat mournful in its picture of settled suburban calm, other writers found ways of celebrating suburbia
both in its physical newness and in the living patterns it pro-
moted. Keble Howard's *The Smiths of Surbiton* sets out explicitly
to write, against the contemporary grain, not merely about
suburbanites but for them, to give expression to vitality and
interest in the ordinary lives newly lived in suburbia:

The Smiths are neither superior nor fashionable. They are suf-
ficiently humdrum, indeed, to take a cheerful view of life, to be
fond of each other, to have children, read the books they like,
visit the theatres they like, and whistle the music they like.[56]

In Howard's deliberately anti-élitist text, the Surbiton that
Crosland sneeringly defined as 'that paradise of all that is suburban'[57] becomes a cheerful locus of domestic foundations
and public celebration, 'all Surbiton was gay with wonderful
window-boxes and bright sun-blinds'.[58] Similarly, Conan
Doyle's sprightly comedy *Beyond the City: An Idyll of a Suburb*
represents suburbia as bracingly modern both in its capacity
to adjust to new social values and in its environmental aesthetics. In Norwood young couples on bicycles are shown 'flying along the beautiful smooth suburban roads'.[59] and a
second-generation New Woman forms an Emancipation Guild
to which 'all the maids and matrons of the southern suburbs
had rallied'.[60] The young male commuter whose working and
domestic habits seemed to writers like Gissing so fatally fractured is here shown to benefit both morally and spiritually:

As he goes back every evening from the crowds of Throgmorton
Street to the tree-lined peaceful avenues of Norwood, so he has
found it possible in spirit also to do one's duties amid the babel
of the City, and yet to live beyond it.[61]

Both Conan Doyle and Howard portray suburbia as vitally
modern as well as reassuringly ordinary. For them, the new

environment can incorporate modern ideas without succumbing either to decadence or to radicalism. Theirs are, however, comparatively lonely voices. The prevailing imaginative response to suburbia in this period was to use its physical qualities as signifiers of pervasive cultural and social anxieties: social disintegration, mass culture, gender roles and class conflicts could all be projected onto a set of demarcated spaces which readily elide into cultural constructs. This construction, as we have seen, was less concerned with social-realist analysis than with representations of fears and prejudices. The perception of Bennett's 'Man from the North', that 'none had suspected that the suburbs were a riddle, the answer to which was not undiscoverable,'[62] clearly resonates with writers of the period, and their decodings of the riddle are energetic and imaginatively varied. However, a solution to the riddle which accorded suburbia the kind of truth in ordinariness that Bennett proposed would be a project antithetical to modernism. The full 'Psychology of the Suburbs' remained to be written.

Notes

1. Walter Besant, *South London*, London, 1899, 308.
2. William Cowper, *Retirement*, 1782, ll. 481ff.
3. F.M.L Thompson, *The Rise of Suburbia*, Leicester, 1982, 3.
4. T.W.H Crosland, *The Suburbans*, London, 1905, 8.
5. Crosland, *The Suburbans*, 9.
6. John Carey, *The Intellectuals and the Masses*, London, 1992, vii.
7. Carey, *The Intellectuals and the Masses*, 53.
8. H.G. Wells, *The New Machiavelli*, London, 1911, 44.
9. Besant, *South London*, 318.
10. Crosland, *The Suburbans*, 144.
11. Crosland, *The Suburbans*, 35.
12. See H.J. Dyos, *Victorian Suburbs: A Study of the Growth of Camberwell*, Leicester, 1961.
13. H.G. Wells, *Tono-Bungay*, London, 1909, 207–8.
14. Wells, *Tono-Bungay*, 229.
15. Wells, *Tono-Bungay*, 227–8.
16. Wells, *Ann Veronica*, 258.
17. H.G. Wells, *Ann Veronica*, London, 1980, 14.
18. Wells, *The New Machiavelli*, 20.
19. Wells, *The New Machiavelli*, 32.
20. Ella D'Arcy, 'At Twickenham', *Modern Instances*, London, 1898, 4–5.
21. George and Weedon Grossmith, *The Diary of a Nobody*, London, 1965, 103–4.
22. Grossmith, *The Diary of a Nobody*, 182.
23. George Gissing, *The Paying Guest*, London, 1895, 127–8.
24. Wells, *Tono-Bungay*, 227.

25. Wells, *Tono-Bungay*, 227.
26. Amy Levy, MS letter (undated), Miller Library, Colby College, US. I am indebted to Christine Pullen for drawing my attention to this letter.
27. Crosland, *The Suburbans*, 54.
28. Ibid., 55.
29. Ibid.
30. Ibid., 50.
31. D'Arcy, 'A Marriage', *Modern Instances*, 40–1.
32. Arnold Bennett, *A Man from the North*, London, 1898, 84.
33. George Gissing, *The Whirlpool*, ed. W. Greenslade, London, 1997, 27.
34. Gissing to Eduard Bertz, 9 May 1896, in *The Collected Letters of George Gissing* eds P. Mattheisen, A.C. Young and P. Coustillas, Athens, Ohio, 1990–7, VI, 100–1.
35. Gissing, *The Whirlpool*, 110.
36. Ibid., 134.
37. Ibid., 174.
38. Ibid., 175.
39. Ibid., 174.
40. Ibid., 354–5.
41. George Gissing, *In the Year of Jubilee*, ed. P. Delaney, London, 1994, 16.
42. Ibid., 17.
43. Ibid., 5.
44. Ibid., 39.
45. Ibid., 15.
46. Ibid., 304.
47. Ibid., 184.
48. Ibid., 341.
49. Ibid., 366.
50. Ibid., 274–6.
51. His London suburb of Saffron Park, for example, is an 'insane village' with 'extravagant roofs' where 'Chinese lanterns glowed in the dwarfish trees like some fierce and monstrous fruit'. G.K. Chesterton, *The Man Who Was Thursday*, London, 1944, 6.
52. Bennett, *A Man from the North*, 101.
53. Ibid., 102.
54. Ibid., 108.
55. Ibid., 264.
56. Keble Howard, *The Smiths of Surbiton*, London, 1906, viii.
57. Crosland, *The Suburbans*, 11.
58. Howard, *The Smiths of Surbiton*, 123.
59. A. Conan Doyle, *Beyond the City: An Idyll of a Suburb*, London, 1912, 70,
60. Ibid., 76.
61. Ibid., 124.
62. Bennett, *A Man from the North*, 110.

CHAPTER 4

POISONED MINDS: SUBURBANITES IN POST-WAR BRITISH FICTION

Dominic Head

'Suburbia is a dirty word' writes Arthur Edwards, at the outset of his environmental history, alerting us to a shared pool of pejorative associations;[1] it is true that, for many people, the adjective 'suburban' defines a state of mind characterised by narrow middle-class aspirations. This is a legacy of the rise of the Victorian suburb, where rapid speculative development often swamped the aristocratic pretensions of the new bourgeoisie.[2] Conceived in ideological terms, the 'suburban state of mind' can be ridiculed and consigned to the intellectual margins, just as its actual physical space notionally occupies the urban margins. Miranda Sawyer's recent *Park and Ride: Adventures in Suburbia* (1999) confirms all of the familiar stereotypes. In this piece of popular (but contemptuous) autobiographical journalism, suburbia is Middle England; it is preoccupied with shopping and cars; it breeds narrow attitudes, and wears naff styles; it is mystified by artistic endeavour. Sawyer's easy target is principally ideological, 'a manner of living, an attitude to life, an atmosphere'. As she acknowledges, the geographical location of suburbia is hard to pin down.[3] The reason, of course, is that suburbia constantly relocates itself. Each wave of development corresponds to particular social aspirations, and may be dismissed (unreasonably) by those whose ambitions have already been fulfilled, and whose personal 'suburbia' has, perhaps, evolved into something more chic.

The reputation, then, is unreliable, although the social contradictions that generate the prejudicial view are worth investigating. This is particularly so given the rapid development of
suburbia as a constant fact of recent human geography, and
the tendency of commentators to assign it a central place in
the explanation of twentieth-century experience.[4]

The postwar novel in Britain, however, has not shown itself
fully alive to the sociological importance of suburbia, which
for many novelists is an object of ridicule. In the provincial
novel of the 1950s and 1960s suburbia figures as the index of
a deadening culture which threatens to absorb energies that
are more vital. In *A Kind of Loving* (1960), for example, Stan
Barstow's Vic Brown marries a girl from a 'little modern semi',[5]
and finds the values of his mother-in-law's house – the mud-
dled snobbishness it seems to enshrine – a serious threat to his
marriage, and his sanity. In Alan Sillitoe's *Saturday Night and
Sunday Morning* (1958), the engagement of Arthur Seaton also
signals a capitulation. His fiancée Doreen, who lives on an
estate of 'nice new houses', inhabits the space of new prosperity.[6] As the novel ends, Seaton self-consciously compares himself to a caught fish. Both Arthur Seaton and Vic Brown are
contradictory figures, whose rebellious energies are unfocused,
driven partly by adolescent male desires. Yet, their pursuit of
self-interest serves, in different ways, to collude with the
emerging culture they would reject.

Television is a focus of the rejection of suburban culture for
both protagonists. The most lucid aspect of Vic Brown's anger
is his irritation at the quiz-show culture that inspires a mindless
acquisitiveness, especially in his mother-in-law's house,[7] and it
is this which seems likely to overwhelm the impressionable
Ingrid. However, as Brown anticipates taking over a music and
electrical shop one day, he is clearly implicated in the leisure
culture, which, in certain guises, excites his ire. In Sillitoe's
novel, the ubiquity of television is the principal marker of the
new prosperity, and is roundly condemned, most notably in
Seaton's feeling that this new cultural phenomenon serves to
pacify the masses.[8] If this suggests an instinctive working-class
anger, it is offset by the ways in which Seaton infects others
with the effects of his own alienation.

'The Movement' of the 1950s was ostensibly rooted in a challenge to the metropolitan centre of cultural authority, and yet,
paradoxically, the Movement novelists, Kingsley Amis and
John Wain, seem to have set the tone for the undermining of
provincial culture. The protagonists of *Lucky Jim* (1954) and

Hurry on Down (1953) are lauded for their distrust of London types, yet both are finally rewarded with jobs in London. This drift towards the metropolitan centre undermines the Movement's provincial credentials, and anticipates the difficulty later novelists have had in resisting the centripetal pull of postwar literary fashion.[9] Moreover, the contradictions which make these novels troublesome seem almost exclusively *symptomatic*, rather than necessary or incorporated features of the writing.

Perhaps a descriptive treatment of suburbia might help to locate novelistic renderings which are more exacting. In trying to get beyond the perception of suburbia as a dirty word, Arthur Edwards establishes a broad definition which embraces the 'new build' of 'an estate-developer', whether city council, new-town corporation, builder, or farmer.[10] A sense of the difficulties of definition emerges when this catch-all understanding is compared with David Harvey's remark about urban planning in postwar Britain: strict legislation was adopted, he suggests, the effect of which 'was to restrict suburbanisation and to substitute planned new-town development or high-density infilling or renewal in its stead'.[11] 'Suburbanisation' is here used to denote unchecked development on the peripheries of existing towns and cities, a trend which stands in *opposition*, not just to urban renewal, but also to the planning of New Towns. As it turned out, of course, British New Towns proved to be definitively suburban for the postwar era, comprising residential zones for car owners, loosely connected by new road systems, an aggregation with a focal point in the shopping centre. Milton Keynes is the prime example, a place which 'even at its core ... remains stubbornly suburban'.[12]

If suburbia has come to represent the intersection of the domestic and the commercial, it embodies a crucial nexus, especially from the perspective of the 1990s: 'the suburbs are where the people are, and the money is,' writes Paul Barker, in arguing that 'the mall is a magnet for development in the same way that cotton mills or docks once were'.[13] This locates the central difficulty in any new development, the problem of balancing those human and financial interests which may be in conflict. In theory, this ought to involve the resistance of external commercial concerns, while some conception of a living community is consolidated. Raymond Williams's novel *The Fight for Manod* (1979), concerning a planned new city in mid-Wales, is conceived as a dramatisation of this complex dilemma. In its idealistic conception, the Manod development is an example of the postwar planning described by Harvey.

Initially posited in the early 1960s, Manod represents an alternative to suburban infill and stands in contradistinction to the 'great sprawling and jammed conurbations' in which 'life is simply breaking down'. Beyond this, Manod (which remains unbuilt) is extraordinarily ambitious, designed as a 'dispersed' city of 'hill towns', each divided by several miles of open farmland. A utopian future is glimpsed, where the investment will be social, rather than economic, for this, 'one of the first human settlements' conceived in 'post-industrial terms'.[14]

Discerning the idealism of the Manod project, Tony Pinkney alerts us to its connection with that theoretical postmodernism which is characterised by social purpose. He shows how Williams taps in to the spatial turn of this postmodernism, together with its willingness to embrace 'Nature, local traditions and popular tastes'.[15] Pinkney appropriately identifies the green hue of Williams's ordinary culture, which here also locates an *urban* ideal, and one which stands in opposition to actual postwar development. However, the novel finally suggests that a realised Manod would *conform* to this postwar experience, where fiscal questions crowd out the idealism, generating a principle of development which is less magisterial, more recognisably suburban. The local speculator John Dance has a narrow, opportunistic vision of 'modern houses' built 'six or eight to the acre' in 'one or two standard designs'. Dance is skilled at producing personal inducements that tie the locals in to his scheme. Significantly, he is also an agent for more than one international oil company; he secures franchises for the conversion of wayside petrol stations.[16] As the agent of external commercial interests, Dance seems set to preside over the devaluation of the Manod project, and the supplanting of genuine community-centred needs.

The stress of standing up for the dream of Manod gives protagonist Matthew Price a near fatal heart-attack, and this last gasp of principled public action (for the character) is pointedly placed in what Pinkney calls 'a realist "limit-text"': its limitations – those of traditional realism – in encompassing 'the complexities of paranational space' are implicitly acknowledged.[17] While this seems to me partially true, the novel also serves the less ambitious function of tracing (in a realist mode) the undermining of community values and the defeat of an urban ideal, all predicated on the eventual triumph of commercial suburbia.

An earlier treatment of the New Town theme, by a writer usually deemed to be more closely wedded to the goals of realism, represents a rather different test of the novel's capacities. Angus Wilson's *Late Call* (1964) offers a satirical portrait of life in Carshall, a New Town in the Midlands, exposing the contradictions and inadequacies of the New Town philosophy. Sylvia Calvert and her deceitful, sponging husband come to live with their recently widowed son Harold and his family. The novel clinically undermines the 'social experiment' of Carshall, particularly through the gradual collapse of Harold, a local headmaster and Carshall's most stalwart proponent. An ideal of classlessness lies behind this advocacy, as he explains to his mother, 'Carshall must develop its own mixed society – status wise, I mean, nothing to do with class – or it must die of atrophy'. Harold's is a 'ranch-type house', one of those 'built to try to persuade our industrial executives to stay in the community'.[18] The point, of course, is that a community cannot be instantly produced, and especially not by seeking both to blur and sustain 'status' differentials. Neither, it seems, can inherited perceptions of class be expelled from the utopia: Harold's daughter Judy, much to his chagrin, is enchanted by the county set. Other social pressures and prejudices intrude. Harold's elder son, the homosexual Ray, feels himself to be hounded out by the scandal that drives his friend Wilf Corney to suicide. (Cosmopolitan London supplies the tolerance he finds lacking in the new suburbia.)[19] Only Mark, the younger son, is likely to make a life (in industry) in the New Town; but this is presented as a betrayal of his political ideals – a self-sacrificing response to his father's breakdown – and as a hollow parody of the embittered ambition of John Braine's Joe Lampton.[20]

The crucial episode in the implicit debate about cultural forms is Harold's production of *Look Back in Anger*, where Wilson makes a wry point about the limitations of the 'Anger' generation. At the same time however (as with the allusion to John Braine), Wilson seems fascinated by the propensity of Carshall to nullify once challenging social texts, and reduce them – almost overnight – to clichéd period pieces. For Harold, Osborne's play is an attack on 'the sort of old-fashioned … Midland town that the New Towns are going to replace'. The production is thus self-congratulatory, utilitarian, and tendentious.[21]

Sylvia's untutored response to the play, however, is far more sensitive to the ambivalent anger of Jimmy Porter (portrayed by grandson Ray). This residual sensitivity is significant since Sylvia's identity in Carshall is swamped by the popular novels and 'tele' serials, which fill her days. Margaret Drabble has astutely observed that the novel's 'subject matter is positively banal', and that 'the whole thing is like a parody of the soap operas to which Sylvia herself is addicted'.[22] This parodic impulse is manifest in the novel's conclusion. Following a breakdown, Sylvia is redeemed (in a rather false sequence) when she is shocked out of her self-absorption by the need to save a child in a lightning storm. This avowedly fictional solution nods at the easy resolution of popular narrative forms. It is also an episode which confirms Sylvia's intrinsic antipathy to Carshall: her good work is chanced upon, whereas the Carshallites' acts of social conscience are a studied compensation for their narrow materialism. Even so, the 'redemptive' ending implies a stable kind of 'social manners' novel that is not there to be found, and this is what makes the novel challenging. Sylvia does not embody a set of values; rather, after her residual resistance is overcome, she is thrown a lifeline, which is to haul her off the sinking ship, and effect her escape. (She has plans to move to 'somewhere near' the more human town centre.)[23] A vision of nullity is glimpsed at the heart of the New Town ideal, and Wilson, refusing to offset this analysis, chooses to mimic its effects.

The ability of suburbia to absorb and distort earnest literary projects has far-reaching implications for the suburban novelist. In making this capacity a theme, Wilson highlights the problem of purchase which *Late Call* is unable to solve; it is partly colonised by the popular forms it seeks to parody. For the more overtly comic writer, this lack of purchase can be a source of humour in itself, where the pretensions of the suburbanite may be matched by the pretensions of the writer. In *The Wimbledon Poisoner* (1990), for example, Nigel Williams makes the ostentatious appreciation of literature part of the suburban identity he seeks to satirise, here in 'poisoner' Henry Farr's attitude to his wife Elinor's friends:

> Many of them, to Henry's horror, openly smoked drugs. One of them wore a kaftan. Two wore sandals. And they still trooped in and out of his house occasionally, looking at him pityingly, as they talked of foreign films, the latest play at the Royal Court and the need for the immediate withdrawal of armed forces from Nicaragua. Sometimes they sat in the front room reading aloud from the work of a man called Ian McEwan, an author who, according to Elinor, had 'a great deal to say' to Henry Farr.

Farr's unvoiced retort is that he 'had a great deal to say to Ian McEwan as well',[24] an assertion of an undeveloped independence in the face of a nullifying conformity. McEwan, of course, is noted for the revelation of psychological and emotional disturbances beneath an ordered social veneer, a challenge here rendered meaningless. In its place Williams produces a comic send-up of suburban mores, which, in the final analysis, seems built on shifting ground. Would-be poisoner Henry Farr is the focusing eye for the novel's satirical portrait of Wimbledon types, such as 'Unpublished Magic Realist', and 'Jungian Analyst with Winebox', so that his focalisation generates the humour. Finally, however, he is the principal butt, staunchest proponent of this, 'the most important suburb in the Western world', of which he is writing the 'Complete History'.[25] The murderous hatred he hatches for his wife is the product of his own mid-life crisis and suburban malaise, a misogynistic 'phase' which jars with the appreciation Elinor elicits from everyone else. The reconciliation of Henry and Elinor, and the discovery that he is not the true poisoner, allows this comedy of suburban recognition to find some kind of balance. However, Farr has *intended* to commit murder, to destroy the cosy world he also documents and celebrates, and which defines him. In this sense, the novel reveals its brutal subtext, the comedy, if comedy it is, of self-hatred and of a poisoned mind.

The philistinism of Henry Farr seems to underscore the antipathy between suburbia and socially coherent fiction, an antipathy which, in *The Wimbledon Poisoner*, results in the disruption of the writer's objective. Julian Barnes discovers a related impasse, albeit in richer terms, in *Metroland* (1980), where suburbia is articulated as the pressure to conformity felt, and resisted, by two intelligent schoolboys: narrator Christopher and his friend Toni. This sense of resistance stems from a familiar adolescent precocity, but is defined as the assertion of aesthetic sensibility, as in Christopher's condemnation of the orange sodium lighting which turns everything brown or orange in London's Metroland. 'They even fug up the spectrum', he complains, glossing 'they' as 'the unidentified legislators, moralists, social luminaries and parents of outer suburbia'.[26] It is this social network which the two boys seek to attack in their arrogant jests to *épater les bourgeois* (as when Toni goes into a boutique named 'Man Shop' and requests 'one man and two small boys'[27]). Again, the impulse is distinctly adolescent, yet it is indicative of a broader aesthetic linked to the possibilities of literary expression. In an echo of Wilson, Barnes has Christopher worry about studying Osborne at school, and about the apparent institutionalisation of 'the

Anger generation' with which the two friends identify. He also
has them engage in a conversation about how parents 'fug
you up', which paraphrases the first stanza of Philip Larkin's
famous poem on this theme, 'This Be The Verse'.[28] This is a
revealing moment, and not merely the knowing ironic
exchange of literary banter between schoolboys that it appears
to be. This section of the novel predates the Larkin poem in fact
(1963 against 1971), so Barnes offers the allusion for the
reader's recognition, implying that Larkin's observation is a
truism that his characters can arrive at themselves.[29] This glim-
mer of a literary sensibility – defined against the deadening
effect of suburban conformity – is dignified by Christopher during his Paris sojourn as the search for 'some vital synthesis of
art and life'. The ironic undercutting persists, however, particularly in the Paris section where the spuriousness of Christopher's idealism is exposed: despite his desire for that 'vital
synthesis', les événements pass him by entirely (to his later
embarrassment), absorbed as he is in his first love affair.[30]

In the final section (set in 1977) Christopher, at the age of
thirty, has been incorporated into Metroland: he is married
with a child, a mortgage, and a good job in publishing. When
inserted into this scene of domestic harmony, Toni is brash
and resentful of his friend's capitulation. Toni has pursued a
career as a minor writer, and has published a monograph on
how all 'important books' are misinterpreted when they first
appear. Now more politically aware, Toni appears driven to
understand why that vital art/life synthesis seems unattain-
able. Christopher, by contrast, has plans for a 'social history of
travel around London', a project he conceals from Toni, and
which he seems willing to advance by utilising the 'Old Boy'
network. The final scene shows Christopher at home, unable
to sleep, reflecting 'to no particular end' on how the orange
light from the street turns all his pyjamas brown. The reader
recognises that he has, indeed, become one of 'them', but this
sense of a sell-out is mitigated by the air of calm and contentment which now pervades the narrative, a mood reflected in
Christopher's outwardly calm acceptance of the news of his
wife's past infidelity.[31] Thus, the novel ends with a simple
choice, which seems a gloomy conclusion on reflection,
between the embittered idealistic commitment to the literary
life, and the suburban conformity which suffuses the final
pages like the streetlamps of Metroland itself. The major
theme of Metroland – the impasse which suburbia represents
for the writer – typifies the postwar perspective.

My examples thus far reproduce the familiar stereotype of postwar suburbia to a greater or lesser degree: the conviction that suburban life is deadening, unimaginative, representative of a low or restricted common denominator. There are two issues that are concealed in this dominant impression. First, the fact that there is actually something unplanned in the configuration of suburban living, unpredictable consequences of even the most rigorous (or cynical) social planning. The second concealment stems from the common experience of suburbia. A mode of living shared by so many people can surely only be seen as trivial if social life is trivial in general. Can such a common mode of living really be homogeneous to the core? Perhaps a more diverse culture is to be found beneath the surface uniformity. These two factors are necessarily linked, as the centrality of suburbia hinges on the paradoxes and contradictions it promulgates and sustains. These are the fissures that make suburban life exemplary of contemporary experience, and make it more surprising than it appears.

Of course, the excavation of the truth beneath the surface is a recognisable process in many representations of suburbia, a process which usually involves peeling away the veneer of civilised respectability to uncover the turmoil of repression or violence seething beneath. (In outline, the method is common to practitioners as diverse as David Lynch and Henrik Ibsen.) In postwar British fiction there have been some notable examples of this engagement with ideological contradiction, though the treatment has often been uncertain. One recent and noteworthy book, which utilises the 'probing' method, is Simon Mason's *Lives of the Dog-Stranglers* (1998). Mason's work is interesting because the discovered fragmentation of suburban lives becomes itself a structural principle. The inhabitants of Parkside, a Victorian suburb of a southern English city, are Mason's protagonists, whose disconnected and alienated lives are described in a short-story cycle. The chosen structure facilitates the use of a variety of voices, but this is done in such a way as to stress the isolation of self-absorbed individuals who fail to connect. When a known character reappears in a subsequent episode, for example, the reader is surprised by new revelations of their actions or attitudes. There is a modernist emphasis on the inner life, but this does not produce a Woolfian sense of a diverse community, built by accretion. Rather, there is a gathering despair at the unknowability and instability of individual identities. The mood is succinctly summarised by one exasperated character: 'We're all figments of our neighbours' imaginations. That's what it's come to. We're anything they want us to be – murderers, red-heads, philanderers, dog-stranglers, whatever suits them'.[32]

In Parkside the simmering suburban violence constantly boils over. There is the woman who beats her husband's face with her shoe at a dinner party; a member of an ad-hoc vigilante group turns against his own neighbour, an abandoned husband plans his wife's murder. There is something unmotivated about the extremity of the violence, and this serves to generate a picture of profound psychological disorder. Since much of the book is also comic, a compelling hybridised mode emerges. The author's note announces that the book 'is written in the mode of farce', and this identifies one element of Mason's hybrid, which, combined with the air of disintegration, produces a particularly bleak brand of humour. A good illustration of this kind of farce is the episode 'Monkey' in which a former owner of a design agency, now bankrupt, takes a job at a funfair, dressed as a gorilla. This protagonist and his wife were once the paragons of suburban affluence, yet, as Parkside's only unemployed resident in a disintegrating marriage, he now imagines that he is 'what all the other Parkside residents fear becoming', and so represents 'their nemesis'.

Dressed as an ape, the ex-designer becomes a symbol of elemental man, divested of his trappings. The farcical scene is the one in which his wife, young son, and mother-in-law – who are unaware of his lowly casual work – visit the funfair. Realising that they do not recognise him in his gorilla suit, he dances for them. Initially he terrifies his son, but finally succeeds in making them all laugh. The scene is signalled by the protagonist-narrator as an epiphany of self-realisation, which he characterises thus: 'we're not what we seem; we're men changed into monkeys, or monkeys changed into men. We're strangers to ourselves'. The essential point about his fluid and uncertain identity is that he can only bring pleasure to his wife and family whilst in 'disguise' as the elemental self he has, in a material sense, become. This farce of misrecognition ends on a depressing note because of the collapsed distinction between the suburbanite and the notionally unfettered man, where each (adopted) role is governed by aggressive self-interest and desire. The point is underscored in the final scene when this archetypal Parksider repeats his dance, this time as a prelude to making an opportunistic pass at a teenage girl with a brace. 'You *are* a monkey' exclaims the girl, as he paws her leg.[33]

Mason's book is formally interesting, but no less bleak than the other works considered here. The exposed contradictions are unproductive since they corroborate the point of view of the horrified observer, revealing the fantastic freak-show embedded in the mundane. What kind of stance, then, might produce a more forgiving or insightful view of suburbia? Is it possible to inhabit this space genuinely and imaginatively, to live and write its contradictions whilst holding off the compelling motif of imprisonment versus escape (literal or psychological)?

In a ground-clearing essay, Stefan Collini hints at such a stance. His aim is to define the historical perspective that would produce 'a story ... "relevant" to the experience of living in contemporary Britain'.[34] He draws an implicit comparison between his own position and that of the eminent historian G.M. Trevelyan (1876–1962), best known for his *English Social History* (1944). Trevelyan's influence, suggests Collini, 'nourished and depended upon the widespread nostalgia' prevalent 'in Britain since the end of the First World War'. This dual relationship to nostalgia indicates a lack of historical responsiveness which leads Collini to summarise his writing in these terms: 'English history as told by Trevelyan was rather like a tour of a beautiful country house conducted by one of the last surviving members of the family'. Wallington Hall, the Trevelyan family home (a Northumbrian mansion, now owned by the National Trust) consequently seems the appropriate source for such a project. Collini contrasts Wallington Hall with his own childhood home, a 'graceless 1950s bungalow on the edge of the Shirley Hills beyond Croydon'. This other location is much more representative, indicative of 'that ribbon of settlement' which 'represented the second wave of suburban expansion, fed by car-ownership rather than the railway'. This suburbia expressed 'values of individualism, privacy, and ruralist nostalgia'; nostalgia partly inspired by writers like Trevelyan, as Collini wryly observes.[35]

Collini's purpose in making this 'symbolic contrast between the Northumbrian mansion and the suburban bungalow' is to suggest that the perspective available from the latter is less disabling than that afforded by the former. The historian from the suburbs, suspicious of the 'epic sweep' of a Trevelyan, has acquired a distancing self-consciousness that should make him or her alert to 'the contingency of so much that a well-connected Victorian gentleman took to be natural'. This new social historian, Collini implies, is 'formed by modern British culture', and is aware that 'there can be no one authoritative narrative of the national past'.[36] Collini's vantage point is meant to imply a position of self-effacing cultural authority, in which the overturning of traditional hierarchies is a corner-stone of the ethical point of view. It is the position from which a culture in transition can be best understood. In the postwar era, the novel that perhaps comes closest to enacting this stance of recentred authority is Hanif Kureishi's *The Buddha of Suburbia* (1990).

Ostensibly, Kureishi's book is so structured as to stage a flight from suburbia. The personal development of protagonist and narrator Karim Amir is predicated on his progression from the suburbs of south London to the metropolitan centre. (He has formative experiences in New York as well as London.) In this dynamic of growth and advancement some of the familiar stereotypes of the suburban mindset are evoked: the passive enjoyment of popular television programmes; the 'fanatical' approach to shopping; the passion for DIY and a philistine response to the arts. Karim's father Haroon, the Buddha of the novel's title, exposes the spiritual emptiness of the suburbanites on several occasions, as when he ridicules alcoholic Auntie Jean's insistence that her guests remove their shoes before walking on her carpet: 'What is this, Jean, a Hindu temple?' he asks, 'is it the shoeless meeting the legless?'[37]

Karim's career might seem to demonstrate the need for the ambitious individual to exorcise the suburbanite from his or her soul. Part one of the novel, 'In the Suburbs', stresses the essential boredom of suburbia for young people, and the overwhelming desire to escape. 'Our suburbs were a leaving place, the start of a life', remarks the narrator as part one draws to a close, and life in the city is anticipated.[38] For Haroon and Eva also, self-realisa-tion seems to depend on this kind of repudiation.

There is, however, an undercurrent which runs counter to the theme of escape, and which implies the need for suburban roots to be recognised. The most obvious and important instance of this more celebratory strand concerns youth cul-ture generally, and pop music specifically. If popular culture is nurtured in suburbia – not just as an object of consumption, but as a focus of creativity too – there are grounds for arguing that Kureishi's novel might incorporate an implicit celebra-tion, at least, of suburbia's role in fashioning a new cultural mood. The emergence of punk rock is the single significant instance of this in the novel, and especially significant given that commentators are apt to stress the suburban origins of important developments in popular music. Kureishi, drawing on personal experience, seems to make this suggestion too: Karim remembers that David Bowie had attended his school.[39] Eva's son Charlie, of course, emulates this success as the international new wave star 'Charlie Hero' (after Billy Idol). In an important essay on suburbia and British rock and pop, Simon Frith examines the implications of 'the suggestion that British pop sensibility is essentially suburban'. If this is so, the notion that pop creativity is 'streetwise', a challenge to middle-class tastes, may be a myth, 'the rhetoric of class and street and grit', notes Frith, 'is itself the product of suburban dreams'. This is an important contradiction, and one which is central to *The Buddha of Suburbia*, 'the most incisive suburban fiction of recent times', as Frith acknowledges, and a novel 'driven by rock not literary dreams'.[40] Frith shows how Bromley – that 'entirely typical' suburb[41] – links Kureishi's novel with 'the quintessential suburban star David Bowie' and with later Bromley 'art school punk' acts like Siouxsie and the Banshees as well as Billy Idol. It is the mood of *alienation* in suburban pop that is particularly relevant to Kureishi, a mood conveyed by dreams of escape (to London) and of personal success through pop stardom. Yet this mood is necessarily contradictory since the sense of alienation – the actual commodity of suburban pop sensibility – demands that the fantasy of escape be perpetually deferred, that it be contained, in fact, by the probability of never being able to leave. In Frith's account, the songs of the group Suede illustrate this self-divided suburban alienation most emphatically, and apropos of their writing, he goes on to make a surprising claim:

> The suburban pop dream (as is obvious for Suede) is to become a big star as a misunderstood artist; to turn suburban alienation into both aesthetic object and mass cultural commodity. And it could be argued ... that because suburbia lacks a grand theorist (the proletariat can make sense of their lives with Marx, the bourgeoisie with Freud), youth pop, as *the* suburban art form, has filled the gap, feeding airwaves around the world with the sounds of boredom, grandeur, longing.[42]

If the claim here is provocatively overstated, it does alert us to a strange lacuna in social theory. Moreover, Frith is right to assign some degree of authority on behalf of popular culture and its ability to catch the pulse of suburban experience.

Frith's claim has a direct relevance to the contradictory celebration that underpins *Buddha*, although Kureishi manages to gesture beyond the closed circle of escape and entrapment, and the emergence of punk – the most significant cultural moment in Kureishi's novel – does not conform to Frith's overview. In fact, Kureishi is at pains to insist that the impetus of the new wave movement did *not* come from the suburbs. At the gig where Karim and Charlie encounter punk for the first time, they betray a 'provincial' reaction of alienation and restlessness, even remarking on the band's lack of professionalism. Of course, the experience is transformative, especially for Charlie, but the punk mood originates beyond 'suburban boys' like Charlie and Karim: 'we're not like them', says Karim, 'we don't hate the way they do. We've got no reason to. We're not from the estates'. The point is clear: the genuine moment of punk, as an expression of anger at social and economic marginalisation, belongs to these 'council estate kids'.[43] The indication that Charlie's enthusiasm is false; divorced from the relevant social motivation, is confirmed after his success. He produces a solo album from which 'the menace was gone' and where 'the ferocity was already a travesty'. Living in New York, Charlie understands that he is not an innovator, he's 'no Bowie', but he has acquired a taste for work and success of a distinctly tempered kind.[44] Kureishi wryly observes the way in which the music industry appropriates and defuses the social impetus of new innovations (a common enough point about punk rock), but also the way in which the suburban values of a Charlie begin to resurface in the unlikeliest of places.

Karim's rejection of Charlie, the erstwhile object of his love and admiration, is a crucial marker of his maturation, a process that is only really beginning as the novel closes: 'perhaps in the future I would live more deeply' as narrator-Karim remarks, with a hint of hindsight that implies a gap between the character Karim and his narrating self. The real grounds for this incipient maturity may be rooted in an implicit recognition of his suburban roots. Unlike the self-deceiving Charlie, there are signs that Karim's proper identity is only partly conveyed by his desire to flee suburbia. Charlie's 'big con trick', the 'manufactured rage' which brought success, and which Karim so much admired, is now a sign of inner vacuity.[45]

For Karim, however, there is no explicit repudiation or celebration of his inherited suburban outlook; rather, there is a calm interrogation of its value. It is worth remarking that the observations about suburbia continue throughout part two, 'In the City', so that the model of progression or rejection implied in the overall structure is subtly undermined by the narrator's continuing preoccupation with things suburban. An important reflection occurs when Karim is in rehearsal with Pyke's theatre group, and his relationship with Eleanor is burgeoning. Feeling himself inferior, he defers to her 'sophisticated ideas' and her language, which was 'the currency that bought you the best of what the world could offer'. Acknowledging the necessity of leaving his world, he resolves to lose his accent, to imitate Eleanor, even though he understands that for him, hers 'could only ever be a second language, consciously acquired'. Importantly, Eleanor is another character that Karim will grow beyond, but at this point, he ruminates ruefully on the nature of his own adventures, his own background, 'where I could have been telling Eleanor about the time I got fucked by Hairy Back's Great Dane, it was her stories that had primacy, her stories that connected to an entire established world'.[46] This is a crucial moment of self-reflexiveness which invites the reader's objection. For the memory that Karim denigrates – the episode in which Helen's racist father ('Hairy Back') tries to see Karim off his premises – is entirely representative of the novel's pointed comedy. Karim exposes Hairy Back's prejudice with innocent questions, while the intimidating dog proves amorous rather than aggressive.[47] If this is the stuff of multicultural suburban identity, it is also the stuff of the narrative itself. Karim, besotted with Eleanor, acquires a false set of priorities, priorities that are opposed by the novel's own narrative procedures.

In this connection it may be significant that the most arresting episode of Eleanor's life is a story she finds too painful to tell, the story of her black boyfriend Gene, driven to suicide by the prejudice which blighted his acting career and his life.[48] But this is not 'her' story to tell. The purpose it serves is to locate the extreme effect of an ingrained racism which is directly challenged by the novel's own narrative energy. At the point where Karim decides to make a break with Eleanor, Gene's story, significantly, becomes part of his own:

> Sweet Gene, her black lover, London's best mime, who emptied bed-pans in hospital soaps, killed himself because every day, by a look, a remark, an attitude, the English told him they hated him; they never let him forget they thought him a nigger, a slave, a lower being. And we pursued English roses as we pursued England; by possessing these prizes, this kindness and beauty, we stared defiantly into the eye of the Empire and all its self-regard – into the eye of Hairy Back, into the eye of the Great Fucking Dane. We became part of England and yet proudly stood outside it.[49]

Here the narrator explains how the novel should be read. The post-imperial challenge to Englishness, we are told, is defiance and appropriation, an apposite formulation for the transitional nature of English postcolonial identity. The defining moments of Karim's formative years – exemplified by the episode with Hairy Back and the Great Dane – are explicitly shown to have this serious purport. These adventures in suburbia are the flipside of Gene's capitulation to the prejudice that poisoned his existence and eroded his sense of self. They are adventures, the narrator is telling us, which might have a place in that new construction of Englishness which is the novel's main concern. The kind of 'hybridity' personified by Karim Amir, born of an Indian father and an English mother, is thus a quality that has to be struggled for. This is, of course, unreasonable since it should be taken as a given, a fact of his situation. (Elsewhere in this volume, Peter Childs offers an extended discussion of how British Asian identity redefines Englishness, and he also sees *The Buddha of Suburbia* as a seminal text in registering this process.)

Karim's quest for identity is also reflected in the novel's form. Steven Connor suggests that *Buddha* 'simultaneously summons and rebuffs the *Bildungsroman* with its typical equations between self and society'. For Connor there is also a tendency to 'signal and decline' an allegiance to 'the novel of class mobility and sexual discovery' as exemplified in writers such as Braine, Sillitoe and Drabble. Such ambivalence produces a contradictory work, in Connor's reading, with Kureishi unable 'to resist the effects of typification' in the presentation of 'Indian Britons'. The problem of 'how to celebrate hybridity without regularising it as a form' remains unresolved.[50]

It is possible to view these problems in a more positive light, however, especially if one reads the novel as an 'initiation' story tracing the first steps of an adolescent protagonist towards maturity. Rather than establishing an uneasy, semi-parodic relationship with the *Bildungsroman*, the book can be seen to have adequately delivered an initiation story with more limited goals, and goals more suitable to its essentially transitional worldview. Kureishi's ambivalent affinity with that roll-call of English novelists thus needs to be refocused. The treatment of class mobility in (especially) Braine and Sillitoe is fraught with contradiction, so Kureishi seems actually to have updated the difficulties the postwar novel has had in this area, and with a more purposive exploitation of that distinctive ambivalence.

It is the English comic novel, however, with which Kureishi has the greatest affinity; something which he has acknowledged himself. In interview (quoted here by Kenneth Kaleta), he has given this account of his literary heritage: 'Looking back on the novel – though I might not like to admit it – I was influenced more by books like *Lucky Jim* and early Evelyn Waugh than I was by *On the Road*. You know funny books about boys growing up and getting into scrapes'.[51] The male initiation narrative, in a mode of comic realism, supplies the primary inspiration for the creation of Karim Amir, and in this light the worry about the restrictive effects of typification seems misplaced. Kureishi, in any case, alerts his readers to the danger of seeking to perceive a 'type' in the reception of a character: the censorship of Karim's portrayal of Anwar, while in rehearsal with Pyke, makes this point very effectively.[52] There is also a convention in comic novels of this kind that the central protagonist is the richest and most fully (sometimes the only) developed character. Yet, despite the common ground between *Buddha* and a comic novel like *Lucky Jim*, one needs to recognise the huge advance in the genre that Kureishi's novel represents. Where Jim Dixon's farcical predicaments are partly self-authored, Karim Amir's years of maturation are fashioned, unequivocally, by broader cultural forces, and where Dixon, the progenitor of the postwar provincial hero, happily turns his back on the provinces and heads for London, Amir's metropolitan experiences stage an enriching conflict between urban and suburban influences. When he lands the part of the 'rebellious student son of an Indian shopkeeper' in a new television soap opera intended to 'tangle with the latest contemporary issues', we see Kureishi's topical and formal concerns converge. Amir begins to succeed in the profession that had excluded the talented Gene; and in incorporating this 'new kind of Englishman',[53] popular suburban culture (which is epitomised in the soap opera) is seen to adapt itself; to engage with issues of ethnicity and opportunity. Kureishi, of course, has performed the same task for the English comic novel. Where Dixon's personal success, his luck, is fortuitous, unmotivated, the story of Karim Amir works resolutely through its attendant social and cultural forces, its productive contradictions. The new type of character that emerges is a fresh serio-comic figure, the embodiment of suburban multicultural identity. As a figure of enlightened literary revisionism, and as a character becoming in tune with his state of social being, Karim emerges as the true Buddha of suburbia.

Notes

1. Arthur Edwards, *The Design of Suburbia*, London, 1981, 1.
2. Roger Silverstone, 'Introduction' in *Visions of Suburbia*, ed. Roger Silverstone, London, 1997, 3.
3. Miranda Sawyer, *Park and Ride: Adventures in Suburbia*, London, 1999, 9.
4. It is this perceived 'centrality of suburbia for an understanding of modernity and of the twentieth century' that links the diverse essays in *Visions of Suburbia*. See Silverstone, 'Introduction', 14.
5. Stan Barstow, *A Kind of Loving*, Harmondsworth, 1962, 54.
6. Alan Sillitoe, *Saturday Night and Sunday Morning*, London, 1994, 150.
7. Barstow, *A Kind of Loving*, 128.
8. Sillitoe, *Saturday Night and Sunday Morning*, 184.
9. Blake Morrison, *The Movement: English Poetry and Fiction of the 1950s*, Oxford, 1980, gives a full account of the Movement's origins, and its contradictions.
10. Edwards, *The Design of Suburbia*, 1.
11. David Harvey, *The Condition of Postmodernity*, Oxford, 1990, 69.
12. Tim Mars, 'The Life in New Towns', in *Town and Country*, eds Anthony Barnett and Roger Scruton, London, 1998, 272.
13. Paul Barker, 'Edge City', in *Town and Country*, eds Anthony Barnett and Roger Scruton, London, 1998, 210.
14. Raymond Williams, *The Fight for Manod*, London, 1988, 12, 13, 77.
15. Tony Pinkney, *Raymond Williams*, Bridgend, 1991, 87.
16. Williams, *The Fight for Manod*, 122, 113.
17. Pinkney, *Raymond Williams*, 71, 76.
18. Angus Wilson, *Late Call*, Harmondsworth, 1968, 120, 135, 66.
19. Ibid., 287.
20. Ibid., 290.
21. Ibid., 125.
22. Margaret Drabble, '"No Idle Rentier": Angus Wilson and the Nourished Literary Imagination', reprinted in *Critical Essays on Angus Wilson*, ed. Jay L. Halio, Boston, 1985, 182–92 (187).
23. Wilson, *Late Call*, 303.
24. Nigel Williams, *The Wimbledon Poisoner*, London, 1994, 6–7.
25. Ibid., 55–6.
26. Julian Barnes, *Metroland*, London, 1990, 14.
27. Ibid., 18.
28. Ibid., 41, 39.
29. Anthony Thwaite gives a completion date of 'April ?, 1971' for Larkin's 'This Be the Verse', with no periodical publication prior to its inclusion in *High Windows*, 1974. See Philip Larkin, *Collected Poems*, ed. Anthony Thwaite, London, 1988, 180.
30. Barnes, *Metroland*, 128, 75–7.
31. Ibid., 170, 153, 176, 163.
32. Simon Mason, *Lives of the Dog-Stranglers*, London, 1998, 24–5.
33. Ibid., 124–5, 129, 134.
34. Stefan Collini, *English Pasts: Essays in History and Culture*, Oxford, 1999, 19.
35. Ibid., 23–4, 24–5.
36. Ibid., 27, 25, 27–8.
37. Hanif Kureishi, *The Buddha of Suburbia*, London, 1990, 41.
38. Ibid., 117.

39. Ibid., 68.
40. Simon Frith, 'The Suburban Sensibility in British Rock and Pop', in *Visions of Suburbia*, ed. Roger Silverstone, 269, 271.
41. Silverstone, 'Introduction', *Visions of Suburbia*, 4.
42. Frith, 'The Suburban Sensibility', 278.
43. Kureishi, *The Buddha of Suburbia*, 129–130, 132, 130.
44. Ibid., 247.
45. Ibid., 284, 154.
46. Ibid., 178.
47. Ibid., 40–1.
48. Ibid., 201.
49. Ibid., 227.
50. Steven Connor, *The English Novel in History, 1950–1995*, London, 1997, 94–5, 98.
51. Kenneth C. Kaleta, *Hanif Kureishi: Postcolonial Storyteller*, Austin, 1998, 77.
52. Kureishi, *The Buddha of Suburbia*, 180–1.
53. Ibid., 3.

CHAPTER 5

SUBURBAN VALUES AND ETHNI-CITIES IN INDO-ANGLIAN WRITING

Peter Childs

> I began to wonder: what was so terrible about coming from suburbia? More to the point: how would you find your way back again? None of the ex-suburbanites seemed to know where suburbia was, exactly, other than it included the particular town that they'd run away from …. In the end, suburbia didn't seem to be a geographically distinct place at all. It was instead a manner of living, an attitude to life, an atmosphere. (Miranda Sawyer)[1]

In discussing suburbia, contemporary writers are no longer simply dealing with the suburbs. Instead, they are concerned with the lives and attitudes found in geographically imprecise places that, although located away from land-based agricultural communities, only orbit the financial, political, cultural, and social centres of a metropolis. The spatial tropes of 'satellite thinking' – centre and periphery, marginalisation, distances and connections – are also applicable to perceptions and writings about the British colonies as varied and amorphous places that can nevertheless be named and recognised, and which are similarly associated with the parochial shortcomings of suburban perspectives.

The connection between suburbia and Empire is first apparent in their parallel history in terms of consolidation and expansion in the eighteenth and nineteenth centuries alongside enormous financial investment, shifting hierarchies of snobbery and ever-present, if evolving, frontier mentalities. The building boom that created suburbia between 1815 and 1939 was funded by the profits of imperial traders who were also instrumental in establishing insular English suburbs beside Indian cities during the nineteenth century. In parallel, Empire and 'metroland' were praised in the twentieth century pre-war and lamented for reasons of finance and fashion after 1945, and both have been positioned as outposts to the imperial capital.

There are further bases for theoretical and metaphorical comparisons in colonial and metropolitan histories, but I want to consider the colonial visions and postcolonial revisions of histories and suburbs in the work of such varied writers as Meera Syal, Amit Chaudhuri, Firdaus Kanga and particularly Hanif Kureishi. For example, Kureishi has written that 'England is primarily a suburban country and English values are suburban values',[2] but in the writing of Kureishi and others, English values and 'Englishness' have been reimagined from a monolithic to a variegated identity which itself has often been positioned in, and in terms of, suburbia. As John Clement Ball has argued, suburbia, as a liminal space between the country and the city, often serves as an image of postcolonial identity between the (old) country and the (new) metropolis, especially as they are inextricably tied to images of travel (the daily migrancy that is commuting as a two-way daily diaspora).[3]

Up until 1700, the London satellite towns were not only considered to be the outskirts of the city but also the hotbed of its criminal classes. By the end of the eighteenth century the idea of the suburbs as a haven from the city had been established, whereas in the nineteenth century the suburbs were chiefly recorded in terms of their unprecedented proliferation; this was also the century in which perceptions of, and pronouncements on, Indians in British cities began to appear in any number. By the middle of the nineteenth century, there were Indian communities in London, Southampton and Liverpool, although these were smaller than other black communities in Britain. In keeping with prejudicial reports from the British in India, Mayhew, in his mid-nineteenth-century survey of the London poor, referred to 'snake-eyed Asiatics' who were 'as cunning as they look' and had 'a mendacity that never falters'. Indians were said by others to be degrading the morals and the colour of the native English.[4] In terms of organisations, the British India

Society was established in 1839, under the influence of 'the first Indian nationalist' Rajah Rammohun Roy, and the London Indian Society was set up in 1872.

It is characteristic of the suburbs that they are shifting and under constant revision. As new building takes place, and the suburbs expand further from the 'centre', they increasingly ring the city like a corona, becoming satellites linked first by A roads and then by motorway corridors, just as the shipping lanes used to link Britain to her colonies. It is also true that locations which are initially suburban can become thought of as increasingly urban when further civic or suburban expansion leaves them so much nearer to the city's centre than its fringes. While the city is associated with the intensities of work and pleasure, the suburb is characterised by leisure and languor. As early as 1876, the 'modern suburb' was characterised by a writer in *The Architect* as 'a place which is neither one thing nor the other; it has neither the advantage of the town nor the open freedom of the country'.[6] According to Kate Flint, a 'distinctive fiction of suburbia' develops from the 1890s onwards, in the work of Gissing, Bennett, Keble Howard, Shan Bullock, and William Pett Ridge.[7] A century later, many English writers continue to set their novels and plays in suburbia, but their work is generally speaking in a recognisable line of English stereotypical experience that runs from the schizophrenic Wemmick's commuting between London and his home-as-castle in Dickens's *Great Expectations* (1861) to David Nobbs's bored and trapped office worker in *The Fall and Rise of Reginald Perrin* (1975). The images of train platforms, twitching blinds, manicured gardens, car washing, DIY, hobbies, societies, groups and Tupperware parties abound alongside visions of neat rows of identikit semis housing the parochial middle classes, creating the impression of suburbia as an English dream decayed into a tedious but oppressive *sub* urban nightmare (consider Nigel Williams's *The Wimbledon Poisoner*, Julian Barnes's *Metroland,* Graham Swift's *The Sweetshop Owner,* Fay Weldon's *Life and Loves of a She-Devil*, or Mike Leigh's play *Abigail's Party).*

Since London was made 'indisputably the West Indian literary capital', in Kenneth Ramchand's phrase, by such writers as Sam Selvon and George Lamming in the 1950s, postcolonial renditions of the imperial centre have continued to figure in migrant writing by David Dabydeen, Timothy Mo, Buchi Emechta, Anita Desai, Caryl Phillips, Salman Rushdie and others. However, within recent travel writing and fiction, extended accounts have also appeared of suburbia seen from the perspective of second-generation diasporans, especially those of Indian descent, such as Farrukh Dhondy, Sunetra Gupta, Amitav Ghosh, and, via the Caribbean, V.S. Naipaul. Such texts represent the view of a recognisable, though not homogenised, group of writers whose perceptions are based on cultural difference and, in many instances, discrimination (according to the census, there were about 1.5 million South Asians in Britain in 1991, 2.1 per cent of the population).

To begin with, I shall note some views of British life in the autobiographical and travel writings of visiting Indians. In the 1950s, Nirad Chaudhuri made his first trip to England to record his impressions for a publisher. In the middle decades, there was Prafulla Mohanti's account of his life in postcolonial Britain from the early sixties to the mid-1980s, *Through Brown Eyes* (1989), while Firdaus Kanga's record of his first visit to Britain in *Heaven on Wheels* (1991) describes more recent experiences. Unlike the texts by English writers mentioned above, these texts that do not give accounts of the claustrophobia of metroland from the inside but offer perspectives on the 'atmosphere' that Miranda Sawyer identified as characterising suburbia and its 'attitude to life'.

One of the important features of Indian writing is its assertion of a competing and in many ways antagonistic body of commentary on English identity and Indian difference, and vice versa. Ten years after Independence, for example, Chaudhuri wrote after his tour of Britain 'I should like the English people to take my word for it that there is no greater myth than the much-talked-about Indo-British friendship since 1947'.[8] For Chaudhuri in the late 1950s, travelling for the first time from India to Britain conjured up a series of differences: geographical, social, and cultural contrasts between the two countries, distinctions between Indian and English identity, and variations between both old and modern England, and old and modern India. Of the Indians living in England he wrote:

> There is no doubt that old John Bull is still alive for a very large number of my countrymen in England, who are there for education, business, or other purposes. Even after staying there for a relatively long time most of them remain without English friends. They live a lonely and at times very unhappy life, grumbling about everything from food to social customs. They have friends only among their countrymen, and feel that the English are a proud, cold, and even snobbish people. Many of them develop into a type which is complementary to the old

Anglo-Indian, living in a country and yet nursing a grievance against it. Not a few turn rabidly anti-English.[9]

The domiciled Indian's impression of English life, according to Chaudhuri, is that it is lacking in both community and conversation (Firdaus Kanga also writes in his book of the rumour circulated back in Bombay that 'the British have no family life; they lead an existence of miserable loneliness'[10]). Chaudhuri is unsurprised to read a letter in an Indian paper complaining 'about the silent habits of the English people. [The correspondent] wrote with burning hatred of their behaviour in the Underground trains where they could think of nothing better to do than to bury their heads in the newspapers'.[11] As an Anglophile, Chaudhuri's experience of England and his perception of Indian experience of living in England was profoundly sobering. It is also representative. Prafulla Mohanti's more recent narrative of his experience in postcolonial Britain, spanning the early sixties to the mid-1980s, is equally characterised by disaffection. *Through Brown Eyes* is a book shot through with Indo-Anglian contrasts that situate English self-conceptions against a background of legal discrimination, racist abuse, and National Front speeches that seem to give the lie to the exported imperial vision in India 'of England as a land of daffodils, crocuses, passing showers, and floating clouds.... There was no poverty and people were fair'.[12] One salient aspect of Mohanti's artful reportage is the reversal of many of the key symbolic scenes of Imperial writing. For example, Adela Quested and Mrs. Moore's bafflement at Mrs.Bhattacharya's absence when they go to visit her in Forster's *A Passage to India*, is reinscribed in Mohanti's experience of invitations from British people in London: 'They would go on telling me about themselves and their families. Sometimes I was even given their telephone numbers and asked to look them up. At first I took their invitations at face value, but when I rang and heard the surprised tone, "Who?", I felt embarrassed and pretended I had got the wrong number'.[13]

For Firdaus Kanga, an Anglophile like Chaudhuri, the condition of Britain he finds towards the end of the Thatcher years is also a few removes from that which he expected, but it is additionally a condition which reminds him of India:

The streets of Cardiff seemed like a foreign land.... There was an unmistakable colonial air about the city, and it could have been my imagination, but the people seemed robbed of their pride, so that they moved slowly, gently, like victims. Again and again I was reminded of India. An imperial occupation had done something to the people, ruined their sense of efficacy, of being able to run things, so that they had withdrawn to an area of self where they were still effective.[14]

Kanga's impression of Liverpool is even worse. He says of the people that 'a remarkable number seemed to be overweight. I wondered if that was a symptom of poverty, the diet too rich in fats, low in protein. Buildings were dirty, black with pollution, signs on shops played fill in blanks, and the streets were littered, puddled. Liverpool did not seem to live in 1989 at all but in some other, darker era'.[15] Overall, postcolonial Britain is divided for Kanga between the prosperity of towns and cities in the south-east, along with that of heritage sites like Edinburgh and Stratford, and the austerities of lives bordering on poverty in the inner cities and the less prosperous suburbs.

In fiction, the new arrival's view of urban decay and suburban tedium is equally bleak. Kripal/Ralph Singh, in Trinidadian V.S. Naipaul's *The Mimic Men* (1967), attaches a prison-sentence's dreariness to London suburbia, considering it the epitome of mundanity and a suitable backdrop to the low-point of his own life:

> There are many of us around living modestly and without recognition in small semi-detached suburban houses. We go out on a Saturday morning to do the shopping at Sainsbury's and jostle with the crowd ... in the lower-middle class surroundings to which we are condemned ... sitting in the train, going past the backs of tall sooty houses, tumbledown sheds, Victorian working-class tenements whose gardens, long abandoned, had for stretches been turned into Caribbean backyards ... idling on a meagre income in a suburban terrace.[16]

More recently, but in the same vein, Amit Chaudhuri's *Afternoon Raag* (1993) contains one chapter devoted to what he calls 'the other Oxford', away from the dreaming spires of the University, down back streets and side alleys, where 'small, jaunty families live ... side by side with the Bangladeshis and Pakistanis'.[17] To Chaudhuri this is the 'aboriginal community' who live the life of an underclass akin to the colonised, whose descendants they now live alongside:

> the young men white and unnaturally fat on baked potatoes and cheddar cheese, still pathetically dependent on their moth-

ers, the women wearing dresses, their feet either in high-heels or sandals in the cold, their legs unstockinged in winter, secretly shaved, with faint blue and purple veins, the older men with long, combed, wavy hair, wearing coats and flared trousers, seldom unshaven, never tying their hair in a pony-tail like the students, rarely seen in corduroys, the last chain-smokers and meat-eaters of England ... white men leading black lives. White niggers, they fought the war, sang drinking songs, married, died.... They are the ones who lived in a world of horrible and immediate prejudices, coined the terms 'Paki' and 'wog', and then lived side by side with the Patels and Muslim Bangladeshi families, and worked for their sons who look like Latin Americans and chatter in Cockney amongst themselves.... The young men and women ... had never been to the orthodontist as children; raised teeth, and lines around their mouths, gave their faces an odd softness. Their complexion, too, was white; they seemed like Madame Tussaud's waxworks, a lost world, remade and fixed. And yet this was their world.[18]

Consistently, the view of the Indian visitor focuses on average English life in terms of unexpected poverty, xenophobia and a marked contrast with the 'England of the Mind' pictured in India. The middle-class middle-income suburbs of English fiction are rarely directly encountered, largely because their insularity seals them off from the experience of the cultural tourist and casual visitor. For accounts of this world it is necessary to turn to second-generation Indian writing which represents the ethnic outsider's position inside suburbia.

Miranda Sawyer's quotation, with which I began, defines suburbia for the ex-suburbanite as a geographically amorphous place, but one that definitely 'included the particular town that they'd run away from'. This desire to escape or to have escaped is repeated in the accounts of the Indian visitor summarised above, but it is also a trope in the fiction of British Asian writers. There are few English novels of suburbia whose plots, fuelled by fears of incorporation, stagnation, and resignation, do not turn on the yearning of one or more characters to flee to the city. In British Asian fiction, the threat suburbia poses is also that of an enervating sameness that reduces life to a predictable homogeneity, but its menace is doubled by the routine persecution of difference in a society founded on conformity. For Meena Kumar, the narrator of Meera Syal's *Anita and Me* (1996), the possibility of absorption into the suburban sprawl of English lower-middle class life represents the close of her childhood and is synchronous with the end of another innocence in her first experiences of racism. Shortly before the conclusion of her narrative, Meena declares:

> I began to notice more strangers hanging round Tollington now. The park, once the domain of under-tens and curious stray dogs, became a hang-out for various groups of teenagers who took over the swings and roundabouts, smoking and flirting together in separate clans. Mrs Worrall told me about how the Bartlett estate had now spread as far as the edge of the cornfields and that 'all these townies get on the bus to come and sniff our fresh air'.... Now the cornfields were the only stretch of land separating us from the 'townies' we so often mocked, the day trippers, the girls in their high heels which kept sinking into the muddy edges of the pavements and the lads all swagger and brash, jingling their loose change and scaring the birds.[19]

This awareness of imminent change, of incorporation into suburbia, occurs shortly after the local 'bored biker' Sam Lowbridge rides up to a *Midlands Today* reporter filming in Tollington and yells 'If You Want A Nigger For A Neighbour, Vote Labour!' Meena finds: 'The next morning, the cracks appeared which would finally split open the china blue bowl of that last summer. They began when papa read out a report from our local paper to mama over breakfast. It was tucked away on page eight, under the headline MAN ATTACKED IN TOLLINGTON:

> The victim, a Mr Rajesh Bhatra from Tettenhall was found in a ditch on the side of the Wulfrun Road. He was suffering from head injuries and broken ribs and had been robbed of his suitcase and wallet'.... Nothing special, papa said. But mama, papa and I knew just how special this was – we betrayed ourselves in the way we avoided each other's eyes. This was too close to home, and for the first time, I wondered if Tollington would ever truly be home again.[20]

Consequently, in much South Asian writing, suburbia appears as a place to be escaped. The familiar English narrative of suburban aspiration, of ambitions to succeed fuelled by the claustrophobia of daily routine and semi-detached incarceration, recurs in Indian writing, and becomes allied to the experience of parochial racism and provincial or suburban prejudice. As we will see in Kureishi's *The Buddha of Suburbia*, this is also linked to a desire to reinvent the self, an inclination to fantasise, a penchant for 'acting', and a displacement of the craving for a new identity onto a spatial relocation, a desire to be somewhere else; a flight from self, transmuted into an escape from place. For Meena Kumar in Syal's novel:

It was all falling into place now, why I felt this continual compulsion to fabricate, this ever-present desire to be someone else in some other place far from Tollington. Before Nanima arrived, this urge to reinvent myself, I could now see was driven purely by shame, the shame I felt when we 'did' India at school, and would leaf through tatty textbooks where the map of the world was an expanse of pink, where erect Victorian soldiers posed in grainy photographs, their feet astride flattened tigers, whilst men who looked like any one of my uncles, remained in the background holding trays or bending under the weight of impossible bundles, their posture servile, their eyes glowing like coals.[21]

To a degree, the suburbs are equated with the oppressive views of English colonial prejudice, while 'elsewhere', frequently the cosmopolitan city, is venerated as a place of liberation. Alienation from suburban living is allied to the minority experience of discrimination, and London is the favoured destination for the suburban escapee. Meera Syal herself, born two years after her parents came to England in 1961, has moved far from her West Midlands childhood to east London, and the capital is the setting for her second novel, *Life Isn't All Ha Ha Hee Hee* (1999).

In terms of the conscious escape from suburb to city, the example I will now consider in detail is the first novel by Hanif Kureishi, an author born in England of an English mother and a father who came to England from Bombay in 1947. As Dominic Head demonstrates in his chapter, *The Buddha of Suburbia* (1990) is a novel that casts the rebelliousness of its prime exemplar of emergent popular culture – punk – in terms of both the city and the suburbs; an urban movement which became a means of protest or escape for bored suburban youth. Thus, punk is positioned in the novel as a hybrid forged in two locations, just as *The Buddha of Suburbia* itself is an amalgam of its two halves: 'In the Suburbs' and 'In the City'. The novel's treatment of popular music can consequently be considered in terms of its overarching concern with newness conceived through transculturation. The narrator, Karim Amir, begins his story by announcing 'I am an Englishman born and bred, almost.... Perhaps it is the odd mixture of continents and blood, of here and there, of belonging and not, that makes me restless and easily bored'.[22] Questions of belonging and hybridity pervade the book, which in several ways concerns Karim's movement between polarised places – between 'here and there', a journey which most explicitly takes place between the different settings of the two halves of the novel. *The Buddha of Suburbia* deals with identity primarily in terms of location, as does Kureishi's earlier essay 'The Rainbow Sign', which is divided into these parts: 'One: England', 'Two: Pakistan', and 'Three: England'. This structure has two significances I want to mention here. On the one hand, it signals the move away from unitary subject positions, and on the other, it locates identity in terms of an oscillation, a movement back and forth. As Homi Bhabha says, there is a 'need to think beyond narratives of originary and initial subjectivities and to focus on those moments or processes that are produced in the articulation of cultural differences. These 'in-between' spaces provide the terrain for elaborating strategies of selfhood – singular or communal – that initiate new signs of identity ... in the act of defining the idea of society itself'.[23] *The Buddha of Suburbia* operates in this in-between space, but it also charts a specific trajectory across it. By the book's close, the sexual and racial prejudices of English society are shown to accommodate the resurgence of the political New Right, as Karim and others celebrate their personal lives and successes in a restaurant on the night of the 1979 general election. Throughout this process, the primary method that Kureishi uses to indicate cultural shift is that of relocation: from India to England, from England to the US, from Orpington to West Kensington.

In 'The Rainbow Sign', Kureishi plots his youthful development against the rising tide of Powellism. He quotes such examples of institutionalised racism as the comment by Duncan Duncan-Sandys, Secretary of State for the Commonwealth and Colonies from 1960 to 1964, that in Britain in 1967 'The breeding of millions of half-caste children would merely produce a generation of misfits and create national tension'.[24] Such views circulated widely in the late sixties and early seventies but Enoch Powell stands as the icon of the New Right against immigration and for Englishness in a restricted, exclusivist sense. While the serious political engagement with racism is only undertaken by his friend Jamila, it is against this background that Karim grows up, as well as the thriving local scene of gauche suburban pick-and-mix appropriations of Indian culture, of the kind satirised and attacked in Gita Mehta's book on American fads and 'the mystic East', *Karma Cola*. Kureishi's novel presents a series of restless characters seeking to move beyond their suburban roots through mysticism, music, class, politics and relocation.

Initially, *The Buddha of Suburbia* rests on a tension. On the one hand, Karim wants to be 'English' and not at all 'Indian'. Until the end of the book, he cannot see how he has any significant connections with Indian culture. On the other hand, Karim will not be allowed to be 'English' by the suburban English. He is therefore constantly denying and denied a position as Indian or English, and it is only towards the end of the narrative that he realises that these are not either/or positions, and that the terms can contain each other.

The second half of the novel is set in the capital, the cosmopolitan promised land for many of the book's characters, but the first half is set in and around Bromley, the Kentish market town ten miles from London Bridge which developed into a London suburb in the second half of the nineteenth century.[25] In 1911, H.G. Wells characterised Bromley, or 'Bromstead', in *The New Machiavelli* as 'a maze of exploitation roads that led nowhere, that ended in tarred fences studded with nails.... It was a sort of progress that had bolted; it was change out of hand, and going at an unprecedented pace nowhere in particular'.[26]

It is this sense of rootless, restless aimlessness that characterises Karim's position in the first half of Kureishi's novel (he is described by another character as 'belonging nowhere, wanted nowhere') and which fires his stated ambition at the opening of the book that he is, 'from the London suburbs and going somewhere'.[27] Karim, however, initially sees his anomie in terms of hybridity and not suburbia, 'Perhaps it is the odd mixture of continents and blood, of here and there, of belonging and not, that makes me restless and easily bored'.[28] In his experience of suburbia in Bromley and Beckenham, Karim is constantly positioned as Indian by people ranging from racists in the streets to avant-garde theatre directors. Kureishi, to an extent, characterises these as the positions of the political Right and Left. The Right feeds off a notion of Englishness which excludes all but Anglo-Saxon people, whether in England or abroad – the term 'English' here does not even in theory include those whose identity it renders invisible through its racial construction of Englishness. The left perceives Karim as simply an 'authentic' Indian, one who is oppressed as a part of a racial underclass: 'his own community'. (Parallel to these fixings of Karim in the novel, pressures to be dutifully 'Indian' are thrust on his friend Jamila, whose father insists she be a dutiful Muslim daughter and eschews Western culture.) At the start of the book, the suburban liberals also want Karim, and more particularly his father, to be genuinely 'Indian' because they see them as their shortest route to transcending materialism in Bromley. In this sense, India is once more portrayed as a spiritual touchstone rather than as a country. Carl and Mar-

ianne, the Chiselhurst couple, epitomise this attitude by arguing that there are 'two sorts of people in the world – those who
have been to India and those who haven't'.[29] This of course
would make Karim one of 'the others' because he has not been
to India – and for almost thirty years neither has his father,
the Buddha of suburbia. The notion of a hybrid identity – of
Karim as a black English person – is constantly denied. It is
denied on the one hand by those who want to have a subclass
they can abuse and on the other by those who want to have
an authentic 'Indian' they can use in attacks on 'Englishness',
as when Karim cultivates a different way of speaking to create
'someone from his own background' for a play: 'At night, at
home, I was working on … the accent, which I knew would
sound, to white ears … characteristic of India'.[30]

Kureishi uses suburbia in the novel as a breeding ground for
stereotypes and a repository of unreconstructed attitudes
towards class, ethnicity and religion, combined with a reactionary stance on sex, especially inter-racial sex. Tradition
stands as a synonym for outmoded beliefs, while youth culture
or sexual transgression (by both Karim and Jamila) appear as
means of escape from suburbia rather than as means of rebellion. *The Buddha of Suburbia,* often discussed in terms of the
picaresque, is therefore organised around character types, some
of whom are stapled into a stereotype of national/racial/class
identity, and others who subvert their types through sexual or
racial nonconformity.

One starting point for Karim's character would seem to be
Eurasian equivalents in Raj fiction. David Rubin's conclusion
on *Bhowani Junction,* John Masters's novel of British Indian
identities part-narrated by two Eurasian characters, is that it
'appears to suggest that, even when he is half-English, a person cannot become an Englishman'.[31] Karim is 'an Englishman born and bred, almost' and so is constantly both abused
and artificially valued for his difference, for the cultural
investment that various factions have in that 'almost'. A cor-
relation between appearance, identity and location is also
expressed by the first theatre director he works for, Shadwell,
who is appalled that Karim has never been to India and cannot speak Urdu or Punjabi. Shadwell, who wants Karim to
play Mowgli, says to him disapprovingly: '[Eva's] trying to
protect you from your destiny, which is to be a half-caste in
England. That must be complicated for you to accept –
belonging nowhere, wanted nowhere'.[32] To combat these cer-
tainties of physical identity, attached to skin colour, gender,

and sexuality, Kureishi employs irony and occasionally, in the style of the picaresque, *naiveté*. When Karim is asked by the second theatre director, Pyke, to come up with a black character, 'someone from your own background', he thinks: 'I didn't know anyone black. I'd been at school with a Nigerian. But I wouldn't know where to find him'.[33] Similarly, Karim uses parody as a way of subverting orthodoxies and stereotypes. At the last performances of *The Jungle Book* Karim mocks his own stage character: 'I sent up the accent and made the audience laugh by suddenly relapsing into cockney'.[34] By combining in one performance Indian and London accents, Karim adds a further layer to his self-distancing from his suburban roots.

Another character embroiled in stereotypical myths of Indian identity is Karim's father. His incongruous position as the suburban Buddha, appointed to lead those locals seeking enlightenment to a higher plane, establishes the book's central attitude towards suburbia as a soulless world of materialism to be transcended, if not physically left. Haroon is a full-time British Civil Servant (a reversal of the stock figure of the Indian Civil Servant under the Raj) and an Eastern mystic in his spare time. His idea, on coming to England at India's independence, was to follow the path of Gandhi and Jinnah: 'Dad would return to India as a qualified and polished English gentleman lawyer and an accomplished ballroom dancer'.[35] He becomes instead the Civil Servant who is also the Buddha of Bromley, conforming to the stereotypical image of the commuting Civil Servant whose suburban boredom has to be enlivened by exoticism and extramarital sex. Karim himself comments ironically on the fact that his father is supposed to be a spiritual guide but cannot even find his way around Beckenham (the stereotype of the Indian mystic is apparent here). Haroon, who has spent his life becoming 'more of an Englishman', now exaggerates his accent and manner to seem more Indian when he is cast in the role of enlightener.

Karim's mother, Margaret, is a caricature of British reserve and sensual denial who meets her equivalent in Jimmy, the pale, earnest, lower middle-class Englishman who is steady, calm and unemotional. Equally familiar figures are Karim's auntie Jean and her husband Ted, who run the gamut of suburban lower middle-class habits that echo the jingoism of the Empire, from drinking gin and tonic (their nicknames) to participating in football hooliganism which spills over into racist aggression. Eva, for whom Haroon leaves Margaret, is initially cast as an avant-garde Bohemian suburbanite of the early 1970s. She latches on to a Fry's Turkish Delight version of 'Eastern culture' as an extension of her rejection of English middle-class values and a focus for her hippie's quest for the unconventional and the creative. However, she is one of the characters who move with the times, like her son Charlie, and she is seen to be constantly tuning into new trends such that by the end of the 1970s she has become 'businesslike' and, after having rejected suburban middle-class sensibilities, believes she has successfully achieved urban ones. Karim finds her proudly taking journalists around her house, having 'risen above herself'.[36]

Eva's son, Charlie, is Karim's idealised love-object for most of the book, although, for a period, this fixation is transferred to Eleanor. Both represent a kind of ideal for Karim. Each is quintessentially 'English' in a way attractive to Karim. Charlie is an example of the cold and beautiful street-punk or ambitious youth rebel; a cross between David Bowie and Billy Idol, seeking escape from his family and his anonymity in suburbia through sex, drugs, and rock and roll. Charlie later says that he is selling Englishness in America, but it is now a kind of Anglo-American urban stereotype based on a Cockney accent alien to his own suburban background. Eleanor, by contrast, represents everything alien to Karim's suburban upbringing: English privilege, influence and effortless high culture. Karim says about both himself and Eleanor's previous boyfriend, Gene, a black actor who committed suicide: 'we pursued English roses as we pursued England; by possessing these prizes, this kindness and beauty, we stared defiantly into the eye of the Empire and all its self-regard.... We became part of England and yet proudly stood outside it'.[37]

Karim's theory here is similar to Fanon's view of the colonised's search for a position in the coloniser's domination. In *Black Skin White Masks*, Fanon argues that it is through sexual possession that transference of identity can seem to be accomplished. If outsiders cannot be members of the elite, they wish to possess someone who is. It is again an impulse that Karim has to move beyond by the end of the book in recognising his self-worth. Fanon later, in *The Wretched of the Earth*, talks of the need for recognising and reclaiming one's own history, which is something Karim gleans from his sudden comprehension that his relationship with Eleanor has been based on his own self-denial. He realises that he spends all his time with Eleanor discussing her family and problems, going to her friends' parties, while his own history, in terms of ethnicity and class, India and suburbia, has been made secondary.

Changez, the Indian imported to marry Jamila, plays the traditional role of the 'innocent' or fool in comic writing. He has been reading Sherlock Holmes and the Saint for his picture of Englishness and so is dismayed by modern suburban English society, making him reminiscent of writers like Chaudhuri and Kanga. At one point Changez says, 'how much he liked English people, how polite and considerate they were ... "They don't try to do you down like the Indians do"'. On the next page, Jamila rings up Karim to tell him that Changez has been attacked by a National Front gang.[38]

Jamila, who is emotionally blackmailed into marrying Changez, is the character that is most sure of who she is and what she wants to achieve. Her attempt to break free from the narrow world of suburban mores, English racism and Indian tradition, stands alone against the other characters' capitulation to Thatcherism: the political force seeking to reanimate English society and return it to the heyday of Imperial capitalism and suburban life in the late Victorian period. This is forcibly illustrated by the conclusion of the book, which pointedly ends on the night of the election that brings the Conservatives to power in 1979. Generally, the characters appear oblivious of this change while at the same time epitomising its values – Karim sells out his acting ambitions for a new job in a soap opera, which will mean recognition and money, while Haroon and Eva, the Bohemian couple of the 1970s, announce they are going to get married. Around them, in a transition which parallels the end of *Animal Farm*, London has changed, 'Everyone was smartly dressed, and the men had short hair, white shirts and baggy trousers held up by braces'.[39] In amongst this celebration of prosperity and family values, only Jamila continues to live in a squat, develop a lesbian relationship, have a child outside of her marriage, and spend the night of the election campaigning for the Labour party. Jamila doesn't go to the restaurant party but, as Karim recognises at one point, 'went forward, an Indian woman, to live a useful life in white England'.[40]

Kureishi has written that 'It is the British, the white British, who have to learn that being British isn't what it was. Now it is a more complex thing, involving new elements. So there must be a fresh way of seeing Britain and the choices it faces: and a new way of being British after all this time'.[41] This view is correlative to Stuart Hall's essays, which have repeatedly interrogated how 'Black culture ... is, in a complicated way, engaged with the redefinition, from the inside, of what it is to be black and British at the end of the twentieth century. It does have profound implications for Britain's mainstream negotiation of itself, in relation to its own imperial past.'[42] In the writing I have examined above, there is an attempt to place Englishness and British Asian identity in to a context where the former is redefined by the emergence of the latter. In terms of suburbia, however, familiar perceptions of metroland are repeated from white English fiction. The earlier migrant writing I considered replicated the view that suburbia is a routine and restrictive environment, both claustrophobic and in many ways shabby in comparison with imperial visions of English life and identity. Again, like much white English writing on suburbia, the later semi-autobiographical fiction by second-generation Indians whose parents came to Britain from 1947 onwards, also evinces tropes of a humdrum existence from which the protagonists sooner or later seek to escape. However, the flight to the metropolis is not here simply a reaction to suburban conformity but also an expression of a desire to flee parochial racism and forge a new identity through the freedom and anonymity of the more cosmopolitan city whose racism, though nonetheless oppressive, is less able to target migrants within little England.

Notes

1. Miranda Sawyer, *Park and Ride: Adventures in Suburbia*, London, 1999, 9.
2. Hanif Kureishi, 'Some Time with Stephen', in *London Kills Me: Three Screenplays and Four Essays*, New York, 1992, 163.
3. John Clement Ball, 'The Semi-Detached Metropolis: Hanif Kureishi's London', in *Ariel* vol.27, no.4, (1996).
4. See Rozina Visram, *Ayahs, Lascars, and Princes: the Story of Indians in Britain 1700–1947*, London, 1986.
5. See Peter Fryer, *Staying Power: The History of Black People in Britain*, London, 1984.
6. Quoted in F.M.L. Thompson, 'Introduction' in *The Rise of Suburbia*, Leicester, 1982, 3.
7. Kate Flint, 'Fictional Suburbia', in *Literature and History*, vol.8, no. 1, (1982): 70.
8. Nirad Chaudhuri, *A Passage to England*, London, 1994, 2.
9. Chaudhuri, *A Passage to England*, 128.
10. Firdaus Kanga, *Heaven on Wheels*, London, 1991, 5.
11. Chaudhuri, *A Passage to England*, 81.
12. Prafulla Mohanti, *Through Brown Eyes*, Harmondsworth, 1989, 24.
13. Mohanti, *Through Brown Eyes*, 50.

14. Kanga, *Heaven on Wheels*, 122.
15. Ibid., 144.
16. V.S. Naipaul, *The Mimic Men*, Harmondsworth, 1989, 8–9.
17. Amit Chaudhuri, *Afternoon Raag*, London, 1994, 92.
18. Ibid., 93–95.
19. Meera Syal, *Anita and Me*, London, 1996, 298–9.
20. Ibid., 275.
21. Ibid., 213.
22. Hanif Kureishi, *The Buddha of Suburbia*, London, 1990, 3.
23. Homi Bhabha, *The Location of Culture*, London, 1994, 1–2.
24. Hanif Kureishi, 'The Rainbow Sign', in *My Beautiful Laundrette and The Rainbow Sign*, London, 1986, 11.
25. See J.M. Rawcliffe, 'Bromley: Kentish Market Town to London Suburb, 1841–1881', in *The Rise of Suburbia*, ed. F.M.L. Thompson, Leicester, 1982.
26. H.G. Wells, *The New Machiavelli*, Harmondswoth, 1946, 33–9.
27. Kureishi, *The Buddha of Suburbia*, 1.
28. Ibid.
29. Ibid., 30.
30. Ibid., 188–9.
31. David Rubin, *After the Raj: British Novels of India since 1947*, London, 1986, 49–50.
32. Kureishi, *The Buddha of Suburbia*, 141.
33. Ibid., 170.
34. Ibid., 158.
35. Ibid., 24.
36. Ibid., 261.
37. Ibid., 227.
38. Ibid., 223–4.
39. Ibid., 270.
40. Ibid., 216.
41. Hanif Kureishi, 'The Rainbow Sign', 38.
42. Stuart Hall, 'Aspirations and Attitudes … Reflections on Black Britain in the Nineties', in *New Formations*, no. 33, (1998): 45.

CHAPTER 6

AN INCIDENT IN THE NEIGHBOURHOOD: CRIME, CONTEMPORARY FICTION AND SUBURBIA

Linden Peach

Suburbia is neither singular nor unchanging. Architectural and landscape styles vary from one suburban environment to another, from the tight semi-detached estates of the unplanned suburbs of 1930s Britain to the more expansive unfenced tract housing of middle America, from the elegant villas of early Victorian London to the clapboard and brick of 1950s Sydney.[1]

Contemporary British and American writers have used crime fiction to reconfigure suburbia and to highlight its contradictions and paradoxes. Although they are not all 'crime novels' in the accepted sense of the term, the texts discussed in this chapter reflect the diversity and complex nature of suburbia in modern/postmodern Britain and America, and the different ways in which suburban crime might be deployed and interpreted.

The American writer Suzanne Berne's *A Crime in the Neighborhood* (1997) is narrated by a suburban 'insider', an adult woman who looks back to the summer when she was ten years old. Then, out of jealousy, she had been responsible for the arrest on suspicion of child murder of a neighbour of whom her mother had become fond. The opening paragraph of the novel immediately makes clear that suburbia, as an ideal, has been lifted out of context, and out of time, 'In 1972 Spring Hill was as safe a neighborhood as you could find near an East Coast city, one of those instant subdivisions where brick split-levels and two-car garages had been planted like cabbages on squares of quiet green lawn'.[2] In Spring Hill everything changes with the discovery of the body of twelve-year old Boyd Ellison, which corresponds with important changes in ten-year old Marsha's own life, including her parents' separation. For example, the discovery of the boy's body near the shopping mall reconfigures the geography of the area into 'safe' and 'dangerous' territories, while posing the question, 'How safe is safe?'. This is analogous to the way in which the separation of the parents redefines the distinction between 'private' and 'public' space because Marsha's father, once he has left his wife, can only meet his children in parking lots, the bowling alley, the skating rink or the shopping mall.[3]

One of the effects of the murder is not only to defamiliarise what had always been taken for granted but also to place suburbia back into time, change and a larger socio-economic context:

> In 1972, Washington suburbs like ours were dowdy, provincial places, like the city itself. The Whitehurst Freeway still ran past an old rendering plant, which smelled so rankly of boiled hooves in the summer that motorists rolled up their car windows even on the hottest days. The Whitehurst emptied behind the battery-shaped Watergate Complex, still known only as elegant apartment buildings. Locusts banged against the screen doors of houses all the way up Capitol Hill. The spring before, millions of locusts had crawled out of the mud after a seventeen-year sleep, buzzed like madness for a week, then died....
>
> As I remember it, the Washington suburbs didn't get expensive until the Reagan years. During his presidency, money exploded into towns that had been shabby, somnolent, often little more than two gas pumps, a Baptist church, and a post office. Suddenly every backwater had a foreign car dealership, a gourmet grocery and a colonial-style brick bank. Malls erupted.... Little houses became big ones, while big houses became mansions, and the bigger the houses got, the less their inhabitants seemed to know about the people who lived near them. Until finally what you had were 'residential areas', places where someone could be murdered on the next block and you wouldn't know who he was.[4]

Boyd Ellinson's murder reminds the inhabitants of Spring Hill that suburbia is both a product of urban expansion and an attempt to escape it, and, ultimately, that herein lies the failure of the ideal. Serious crime is linked to the expansion of the suburbs, their ever-increasing social complexity and the loss of community within them. However, it is also associated with the return of what was repressed by the ideal of suburbia, represented here by the Watergate scandal, the locusts and the old rendering plant.

If the search for a perfect balance of nature and culture, a comfortable environment in which the relatively prosperous may live comfortable lives, has a long history, so, too, does the anxiety that goes along with it. The occurrence of crime in the suburbs reminds us, as Robert Fishman observes, that they are 'a testimony to bourgeois anxieties and deeply buried fears'.[5] Representations of crime in American suburbia are frequently an opportunity to contemplate what the suburbs have tended to take for granted and to rehearse suburban America's concerns about security. Patricia Cornwell's crime novels featuring forensic investigator Kay Scarpetta are well known manifestations of middle-class America's anxieties. In her debut Scarpetta novel, *Postmortem* (1990), the scientist ponders the security of her own neighbourhood in the wake of a recent wave of serial killings, concerns which prove ironic when the murderer eventually enters her own bedroom:

> My house was in a new subdivision in the West End of the city, where the large homes stood on wooden one-acre lots and the traffic on the streets was mostly station wagons and family cars. The neighbors were so quiet, break-ins and vandalism so rare, I couldn't recall the last time I had seen a police car cruise through. The stillness, the security, was worth any price, a necessity, a must, for me. It was soothing to my soul on early mornings to eat breakfast alone and know the only violence beyond my window would be a squirrel and a blue jay fighting over the feeder.[6]

'How safe is safe?' is a recurring motif in the American suburban crime novel, perhaps echoing the way in which sex, domestic violence and incest in *Peyton Place* defamiliarised American small-town life in the 1950s. In *Body of Evidence* (1991), a text to which I shall return later, Scarpetta contemplates how the district in which Beryl Madison is brutally killed is 'not the sort of neighborhood where one would expect anything so hideous to happen. Homes were large and set back from the street on impeccably landscaped lots'.[7] In another recent exposition of violent suburban crime Lynn Hightower's *The Debt Collector* (1999), a victim's uncle has a similar difficulty in coming to terms with the murder of his niece and nearly all of her family: 'Are you sure you got the right people? She had a nice new house in that new subdivision....'[8] As in *Postmortem*, the horrific suburban murder defamiliarises for the investigator, in this case Sonia Blair, the 'nice' neighbourhood in which she lives:

> She glanced over her shoulder at her own house, curtains still open in the living-room window, Heather curled up on the couch, Tim pacing the hallway, talking on the phone. It seemed so bright inside, cozy, as sunlight drained away and motes of darkness grew thick in the air.[9]

Ironically, Blair's own presence in her Cincinnati neighbourhood is not only perceived as incongruous but 'an object of dread and fascination'.[10] The cause of her neighbours' anxieties is not merely that she is a single parent and a homicide officer but that she has teenage children. Indeed, she admits that 'teenage boys with loud bases throbbing from car speakers used to make her nervous, before she got one of her very own'.[11] 'Teenage boys' here are a suburban configuration of the urban.

The delineation of suburban crime in twentieth-century British and American fiction, however, is not only a testimony to suburban anxieties about the infiltration of crime from outside but to the stresses and strains within the suburbs themselves. Suzanne Berne develops these interrelated strands by turning back to the traditional English detective novel. In 1972, Spring Hill struck Marsha as 'anything but lawless' and 'the most wonderfully inoffensive of places', but with the start of the long hot summer of that year, 'a kind of lawlessness infected everything'.[12] Not only did neat lawns and pruned trees give way to 'a seething tangle of colour' but children's behaviour became bizarre: an eight-year-old decorates herself in toothpaste and runs across the lawn in only her underpants, and the boy who is to be murdered appears at the playground with a bicycle identical to one stolen from a neighbour. At the same time, Marsha's teacher begins to read the class *The Hound of the Baskervilles,* which not only encourages the child to notice and record every detail of life in the suburb but haunts her with its images of the 'boggy, sulphurous moors', fog and gloom.[13] It is a commonplace that Victorian writers, including Conan Doyle, were obsessively aware of the chaos lurking beneath the veneer of civilised life, especially evident in *The Hound of the Baskervilles* which, as Christopher Clausen says, is 'heaving with references to nightmare, madness, the diabolical, and reversions to the primi-tive'.[14] In its imagery. The bulbs drive through the ground 'like spears', reminding us of early peoples who used to live on the moors inhabited by the Baskervilles, the grass looks 'an unearthly green', the smell of 'blooming' gets everywhere like Conan Doyle's fog and, reminiscent of the swamp, 'all the car windshields gathered greenish pollen, frothing against the windshield wipers'.[15] Berne's novel links the swamp and the moors in *The Hound of the Baskervilles* with the lawlessness that apparently erupts from within the neighbourhood.

Berne's novel relies also on another commonplace of the Vic-torian detective story: the provision for its readers of a subli-mated account of their fears, with the discovery of the criminal signifying the restoration of law and order. After the arrest of Mr Green, everything appears to return to 'normal', but we cannot forget that Marsha, in compiling her 'book of evidence', has noted that her family's home 'contained so many damaged things'.[16] While one strain of Victorian science emphasised the logic and deductive reasoning of scientific method, which Mar-sha appropriates from her reading of Sherlock Holmes stories, another, as Stephen Knight has said, stressed the anxiety that 'naked science itself could appear to be a disorderly force'.[17] Darwinism, in insisting that there was no difference between humankind and animals, seemed to endorse the brutality of which people were capable. This is evident in Berne's novel in the section in which, to the disgust of Marsha's brother, the chil-dren mutilate the body of a mantis. Just as Conan Doyle makes us aware of the tenuous hold of reason, morality and law on civilisation, Berne foregrounds the tenuous grasp that law and order have on the suburbs and middle-class America, epito-mised by the sudden devastation and disruption caused by Hur-ricane Agnes. The extent to which middle-class America eschews the fragility of its own social structures is summarised in Marsha's mother's observation that 'real' life happens in the country, 'the suburbs are a *distortion*'.[18]

Child murder undermines the fundamental premise upon which the ideal of suburbia is constructed, that the suburban neighbourhood is a safe environment in which to bring up children. But Berne's novel also challenges the way in which we tend to 'pathologise' child murderers:

> Perhaps he wasn't the worst man in the world. Perhaps he was a man who lived in a neighborhood full of children, a man with a neat lawn and orange marigolds around his front steps,

a man who bought raffle tickets and lent out his jumper cables,
a man who could – if you didn't look closely – resemble any
other neighbor.[19]

All detective fiction is based on masks and deception since its
objective is to unmask, literally, the criminal. However, the
point being made here is not only that dark forces may lurk
behind the mask of respectability but that social interaction
itself may be based upon the constant adoption of masks. In
this respect, modern crime fiction challenges basic assumptions about the way people relate to each other, suggesting at
its most cynical that constantly shifting masks are communicating with other endlessly changing masks.

The mask motif is especially pertinent to fiction based on
suburban crime because it can be taken as an analogue of the
importance of appearance in suburbia. However, it might also
suggest the significance attached to performance in the suburbs. As Lynn Spigel has observed, 'postwar Americans – especially those being inducted into the ranks of middle-class
home ownership – must, to some degree, have been aware of
the artifice involved in suburban ideals of family life'.[20] In
fact, this is as true for British suburbia as for American suburbia; disparity between appearance and reality, and the way in
which communication is often between masks are also recurring motifs in British writing about suburbia.

In Julian Symons's *Something Like a Love Affair* (1992), Judith
Lassiter feels that her detached out-of-town home and suburban mentality have made her life a mask that she puts on
each morning. Indeed, the novel itself is based on the assumption of roles. Plotting against her husband's life is a game for
her and the hitman she thinks she hires with her lover's help
is literally an actor, while for years her husband has had a
secret life indulging in masochist fantasies with gay men.

One of the ironies of Symons's novel is the estate on which
Judith Lassiter's lover lives. It is modelled on privately built,
suburban neighbourhoods informed by the principle that 'the
true-born Englishman was only happy living in his own house
with his own patch of grass and his own front gate'. Called the
Orchard Estate, it is 'a multitude of little red brick houses
which differed only in minor details, in streets all named after
flowers'.[21] However, while the ideal of suburbia promises its
inhabitants safety, Orchard Estate has a reputation of being
'dodgy', especially at night. Suburbia and Orchard Estate are
inverse images of each other, a motif echoed throughout the

novel; for example, one of the gay men that Judith's husband is photographed with has the same name as her lover. Moreover, Judith's hitman, or rather the hitman she thinks she is hiring, is the inverse of his respectable appearance. On the first occasion he looks like a schoolteacher while on the second he is dressed like a candidate for an interview. Her lover's story of how he and his mother were frequently beaten by his drunken father prompts her to admit that after she lost her parents she was brought up by an aunt and uncle who abused her and was made pregnant by their son when she was fourteen. In other words, one becomes mirrored, at least to some extent, in the other.

In *Felicia's Journey* (1994) by the Irish writer William Trevor, the reader is more closely involved with the practice of deception than is usual in the crime novel. Set in the English Midlands with occasional flashbacks to Ireland, the novel concerns a serial child killer who plots to entice a young runaway Irish girl into his company and, eventually, his suburban home. There are many 'Irish' aspects to this text that are beyond the scope of this essay. In preying on young girls, Hilditch is redolent of the Irish folk-tale demon, the King of the Snakes who preyed on children. He may also be thought of as a parodic inversion of the Catholic concept of the Father who searches out lost individuals, especially as he thinks of himself as 'saving' Felicia. In the terms of this essay, it hardly needs pointing out that the novel, like *A Crime in the Neighborhood*, challenges what gives classic suburbia its air of confidence. Although in Trevor's text the proposed crime is never actually committed, details of Hilditch's previous murders are released cryptically in the course of the narrative. It differs from Berne's book, in that the focus is upon the psychology and the modus operandi of a serial killer who is able to maintain the facade of a normal existence. Nevertheless, like Berne's novel, yet with considerably more justification, *Felicia's Journey* highlights anxieties about the single person, especially a man, living in a family-dominated neighbourhood. The numerous references throughout the novel to Duke of Wellington Road anticipate how, when Hilditch's crimes are discovered, this suburban street will become as notorious as Rillington Place. Taken out of its suburban normality, it will become an icon of evil – 'othered' as if to deny its association with its location. Trevor's novel is dual coded, pointing toward the apparent order and respectability of suburbia, while emphasising the abnormality it can belie:

No one passing by in Duke of Wellington Road, no hurrying housewife, or child, or business person, no one who can see Number Three from the top of the buses that ply to and fro on a nearby street, has reason to wonder about this house or its single occupant.[22]

If Berne's novel poses the question, 'How safe is safe?' Trevor's novel asks, 'How normal is normal?'

This is a similar question to that posed by a very different kind of novel about crime and suburbia, Jenny Diski's _Nothing Natural_ (1986). Set in and around a London suburban flat near Hampstead, Rachel, a single parent in her thirties, enters into a sado-masochistic relationship with a sinister man she eventually believes guilty of attacking a sixteen-year-old girl in Scotland. In making sadomasochistic sex the Trojan horse at the centre of both the novel and suburbia, Diski draws on what has become a familiar motif in tabloid newspaper stories: the secret practice of unlawful, unusual sex behind the blinds and net curtains of so-called respectable houses. As Alan Jackson points out, this dates back to at least the Golders Green affair of 1927 in which 'a house of ill-fame' was discovered in a London suburb.[23]

Although the fusion of crime and sexual transgression is a well-established trope in crime fiction, Diski approaches it from an original perspective. The title of Diski's novel is ambiguous, suggesting that there is nothing natural, in the sense of normal, in the sexual practices in which Rachel becomes involved, or that nothing is natural in the sense that everything is unnatural. Whichever way we interpret it, the title may be provocative rather than simply descriptive of the text's position. Certainly it is concerned, as is suggested by the novel's epigraph from Bertolt Brecht, with the implications of labelling anything natural for our understanding of what we might then think of as abnormal:

> Let nothing be called natural
> In an age of bloody confusion
> Ordered disorder, planned caprice,
> And dehumanized humanity, lest all things
> Be held unalterable.[24]

The permeable boundary between natural and unnatural is suggested in the press coverage of the assault on the sixteen-year-old girl. The report says that she was lured into a car by a couple and raped. It then adds that she had been 'forced to take part in other sexual acts with the couple', implying that these were less natural than the rape. Although it is a very different novel from *Felicia's Journey*, it, too, requires us to rethink definitions of normality and abnormality in situations in which people act according to the different masks they assume. Early in the book we are introduced to the possibility that Joshua Abelman is a rapist, so that all his behaviours, and the various identities that Rachel assumes with him, are read through this particular lens.

Again, the point, as Suzanne Berne's novel observes, is that we pathologise the rapist and the child-killer, not willing to admit that he, as is more than likely, might be the seemingly innocuous person next door. In contrast to the image of the mad rapist, Joshua can appear sensitive, caring and witty. Rachel cannot relate these characteristics of Joshua to the man who had beaten and abused her verbally or to the man who must have listened to the pleas and whimpering of his child victim. Moreover, the fact that a couple committed the assault upon the girl also challenges the stereotype of the lone, male predator.

Unlike *Felicia's Journey*, *Nothing Natural* examines what is 'different', in the context that 'a life without shadows and dull grey skies would become tedious'.[25] However, what is different is explored in a dialectical relation to the conventional. When Joshua spanks Rachel in the kitchen, he interrupts her involvement in a typical suburban activity, making dinner. While he beats her, she sees herself simultaneously as subject and object. The eye that watches and the voice that questions her complicity are the eyes and voice of suburbia. Nevertheless, the part of her that is not watching accepts what is happening without getting involved in definitions of abnormality and normality. The text invites us to consider whether the 'different' sex or the suburban normality is 'unnatural'. When Rachel and Joshua eat together after he has spanked and sodomised her they do so without the decorum we might associate with meals in suburbia, 'forks and knives spearing and tearing apart the meat and vegetables which they put directly into their mouths' from the roasting tin.[26] Rachel positions herself between two people who are at the poles of her imagination. The first is Joshua who existed in her imagination before he appeared: 'She had, in the past, had fleeting fantasies ... and they were always with a man without a face. Now Joshua's features had imprinted themselves on the anonymous protagonist'.[27] The second is her friend and 'adoptive mother' Isobel, the voice of respectable middle America:

'She was a woman in her early sixties, dressed in the careful elegance of a successful academic, the clothes expensively designed not to draw attention away from the presence of the substantial woman who wore them, her grey hair subtly cut to a sensible but attractive crop'.[28]

Not surprisingly, the idea of the split self is a recurring trope in suburban crime fiction. In *Something Like a Love Affair*, it acquires a particularly sinister emphasis, blurring the boundary between crime fiction and the psychological thriller. The novel begins by acknowledging: 'There were times when Judith Lassiter felt like two people ... she occasionally found herself looking down at her thin hands and moving the fingers with a feeling of wonder that they had once again obeyed her instructions'.[29] While the inner eye that watches Rachel bend over for Joshua to beat her is the suburban eye, here it is the suburban persona that is being observed. However, like Rachel, when Judith begins her affair she consults her friends as to whether she is doing the right thing. Although a very different character from Isobel, Annabel, too, is the voice of suburban respectability. Like Isobel, she warns her friend that the affair cannot continue.

Isobel's presence in *Nothing Natural* and Annabel's in *Something Like a Love Affair* remind us that the home and the suburb, as John Hartley maintains, is where public knowledge is 'recreated, generalized and personalized'.[30] Rachel challenges public assumptions that women are not expected to admit to rape fantasies. Her involvement with Joshua and sadomasochism subverts the way in which she has always 'pathologised' crime, especially sexual crime committed against women, even entertaining at one point that she would have been aroused by it. Eventually, the casual, sadomasochistic relationship with Joshua begins to take over her life, and all her fantasies.

More conventional crime novels are usually less concerned with how public knowledge is recreated and personalised in the suburbs, and more likely to address whether the ideal suburban family constitutes any kind of social norm. Minette Walters's *The Breaker* (1998) interleaves a conventional police procedural narrative, based on the interrogation of suspects and witnesses, with dysfunctional families that are probably nearer the norm than the suburban ideal of the nuclear family. The contradictory picture that emerges of the victim, a woman washed up naked on a Dorset beach in the south-west of England, is commensurate with the diversity and fragmented nature of late twentieth-century social life generally represented in the book.

The police investigation of the victim's background takes them to Rope Walk, a quiet tree-lined avenue in one of the suburbs to the west of the yacht clubs. It is not classic suburbia – that description applies to the row of 1930s semi-detached houses where the victim once lived – it is a biographical detail that provides an opportunity to introduce some of the suburban stereotypes against which the novel is pitched. The victim herself would appear to epitomise social mobility in postwar Britain. Brought up on a council estate in the English Midlands, she had been inspired by the ideal of suburbia: 'A house of her own. Social acceptance. Respectability.'[31]

Two aspects of her current home, where she lived with her three-year-old child and her husband, are disturbing. All the photographs are of herself or of herself and her daughter, as if her husband is invisible – signifiers of the alternative 'reality' behind the curtains. Moreover, everything is over-embellished with stereotypically suburban frills, as if the victim had been trying too hard to preserve the veneer of respectability. In fact, the different views of her that emerge in the course of the narrative, not only contradict the initial picture that her husband provides of her but also undermine the idealised image of suburban respectability generally. Her mother-in-law regards her as a gold-digger while police statements taken from people with whom she worked, and eventually from her husband, variously describe her as sly and mischievous. One of them displays the prejudiced hostility frequently shown to those moving into suburbia from an underprivileged background: 'She was uneducated, vulgar, manipulative and deceitful, and she was out for anything and everything she could get ... and she was never happier than when she was pulling people down to her own level or below.'[32]

As is evident from Walters's work, the contemporary suburban crime novel foregrounds the contradictions within suburbia while stressing how it is itself changeable and fluid. In the more popular crime novels, such as Colin Dexter's Inspector Morse mysteries, the diversity and fragmentation of suburbia brought about by socio-economic changes are often presented transparently as a backdrop to serious crime. For example, the murder scene in the third Inspector Morse novel *The Silent World of Nicholas Quinn* (1977),[33] concerned with the death of a new member of the Oxford Examinations syndicate, is his North Oxford suburban home. The location appears to have been chosen as one that the reader might expect to be associated with crime. Not only is North Oxford, like Suzanne

Berne's Washington suburbs, fragmented, but the boundaries are blurred between residential and business, between town and gown, between the upper and the lower middle classes, and between home and abroad. Indeed, the confusion of geographical, cultural and class boundaries in the more complex and hybrid suburban areas is an increasingly significant feature of popular suburban crime writing. Dexter and Berne's interest in placing the suburbs within a changing socio-economic context is much more pronounced, for example, in Marcia Muller's work. Muller's *There's Something in a Sunday* (1989) is interleaved with accounts of areas whose spatial complexity defy definition. Often the approach to a particular area, The Castles and the Haight-Ashbury District, is literally a drive through their history:

> The Haight-Ashbury District is best known for the social and psychedelic explosion that took place there in the 1960s, but its history encompasses far more than the brief hippie area. It was originally settled by livestock farmers ... with the expansion of the city's rail service to the area, "suburbanites" followed, building the splendid Victorians that are so prized today.... Long before the hippies discovered the district, bohemians and college students moved there for cheap rents; after the hippies left, hard-case junkies and drug dealers took over.... Today the Haight is a neighbourhood in search of an identity.[34]

However, Muller is not interested in placing the various districts of San Francisco in their architectural and topographical history for its own sake. The central trope in the novel is that the city has become, as Muller's female investigator Sharon McCone observes, more crime ridden, for which the fog is an analogue: 'Foggy dusk enveloped the city, early for September, a forewarning of a long, dark, hard winter. As the shadows lengthened, my depression deepened. For me, San Francisco had always been a brightly lit city, and that illumination mainly came from its good people. But lately it seemed the lights were going out'.[35] The detailed histories of specific neighbourhoods are set against this general sense of change and crime in order to rationalise what McCone feels is happening to the city. Muller's novel also seeks to take comfort in the fact that if change, not stasis, is the underlying reality then things might always change again for the better.

Crime is both implicitly and explicitly associated throughout *There's Something in a Sunday* with domestic disorder through two narrative strategies. The investigation is punctuated with incidents in which Sharon McCone returns to her home, the inverse of suburbia: her backyard is 'weedy, overgrown',[36] and it has a half-completed bedroom in what was once the back porch.[37] Like Minette Walters's *The Breaker*, the novel weaves its way through a patchwork of dysfunctional families and locations. When McCone first visits Vicky, who turns out to have wanted to kill her husband, she senses that she has stumbled across a 'difficult domestic situation' and 'troubled household'.[38] Returning at the end of the novel to Vicky, who is hysterical on realising that she has mistakenly killed the wrong person, McCone observes that the home 'resembled a war zone, domestic variety: Dirty dishes were stacked everywhere, interspersed with empty wine bottles. A paper sack of garbage overflowed onto the floor; next to it another one had fallen over and broken, leaking damp coffee grounds'.[39] While the detail detracts from what is happening to Vicky, it explicitly sets the chaotic reality of family life in contradistinction to the suburban ideal. It also implies that the relationship between the two is comparable to that between the male imaginary of the ideal female body of closed, perfect surfaces and the open, imperfect, real-life body. The real kitchen, like the real body, overflows, leaks and gets damp. McCone observes: 'As I called 911, I stared at the reminders of typical family life posted there. But they were not all commonplace or reassuring; Betsy had drawn Halloween pictures for Daddy, Mom, and Rina, signed with love; the one for Rina had been ripped in half, and part of it lay on the floor at my feet'.[40]

Although crime is employed to interrogate suburban ideals, preconceptions and definitions, *There's Something in a Sunday* appears to have the failing that Sally Munt has found in much New Woman crime fiction, 'the radical content is derailed by the deep structure of conventionality underpinning it'.[41] However, the novel is more complex than this; poised between the suburban ideal of order and the disorder that lies outside, beyond, and often within it. The extent to which this is so often a feature of contemporary suburban crime fiction is evident in the way in which Marcia Muller, Julian Symons and Patricia Cornwell approach the movement beyond suburbia. In *There's Something in a Sunday*, *Something Like a Love Affair* and Cornwell's *Body of Evidence*, those who move out and ostensibly beyond suburbia still inhabit the suburban state of mind. What has changed is the balance that suburbia pretends to achieve between the city and the country, community and privacy. The move out of the suburbs in each of these nov-

els is away from the town or city to the country, and closer to
the wilderness. The Burning Oak Ranch in Muller's novel blurs
the boundaries between ranch house and an upmarket suburban family home. The Lassiter's residence in *Something Like a
Love Affair* is also an American style ranch house about a mile
out of Wyfleet. Set on a piece of high land, from which the
earth shelved deeply, it has views over 'the small neat lawn
and the flower beds of Sussex fields, and the steel gleam of a
river winding in S bends towards the sea several miles away'.[42]
Here seclusion and detachment, too, are privileged over community, an analogue for the way in which the personal space
in which Judith lives has become increasingly detached and
alienating. There is not much physical warmth in the Lassiter's relationship, signified by the croissants which Judith
wraps every morning in a napkin so that they retain 'a memory of heat', and the couple have separate bedrooms. She
desires to return to where they used to live, in a semi-detached
house in a street with numbers. While the ranch house has
wider, more inspirational vistas than suburbia, of which the
neat lawn and flowerbeds are a reminder, the prospect is of an
increasing lack of boundaries, which is both outside and
within Judith Lassiter herself. This lack of boundaries is evident in family relationships that are, from a suburban perspective, even more unconventional than those entertained
by Minette Walters. For example, Judith's housekeeper, Patty,
lives with a lorry driver, has a child by another man and takes
a second lover while the first is on long-haul assignments. She
goes on holiday with both, the second lover taking another
girlfriend with him. Ironically, having ostensibly taken a step
up from suburbia, Judith becomes involved in a world redolent
of hard-boiled, urban crime fiction; she has an affair in a
seedy hotel, hires a hitman and commits murder.

The victim's house in *Body of Evidence* occupies a location
between the suburban, signified by the contents of the living
room – a glass coffee table, magazines, crystal ashtray, art deco
bowls and dhurrie rug – and the country that was destroyed to
enable its construction. It is an appropriate text to draw this
essay to a close, for although it takes us beyond suburbia in
one sense it returns us to the wilderness within the suburban
with which we began. The district in which Beryl lives is
intended to appeal to the suburban dream of the country, as
the forensic investigator's police colleague, Marino, demonstrates: 'Me, I'd love a crib like this. Build a nice fire in the winter, pour yourself a little bourbon, and just look out at the

woods'.[43] But it is the privacy-cum-isolation that a house of this kind provides over and above suburban housing that contributes to the victim's death; her house in particular enjoyed the last position on the lot and the trees that screened her house made it easier for her killer. The country which the house overlooks – 'the ravine of underbrush' – suggests the underside of society and the human psyche to which the horrific murder points. While the text highlights the dark substrata of society that suburbia can never entirely escape, Beryl Madison's house is an aberration in suburban terms; as the kind of property a wealthy young couple might build, having 'a lot of expensive and wasted space', its physical appearance invokes the wildness which suburbia seeks to keep at bay, 'The grass was badly overgrown and spangled with tall dandelions swaying in the breeze.'[44] This sense of anarchy in suburban terms mirrors the discoveries Kay Scarpetta makes about Beryl's life, even though she believed that she knew everything about her.

Writing about crime in suburbia, like suburbia itself, is 'neither singular nor unchanging', and narrative strategies and perspectives vary as do the architecture and landscape from one suburb to another. The most interesting work, poised on the heightened divisions of suburbia, explores and develops deeply-entrenched as well as new-found anxieties: the contradictions and paradoxes in suburbia itself, the return of what suburbia has always sought to repress, the increasing social complexity and fragmentation of the suburbs, the discrepancy between appearance and reality, and the authenticity of what is taken for 'normality' when freed from the habitual familiarisation of convention and routine.

Notes

1. Roger Silverstone, 'Introduction', in *Visions of Suburbia*, ed. Roger Silverstone, London 1997, 4.
2. Suzanne Berne, *A Crime in the Neighborhood*, London and New York, 1998, 1.
3. Berne, *A Crime in the Neighborhood*, 55.
4. Ibid., 49–50.
5. Robert Fishman, *Bourgeois Utopias: The Rise and Fall of Suburbia*, New York, 1987, 154. Cited in Silverstone, 'Introduction', in *Visions of Suburbia*, 6.
6. Patricia Cornwell, *Postmortem*, London, 1998, 41–2.
7. Patricia Cornwell, *Body of Evidence*, London, 1993, 8.
8. Lynn Hightower, *The Debt Collector*, London, 1999, 54.
9. Ibid., 6.
10 Ibid., 5.

11. Ibid.
12. Berne, *A Crime in the Neighborhood*, 48.
13. Ibid., 51–2.
14. Christopher Clausen, 'Sherlock Holmes, Order, and the Late-Victorian Mind', in *Critical Essays on Sir Arthur Conan Doyle,* ed. Harold Orel, London and New York, 1992, 83.
15. Berne, *A Crime in the Neighborhood*, 48.
16. Ibid., 52.
17. Stephen Knight, 'The Case of the Great Detective', in Orel, *Critical Essays on Sir Arthur Conan Doyle*, 203
18. Berne, *A Crime in the Neighborhood*, 80.
19. Ibid., 111.
20. Lynn Spigel, 'From Theatre to Spaceship: Metaphors of Suburban Domesticity in Postwar America', in *Visions of Suburbia*, ed. Silverstone, 220.
21. Julian Symons, *Something Like a Love Affair*, London, 1993, 109.
22. William Trevor, *Felicia's Journey*, London and New York, 1995, 200.
23. Alan A. Jackson, *Semi-Detached London: Suburban Development, Life and Transport, 1900–39*, London, 1973, 185.
24. Jenny Diski, *Nothing Natural*, London, 1987.
25. Ibid., 7.
26. Ibid., 31.
27. Ibid., 37.
28. Ibid., 89.
29. Symons, *Something Like a Love Affair*, 7.
30. John Hartley, 'The Sexualisation of Suburbia: The Diffusion of Knowledge in the Postmodern Public Sphere', in *Visions of Suburbia*, ed. Silverstone, 182.
31. Minette Walters, *The Breaker*, London, 1999, 143.
32. Ibid., 160.
33. Colin Dexter, *The Silent World of Nicholas Quinn,* London, 1978.
34 Marcia Muller, *There's Something in a Sunday*, London, 1995, 51.
35. Ibid., 40.
36. Ibid., 63.
37. Ibid., 123.
38. Ibid., 59.
39. Ibid., 203.
40. Ibid., 24.
41. Sally R. Munt, *Murder by the Book: Feminism and the Crime Novel*, London and New York, 1994, 58.
42. Symons, *Something Like a Love Affair*, 11.
43. Cornwell, *Body of Evidence*, 11.
44. Ibid., 10.

❧ CHAPTER 7 ❧

BETWEEN SUBDIVISIONS AND SHOPPING MALLS: SIGNIFYING EVERYDAY LIFE IN THE CONTEMPORARY AMERICAN SOUTH

Joanna Price

Easter – the optimist's holiday, the holiday with the suburbs in mind, the day for all those with sunny dispositions and a staunch belief in the middle view, a tiny, tidy holiday to remember sweetly and indistinctly as the very same day through all your life.

Richard Ford, *Walker Percy: Not Just Whistling Dixie*

In America the age of the suburbs has arguably already ended, as suburbs are being superseded by 'edge cities'[1] or 'technoburbs'. Technoburbs, according to Robert Fishman, are decentralised 'socio-economic units' made viable by information technology and a network of highways with all the amenities which one needs to work and live, 'shopping malls, industrial parks ... office complexes, hospitals, schools, and a full range of housing types'.[2] The technoburb dissolves the boundaries formerly maintained by the suburbs where, for men, private life is clearly separated from the work in the city to which one must travel.

Nonetheless, the myth of suburbia persists. For writers of the contemporary American South, suburbia provides a fictional locus through which to explore the effects on individuals of the 'Americanisation' of the South. Suburbia offers a lens through which the significance attached to everyday life can be examined, at a time when the meanings ascribed to it by regional cultures are being erased by those conferred by consumer culture. The myth of suburbia constitutes an ideal locus for this exploration, concerned as it is with the production of subjectivity through the spatial and temporal determination of the meaning of everyday life. At the heart of the organisation of the meaning of life in the suburbs, which Roger Silverstone has described as 'the crucible of a shopping economy', is a tension between the fostering of civic, community-oriented behaviour, and the individualism which is cultivated by the 'commoditization of everyday life'.[3] Recent Southern writers have thus turned to suburbia as offering an already mythologized setting for the investigation of large cultural shifts in the lives of their characters, from Walker Percy's New Orleans, to Anne Tyler's Baltimore, Frederick Barthelme's Gulf Coast, Bobbie Ann Mason's western Kentucky, and Richard Ford's New Jersey. In this essay, I will focus on the representations of how suburbia confers significance upon the lives of its subjects, and the effects of this process upon them.

Bobbie Ann Mason's short story, 'Shiloh', concludes with Leroy Moffitt watching his wife, Norma Jean, who has just told him she wants to leave him: 'Now she turns toward Leroy and waves her arms. Is she beckoning to him? She seems to be doing an exercise for her chest muscles. The sky is unusually pale – the color of the dust ruffle Mabel made for their bed'.[4] Leroy is looking out at Norma Jean over the cemetery on the site of the Civil War battleground at Shiloh, but his thoughts retreat to a detail of their marital lives, the dust ruffle made by his mother-in-law. This detail is comforting in its immanence, its intractability for signifying anything other than familiar domesticity.

Critics have categorized fiction such as Mason's as 'minimalist', due to its focus on quotidian details, frequently rendered though 'depthless' tropes such as similes and non sequiturs, which seem to contain, rather than allow for, the elaboration of meaning, as would metaphor. One critic concludes, for example, that writers of such fiction, including Mason, 'give us random and unimaginatively chosen details and events, signifying nothing'.[5] The criticism intended by the term 'minimalism' is that the scope of this fiction is reduced to the ephemeral, private concerns of inconsequential characters who are cut off from the larger processes of 'history'. Moreover, the diminished world of this fiction is informed by a pessimistic philosophy wherein neither the characters, nor the author, believe in the possibility of change.[6]

However, in the case of Leroy Moffitt's dust ruffle, the preceding narrative has inscribed it with a significance that is available to the reader, although not to Leroy. For the reader, the dust ruffle is imbued with Leroy's apprehension of what may already have been lost (domestic union with his wife) and his mother-in-law's attempts to preserve the marriage. The story further construes the dust ruffle by situating Leroy's loss within a context of broad cultural transition, and here, as elsewhere in Mason's fiction, this transition is evoked by the growth of subdivisions. At the beginning of 'Shiloh', Leroy, the now unemployed truck-driver, observes the changes that have occurred in the region of his home town during the years he spent on the road: 'Subdivisions are spreading across western Kentucky like an oil slick'.[7] Through this simile, Mason succinctly evokes the recent transformations of the landscape of western Kentucky which have accompanied the passage from an agrarian to a predominantly consumer-based economy. As he looks at the landscape: 'Leroy can't figure out who is living in all the new houses. The farmers who used to gather around the courthouse square on Saturday afternoon to play checkers and spit tobacco juice have gone'.[8] In this landscape, public and private space are reorganised as agribusinesses replace small family-owned farms, and social connections are replotted around such phenomena as subdivisions, shopping malls and interstates. Superimposed on all of this is the 'hyperreal' grid of television, telephones and information technology. With the removal of a central relation to the land, significant coordinates of identity have been challenged and reconfigured by the popular media and the ideology of consumerism that it disseminates. The former determinants of the significance of everyday life, such as knowledge, gender roles and class structures related to labour on the land have been eroded, as have the traditions and histories which cohered 'community'.

Leroy is stranded in the present, as is exemplified by his failure to respond to the historical specificity of Shiloh, 'The cemetery, a green slope dotted with white markers, looks like a subdivision site'.[9] His disconnection from 'history', which, in an agrarian community, would once have been communicated through collective narratives ascribing meanings to shared memories, leaves him not only unable to plot his place in relation to public events, but perhaps more significantly, unable to interpret the details of his life. He recognises that his nostalgic fantasy of building a log cabin is ill-suited to survival in the subdivisions. By contrast, Norma Jean seems better equipped to adapt to contemporary life. She has embraced consumer culture's rescripting of the American Dream through its cannibalisation of the discourses of, among others, feminism, class-mobility and self-improvement. Through these discourses, the details of her life, such as the food she cooks and her body-building, have accrued new significance, connoting a change in class-position and gender roles.

Most of Mason's characters experience difficulty adapting to the transition from rural or small-town life to a 'lifestyle' dominated by consumer culture. In Mason's topography, subdivisions and shopping malls are the arenas in which the influence of consumer culture on her characters is most concentrated. The lives of these characters are pervaded by commodities whose significance lies in the fantasies conveyed by the images used to promote them, rather than in their use-value. These fantasies are produced by a consumer culture which turns upon 'the aestheticization of everyday life', as Mike Featherstone has put it, whereby a 'rapid flow of signs and images' confronts people 'with dream-images which speak to desires, and aestheticize and derealize reality'.[10]

Many of Mason's characters feel trapped in this culture of 'signs and images', experiencing a sense of 'culture shock' and 'exile' from the traditional cultures which would formerly have determined their identities and the significance of their lives.[11] The only repository of 'authentic' meaning uninscribed by consumerism appears to be 'nature'. In 'Coyotes', for example, Cobb reflects on his girlfriend Lynnette, who is not 'the type who would have wanted a wedding reception at the Holiday inn, a ranch house in a cozy subdivision, church on Sunday'.[12] instead, Lynnette helps Cobb see 'the unusual in the everyday'[13] and believes that 'weeds were beautiful'.[14] Lynnette is disturbed by consumer culture's aestheticisation of the real, and by the equivalence which it creates between images of the real. She works in a photography shop, and observes: 'We get amazing pictures – gunshot wounds and drownings, all mixed in with vacations and children. And the thing is, they're not unusual at all. They're everywhere, all the time. It's life'.[15] The story ends with imagery approximating an epiphany, as Cobb, disturbed by Lynnette's morbidity, watches her sitting beside a creek, into which a blue-jay's feather has fallen:

Cobb watched the feather loosen from the leaf and begin to float away in the little trickle of water in the creek bed. He tried to comprehend all that might happen to that feather as it wore away to bits – a strange thought. In a dozen years, he thought, he might look back on this moment and know that it was precisely when he should have stopped and made a rational decision to go no further, but he couldn't know that now....

Tufts of her hair fluttered slightly in the breeze, but she didn't notice. She couldn't see the way the light came through her hair like the light in spring through a leaving tree.[16]

The significance that Cobb elicits from this moment is, of course, tied to his aestheticisation of the moment, renewed as his perception has been under Lynnette's tutelage. However, the feather, the water and the tuft of Lynnette's hair escape the codification of meaning imposed by consumer culture. These natural objects retain their integrity *as* objects, whilst also sustaining metaphoric associations.

'Nature' receives a similar aestheticisation, apparently uncolonised by consumer culture, in 'Piano Fingers'. In this story, Mason depicts the alienation and sense of dissociation of the unemployed Dean. Dean's wife, Nancy, fantasises about their moving to a 'dream-house' in the Birch Hills subdivision, 'a new development of medium-priced houses on the east edge of town',[17] which, Dean wryly notes, has 'no birches, no hills'. To Dean, the commodified desirability of dream-houses in the subdivisions does not mask their lived reality. As he drives aimlessly around another subdivision, he remarks how 'on this street in the last couple of years one man, a school-board member, was arrested for molesting a child at the playground; a young woman tried to commit suicide; a child died of leukemia'.[18] The story concludes however, with Mason's suggestion of Dean's possible redemption from his aimlessness. Whilst this glimpsed transformation is not contained by his culture's determination of the everyday through consumption, it is facilitated by it. When Dean's daughter is told by her piano teacher that she has 'piano fingers', Dean decides to cultivate her gift by buying her an electronic keyboard. Dean's dissociation momentarily disperses into a sense of wonder as he contemplates his daughter: 'The little girl sitting expectantly beside Dean seems like someone he has suddenly dreamed into reality. He can hardly believe his eyes.... It is starting to snow: big, beautiful splotches – no two alike'.[19] Elsewhere in Mason's fiction, the potential for self-transformation is directly related to the scene of consumption, but to

ambiguous effect. In a 1975 essay, speaking of the spread of the
suburbs in America after the Second World War, Joan Didion
commented: 'The frontier had been reinvented, and its shape
was the subdivision, that new free land on which all settlers
could recast their lives tabula rasa'.[20] In the suburbs of the postwar period, the promise of self-reinvention offered by the neighbourhood shops or shopping centre in traditional suburbs was
constrained by their spatial incorporation into the mundane
routines of everyday life. However, the shopping mall, that
inevitable excrescence of more recent suburbs, which is typi-
cally located outside the suburbs 'at the intersection of major
"feeder" roads',[21] surrounded by parking lots for thousands of
cars, provides in part an escape from daily routines. According
to Rob Shields, the shopping mall is a 'liminal zone', a 'controlled' environment in which the subject is persuaded that,
freed from 'the routines of everyday, proper behaviour', she can
reinvent herself in a perpetual present.[22] Here, the shopper or
browser can observe the spectacle of consumption and participate in the fantasy that the purchase of commodities will
enable the creation of the desired persona and lifestyle. Lauren
Langman has commented that within the shopping mall,
'Everyday life has been transformed into an extension of consumer capitalism and the person rendered a consumer or spectator in whom the commodified meanings, the symbolic and
affective values embedded in the sign system, have been interi-
orized as representations of reality'.[23] As Langman's comment
suggests, however, the modes of perception and ideology which
are cultivated by the shopping mall recast the subject's inter-
pretation of her 'everyday' life when she returns to it.

In Mason's story 'The Secret of the Pyramids', a shopping
mall provides the locus for her protagonist's attempt to rein-
terpret her life, following its destabilisation by bereavement.
Mason describes Barbara's grief when she discovers, via a television bulletin, that her former lover has been killed in a car
crash. Barbara's sense of self-estrangement in her grief is com-
pounded both by the fact that she had previously ended her
affair with her married lover, and that in her illicit position as
Bob Morganfield's former lover, she cannot openly participate
in the rituals of a community of mourners. The shopping mall
where Barbara works and where Bob Morganfield owned a
shoe store both symbolises and has contributed to their alienated lives. Barbara searches through her memories to find
something that will invest her relationship with Morganfield
with significance. She savours her memory of visiting a restau-

rant in Cairo (on the Mississippi in Illinois) with Morganfield, and how Morganfield explained to her 'what the young boys came to Cairo for – to learn the secret of the pyramids'.[24] To Barbara, this exotic piece of apocrypha evokes a key to hidden significances, 'images of secret maps and treasures, hidden away in safe places'.[25] The image leads her to observe to Bob that 'you hide your real self. That's what keeps me interested'. Her remark prompts Bob to volunteer something about himself, but his disclosure reveals a depthlessness and ephemerality which is characteristic of the fantasies of consumer culture to which it relates. He explains how, early that morning, 'I was in the center of the mall, by the fountain, and everything looked so fresh and new, like the whole place was about to bust open like a flower as soon as the stores opened'. Upon seeing a girl in a yellow dress, he 'had one of those realisations – one of those moments you know you'll remember all your life?' Bob's realisation is that 'I hated myself' and that 'what I wanted to do was rollerskate down the mall', which, however, he could not, 'because of my reputation'.[26] Bob's meagre epiphany, wherein the shopping mall stimulates a fantasy of self-transformation, reverberates through the estrangement that Barbara experiences in the shopping mall following the shock of his death. On the one hand, the simulated environment triggers a memory which informs a fantasy of possibility and change: she 'loves the lighting in the mall' which 'makes her think of that sunset on the Mississippi River last year. Something is always happening; it is never the same, like the churning river'. On the other hand, the mall presents a spectacle of alienation: 'It is the only quality mall for more than a hundred miles, and people from the country and the small towns congregate here on the weekend.... Everyone looks dazed'.[27] It seems to Barbara that the alienating mechanisms of consumerism extend even to the rites for the dead. The reifying gaze of the consumer colonises Morganfield's death. To Barbara, reading of the death in the newspaper, Morganfield, 'was a distant figure, like a celebrity'[28] and in the funeral home, his 'body [was] lying in the casket like a store display'.[29]

On her return to her apartment, Bob's absence from Barbara's everyday life away from the mall is revealed when she attempts to 'locate his traces'. These prove to be a tourist's memorabilia, which she has collected from hotels and restaurants they have visited. Barbara decides to dispose of them, yet the conclusion of the story suggests that she can salvage something that signifies, or at least, is usable, from her ephemeral affair. She finds 'a pink Elvis Presley clock shaped like a guitar' which Morganfield had given her, and she recognises that 'it is an absurd clock, but a good one ... it keeps time perfectly'.[30]

The scenes which Mason sets in shopping malls in her novel *In Country* also convey an ambivalence about the fantasies of the transformation of one's everyday life which consumer culture fosters. The narrative recounts the attempt of its protagonist to learn about the identity of her father who died in the Vietnam War, before she was born. To the 1980s teenager Samantha (Sam) Hughes, American soldiers' experiences of Vietnam signify much that her own culture lacks, associated, as the war is for her, with various trends of the 1960s. It connotes, for example, strong (masculine) community and an intensified and extreme experience of 'the real'. By contrast, the opportunities afforded to women by another phenomenon arising in the 1960s, second-wave feminism, hold little promise to Sam. Instead, in a televisual culture where 'Johnny Carson had Joan Rivers substituting.... And it's a rerun. Nothing's authentic anymore',[31] Sam is seduced by the commodification of herself as a means of escaping the quotidian. She and her friend Dawn fantasise about making a video in which they will 'wear black leather pants and sunglasses with bright pink rims',[32] although when Dawn suggests that 'we could go hang out at one of those bars in Paducah where those traveling business men go. We could wear our sexiest outfits and they'd think we were a lot older. Maybe they'd buy us something to eat and give us some money,' Sam demurs, 'I'd be satisfied if we could just go to the mall in Paducah'.[33]

The shopping mall provides an escape variously from the sameness of daily life in small-town western Kentucky, the fetid clutter of the farm life from which she is but one generation removed and the appalling experiences of both the Vietnamese and the American soldiers in Vietnam, with which she is confronted when she reads her father's war diary in the 'safe' and anonymous space of the shopping mall. Aspects of the shopping mall enable Sam, through an act of imaginative transformation, to convert it into a 'microsphere of empowerment'[34] which counters her culture's homogenising processes. The shopping mall in Maryland, which Sam visits as she and her relatives travel to Washington D.C. to visit the Vietnam Veterans Memorial, provides her with stimuli to fantasy, whereby she can transform her everyday life *by* reconnecting it with 'history' – albeit a history which is in part fantasised. The mall is reassuring in its homogenising repetition of the familiar – 'The same store is in Paducah' (Kentucky) – although its products, specifically 'punk outfits', 'bring out that urge in her to be outlandish', to which end she buys some 'black leather-look panties'. This purchase indicates that consumerism recuperates the 'resistance' which it generates, by translating that resistance into a matter of personal style. Further, when Sam imagines that the palm trees growing in the controlled climate of the mall are the foliage of Southeast Asia, her act of historicising projection is recommodified as 'all of these scenes travel through her mind like a rock-video sequence'.[35] A Bruce Springsteen album, however, seems to transcend its own commodification: on the cover of *Born in the U.S.A.* Springsteen is depicted looking at the American flag, 'as though studying it, trying to figure out its meaning'.[36] Throughout the narrative, Springsteen has configured for Sam a contesting voice, both insofar as his songs represent elements of an American underclass, which includes Vietnam veterans, and in his articulation of sexual desire, which although solicited by consumer culture, ultimately becomes unrecuperable by it. When Sam leaves the mall to continue her journey to the Vietnam Veterans Memorial, Springsteen, co-opted as he is by his status as a celebrity, provides her with a model of how to be an interrogative reader of her country's icons.

Mason's fiction variously illustrates and challenges the view, most (in)famously articulated by Jean Baudrillard, that '"consumption" has grasped the whole of life' and that every detail of daily life has been appropriated by a totalising signifying system.[37] In *In Country*, however, Sam Hughes's response to the 'commoditisation of everyday life' could be interpreted as showing that, because consumer culture depends upon the operation of desire, which to an extent it constructs, the signifiers of consumerism, and the subject's response to them, will always be radically unstable.

The determination of the significance of the everyday by consumer culture is at the heart of suburban life, in whose ideologies those of consumerism are embedded. However, in the fiction of at least one writer of the contemporary American South, Richard Ford, suburbia is invoked as the consolatory myth in which the relation between a signifier and its signified is secure, thereby delineating a stable position for the subject. At the same time, he deconstructs this myth, revealing its inherent contradictions.

In his fiction about the myth of suburbia, Ford is concerned with characters whose lives and identities have been profoundly troubled by events that have called into question not only the over-arching structures of their lives, but also their ability to interpret the local details and shapes of their lives. The myth of suburbia is designed to naturalise the meanings ascribed to the everyday; it coordinates how one divides one's time between work and leisure, and the significance given to these activities. In mythologized suburbia, the map onto which everyday life is conventionally plotted comprises 'the commuter schedule for the husband, the nursery and social schedule for the wife, the school day for the growing child'.[38] 'Suburbia' determines the significance one attaches to the space one occupies: the privacy of the home and the 'neighbourly' interactions of the street, the shopping centre, the school, the church and the club.[39] The ideology of consumerism, as disseminated by the media, compounds the naturalisation of the meanings informing everyday life by co-opting its details to the narrative of the progress of the ideal white, middle-class nuclear family, whose survival and prospering provides the ideological and economic raison d'être of the suburbs.

In a discussion of 'suburban culture' in the fiction of Frederick Barthelme, Robert H. Brinkmeyer, Jr. has argued that the representation of suburbia invites the defamiliarisation of the mundane for two reasons. Firstly, the suburban world is a 'frontier world', in the case of Barthelme's Gulf Coast settings, a frontier between land and sea, but more generally, between city and country. The representation of such a world, Brinkmeyer argues, has an 'evocative power' which inherently contains a collision 'between two opposing realms of order and understanding'.[40] Roger Silverstone's proposition that suburbia is a 'social' and 'cultural' 'hybrid,' in that it is 'not nature, not culture; not country, not city',[41] similarly points to the susceptibility of the myth of suburbia to its own denaturalisation. This is particularly so given its dependence on the rather fragile – if fiercely defended – exclusion of all that which is construed and feared as 'other' to the suburban self. Brinkmeyer further proposes that the fact that suburbia is comprised of artefacts also invites its own defamiliarisation. Because Frederick Barthelme's 'suburban world' is 'a postmodernist world of surfaces, textures and signs', rather than a modernist world of perceived essences, it invites the observer of or participant in suburban life to undertake an imaginative act which will 'transfix and transfigure' and 'remake anew'.[42]

Suburbia also provides a consolatory myth which is both invoked and deconstructed in Richard Ford's novels, *The Sports-*

writer (1986) and its sequel, *Independence Day* (1995). Ford was born in Mississippi, but has chosen to live in many states. When asked about the concept of 'Southern' writing, he has commented: 'southern regionalism as a factor in the impulse that makes us write novels … has had its day…. The south has become the regrettable "Sunbelt"…. The south is not a place any more: it's a Belt, a business proposition, which is the nearest thing to anonymity the economy recognizes'.[43] Frank Bascombe, the protagonist of *The Sportswriter* and *Independence Day*, is the ironic champion of suburbia, precisely because it erases regional specificity, amongst other traditional determinants of identity.

Independence Day finds Frank Bascombe working as a realtor in the suburbs. Frank's profession, combined with his attempt to rehabilitate his errant son, and the setting of the novel over an Independence Day holiday, afford the narrative pretexts for his exploration of two of the mythicised strands of American identity that inform the ideology of suburbia. One strand is associated with community, neighbourliness, security and civic behaviour; and the other with independence, self-reliance and individual responsibility – particularly inasmuch as these are connected with the ownership of private property. Weaving these two potentially contradictory strands together, Frank hopes, will enable one to sustain 'the high-wire act of normalcy'.[44] While *Independence Day* is largely concerned with exploring the tenability of the metanarratives which inform concepts of American individual and national identity, as articulated through the myth of suburbia, *The Sportswriter* focuses on the significance of everyday life in the suburbs.

At the opening of *The Sportswriter* Frank Bascombe, the writer of a 'serious' novel, has turned to sportswriting instead, and has embraced life in the suburbs of Haddam, New Jersey. Both of these moves attest to Frank's decision to become a 'proponent of forgetting',[45] to avoid introspection and forget 'history', especially his own. A particular reason for Frank's adoption of this position is that his familiar world has been shattered by the death of his young son, and his subsequent estrangement from his wife 'X', and their two surviving children.

The narrative takes place over an Easter weekend, which begins at five o'clock on Good Friday morning with Frank meeting X at their son's grave to observe the anniversary of his death. As Frank awaits X in the neighbourhood cemetery, the demarcation of time through the quotidian in the suburbs is emphasised by the sounds of his elderly neighbours playing tennis in their yard. To commemorate his son, Frank begins

reading a 'Meditation' by Theodore Roethke, which he interprets as being about 'letting the everyday make you happy –
insects, shadows, the color of a woman's hair'.[46] X interrupts
him, however, expressing her distaste for the poem, which
confirms Frank's belief that 'I don't know how to mourn and
neither does X'.[47]

Frank, an eminently self-reflexive narrator who maintains
an ironic awareness of the discrepancy between what he propounds and what he seeks, concludes that 'transcendent
themes' are a fabrication and the preserve of 'literature', and
that instead he will become a celebrant of the immanent and
the everyday. He develops a lexicon of concepts through which
to elaborate this position, foremost amongst which are 'the fac-
tual' and 'the literal'. A 'literalist' is one who can experience
being entirely within the moment and within oneself, such that
'the distance is closed between what you feel and what you
might *also* feel',[48] unlike Frank, who is 'always able to "see
around the sides" of whatever I was feeling'.[49] Frank illustrates
the distinction between a literalist and a factualist with the following example: 'A literalist is a man who will enjoy an afternoon watching people while stranded in an airport in Chicago,
while a factualist can't stop wondering why his plane was late
out of Salt Lake, and gauging whether they'll still serve dinner
or just a snack'.[50] A literalist is receptive to the 'mystery' of the
everyday, 'mystery' being 'the twiney promise of unknown
things ... which you must be wise enough to explore not too
deeply, for fear you will dead-end in nothing but facts'.[51]

Suburbia provides the ideal habitat for the literalist, in that
it offers 'the most diverting and readable of landscapes', whose
'language is always American'.[52] Through the myth of suburbia, worrisome ambiguity is erased, giving solace to the contemporary subject such as Frank, who finds that nowadays
'it's harder to judge what is and isn't essential'.[53] Suburbia's
foregrounding of the ordinary and the everyday allows 'mystery' precisely because its appearances and surfaces, so closely
guarded by suburban subjects, refract glimpses of depths and
essences. Haddam is 'a town of mailers and home shoppers',[54]
and in the extremity of his 'dreaminess', or self-estrangement,
Frank turns to mail-order catalogues as delivering a pure form
of the suburban mythology. He explains of 'the life portrayed
in the catalogs' that:

> In me it fostered an odd assurance that some things outside my
> life were okay still; that the same men and women standing by

the familiar brick fireplaces, or by the same comfortable canopy beds, holding these same shotguns or blow poles or boot warmers or boxes of kindling sticks could see a good day beyond their eyes right into perpetuity. Things were knowable, safe-and-sound. Everybody with exactly what they need or could get. A perfect illustration of how the literal can become the mildly mysterious.[55]

Frank's life and identity having been profoundly unsettled, he allows himself to be consoled by the apparent stability which is conferred upon the signifiers of consumer culture by the simplifying abstractions to which they refer: the changelessness of everyday life, where the nuclear family exists harmoniously 'into perpetuity', with men and women in their familiar places.

The narrative does not, of course, allow Frank to continue inhabiting the world of suburban appearances. Frank's flight from himself and his past takes him on an odyssey through suburban culture, where he has a series of encounters with the 'otherness' which suburbia purports to exclude. Pursuing his fantasy of the ephemeral and the superficial, Frank dates Vicki Arcenault, a resident of a 'theme-organized housing development', Pheasant Run. Vicki has furnished her condominium 'in a one-day whirlwind trip to the Miracle Furniture Mile in Paramus',[56] and she therefore appears to have created a persona free of 'history'. To Frank, she promises to be 'a girl for every modern occasion', such that he finds 'I can be interested in the smallest particulars of her life'.[57] Vicki resists this construction of herself, however, choosing to disclose to Frank events and relationships from her past which depress him with their 'bedrock factuality'. Frank accepts Vicki's invitation to an Easter Sunday lunch with her family, hoping to salvage their relationship. He is greeted by 'a near life-size figure of Jesus-crucified' hanging on the Arcenaults' house in Barnegat Pines, which he immediately interprets as another example of the retreat of meaning, whether it be historical or religious, from suburban signifiers; the crucifix is simply an example of suburban bad taste, 'Jesus in his suburban agony'.[58] He finds, however, that the members of the Arcenault family espouse diverse philosophies of life which cannot be assimilated to the suburban preoccupation with appearances. Vicki herself ends the relationship, refusing Frank's embrace of ephemerality; of 'every sweet untranscendent little thing we know or think we know'.[59]

A parallel dénouement occurs in Frank's acquaintance with Walter Luckett, a fellow member of the Divorced Men's Club. Frank enjoys his meetings with the other members of the club specifically because they seem to bear out his belief that the suburbs 'are not a place where friendships flourish',[60] but instead are conducive to superficial alliances. Walter Luckett insists on valuing his 'friendship' with Frank, however, which he demonstrates by disclosing to Frank his guilt about a recent homosexual encounter. Walter's subsequent suicide prompts Frank to temporarily relinquish his suburban fantasy, as he asserts: 'Life-forever is a lie of the suburbs – its worst lie – and a fact worth knowing before you get caught in its fragrant silly dream'.[61] The narrative concludes, however, with Frank, who has left Haddam, attempting to sustain the belief that there is merit in accepting that one has 'a past, even an imputed and remote one',[62] whilst also maintaining that 'some life is only life, and unconjugatable'.[63]

The suburbia to which Frank Bascombe assents when he comments that 'nowadays I'm willing to say yes to as much as I can: yes to my town, my neighborhood, my neighbor, yes to his car, her lawn and hedge and rain gutters',[64] has already passed, if it ever existed. Nonetheless, at a time of transition from the diversity of regional cultures to the homogenisation of American consumer culture, the very constancy of the myth of suburbia provides Southern writers such as Mason and Ford with a lens through which to scrutinise the ideological and representational structures by which the significance of the everyday is established. Through this lens, the intrinsic instability of the determination of everyday life by consumer culture is revealed.

Notes

1. Joel Garreau, *Edge City: Life on the New Frontier*, New York, 1991.
2. Robert Fishman, *Bourgeois Utopias: The Rise and Fall of Suburbia*, New York, 1987, 184.
3. Roger Silverstone, 'Introduction', in *Visions of Suburbia*, ed. Roger Silverstone, London and New York, 1997, 8.
4. Bobbie Ann Mason, 'Shiloh', in *Shiloh and other Stories*, 1995, 9.
5. Ben Yagoda, 'No Tense Like the Present', *New York Times Book Review* 10 August 1986, 30.
6. See Barbara Henning, 'Minimalism and the American Dream: "Shiloh" by Bobbie Ann Mason and "Preservation" by Raymond Carver', *Modern Fiction Studies* 35, no. 4 (Winter 1989), 690; Robert Dunn, 'Fiction That Shrinks From Life', *New York Times Book Review* 30 June 1985, 13, 24, 25; and John Barth, 'A Few Words About Minimalism', *New York Times Book Review* 28 December 1986, 1, 2, 25.
7. Mason, 'Shiloh', 3.
8. Ibid., 3–4.

9. Ibid., 15.
10. Mike Featherstone, *Consumer Culture and Postmodernism*, London, 1991, 67, 68.
11. Lila Havens, 'Residents and Transients: An Interview With Bobbie Ann Mason', *Crazyhorse 29* (Fall 1985), 95 and 102.
12. Bobbie Ann Mason, 'Coyotes', in *Love Life*, London, 1990, 181.
13. Ibid., 182.
14. Ibid., 179.
15. Ibid., 192.
16. Ibid., 198.
17. Bobbie Ann Mason, 'Piano Fingers', in *Love Life*, 100.
18. Ibid., 110.
19. Ibid., 113.
20. Joan Didion, *The White Album*, Harmondsworth, Middlesex, 1981, 181.
21. Rob Shields, 'Introduction', in *Lifestyle Shopping: The Subject of Consumption*, ed. Rob Shields, London and New York, 1992, 4.
22. Shields, 'Introduction', in Rob Shields, ed. *Lifestyle Shopping*, 7.
23. Lauren Langman, 'Neon Cages: Shopping for Subjectivity', in Rob Shields ed. *Lifestyle Shopping*, 47.
24. Bobbie Ann Mason, 'The Secret of the Pyramids', in *Love Life*, 87.
25. Ibid., 87.
26. Ibid., 88.
27. Ibid., 90.
28. Ibid., 91.
29. Ibid., 94.
30. Ibid., 95.
31. Bobbie Ann Mason, *In Country*, London 1990, 19.
32. Ibid., 104.
33. Ibid., 43.
34. J. Fiske, quoted by Lauren Langman, in 'Neon Cages', 48.
35. Mason, *In Country*, 237.
36. Ibid., 236.
37. Jean Baudrillard, 'Consumer Society' (1970), in *Jean Baudrillard: Selected Writings*, ed. Mark Poster, Cambridge, 1989, 33, 35.
38. Robert C.Wood, *Suburbia: Its People and Their Politics*, Boston, 1958, 6.
39. See Anthony Downs's discussion of neighbourhood interactions in *Opening Up the Suburbs: An Urban Strategy for America*, New Haven and London, 1973, 61.
40. Robert H. Brinkmeyer, Jr., 'Suburban Culture, Imaginative Wonder: The Fiction of Frederick Barthelme', *Studies in the Literary Imagination 27*, no.2 (Fall 1994), 110.
41. Silverstone, 'Introduction', in Silverstone ed., *Visions of Suburbia*, 7, 8.
42. Brinkmeyer, 'Suburban Culture', 113. Henri Lefebvre makes a similar point about consumer culture in general in *Everyday Life in the Modern World*, trans. Sacha Rabinovitch, London, 1971, 90. He argues that: 'The act of consuming is as much an act of the imagination ... as a real act ... and therefore metaphorical ... and metonymical'. Thus consumption always provides a 'fluid frontier' between 'imaginary consumption or the consumption of make believe ... and real consumption'.
43. Richard Ford, 'Walker Percy: Not Just Whistling Dixie', *National Review 29* (13 May 1977), 561–2.
44. Richard Ford, *Independence Day*, London, 1995, 94.

45. Richard Ford, *The Sportswriter*, London, 1989, 150.
46. Ibid., 25.
47. Ibid., 17.
48. Ibid., 71.
49. Ibid., 70.
50. Ibid., 139.
51. Ibid., 101–8.
52. Ibid., 58.
53. Ibid., 57.
54. Ibid., 55.
55. Ibid., 202.
56. Ibid., 63.
57. Ibid., 61.
58. Ibid., 249.
59. Ibid., 254.
60. Ibid., 85.
61. Ibid., 325.
62. Ibid., 377.
63. Ibid., 375.
64. Ibid., 58.

CHAPTER 8

URBAN THRALL: RENEGOTIATING THE SUBURBAN SELF IN NICK HORNBY'S *FEVER PITCH* AND *HIGH FIDELITY*

Daniel Lea

In his polemical essay on the identification of British pop culture with the concerns of the suburban imaginary, Simon Frith has argued for a delimited definition of suburban demography:

> Suburban culture, whether shaped by pop or the BBC, is white culture, white English culture, white south-eastern English culture; it describes an urban phenomenon, the media domination of London, the concentrated site of both political and cultural power.[1]

Articulated in this statement is the implicit dependency of suburbia on external definitions of the quality of the suburban experience. Discourses of suburbia have repeatedly foregrounded the liminal nature of the suburbs and the consequent fluidity of identity across the boundaries of traditional country and city typologies. For Roger Silverstone the suburbs are 'always defined by what the country and city are not'[2] and cultural expressions of suburban identity are perpetually caught within the paradox of this hybridity. Recent literary versions of suburbia are characterised by their explorations of the condition of 'in-betweenness' reflecting an uncomfortably rootless position ascribed to the suburbs in contemporary cul-

ture. Nick Hornby's writing articulates the problematical negotiation of identity across the borders of urban and suburban
spaces. In *Fever Pitch* (1992) and *High Fidelity* (1995) the equivocal status of the suburbanite is highlighted, but more importantly, the marginality of the suburbs is seen as a direct
reflection of the decentering of the self within urban/suburban
culture. Both texts situate their protagonists firmly in a suburban environment but display their ambivalence towards that
position, and reveal an irresistible urge to return ritualistically
to the city in search of vitality, meaning and direction. It is the
psychosocial distance that exists between these two states, and
not the condition of being either urban or suburban, which is
repeatedly emphasised. It is within this space of penumbra
that the selves of Hornby and Rob Fleming are generated, rendering them quintessentially hybrid, and condemning them
ultimately to identity crisis.[3] The intention of this essay is to
explore the impulse, explicit in Hornby's writing, to discard
the shell of the suburban self in favour of one fashioned
within an urban context. *Fever Pitch* and *High Fidelity* depict an
imperative to return to the metropolitan centre to discover the
limits and parameters of the self. In that reclamation of the
urban, it is possible to discern an attempt to define the suburban by comparison, but also to escape from the perceived class
homogeneity of the suburbs by embracing the traditionally
working-class leisure pursuits of football and rock music.

Fever Pitch details the obsessional relationship that Nick
Hornby has with Arsenal Football Club and constitutes a form
of confessional analysis into the nature of such obsession. The
narrative is intended as an expiation of the guilt Hornby feels
for allowing the club to dominate his thoughts and actions,
but it is also a confused attempt to understand the circumstances which brought about this all-consuming fascination.
The initial identification of the self with the football club
begins the process of transition by which Hornby psychologically associates himself with the city, and by which the city
itself becomes symbolically representative of meaning and
direction. Whereas Hornby's suburban home in Maidenhead
connotes fracture and familial dissonance, the urban environment of north London suggests belonging, support and collective interest. As presented in *Fever Pitch*, football is first raised
in the consciousness of Hornby as a desperate act of palliation
by his father after his separation from Hornby's mother.
Unable to find a suitably involving activity for his infrequent
visits to the family, the father resorts to Highbury as a final

measure. The contiguity of the family's dissolution and Hornby's introduction to football is hardly coincidental, and the narrator openly acknowledges the interconnection.[4] Infatuation is therefore born out of fracture and it is clear that the trauma of separation is mitigated for Hornby through his growing love of Arsenal. The domestic stability, which he has lost within his familial context, is replaced by the solidity and predictability of the football experience. The regular Saturday outings provide a channel of displaced communication through which the father and son can enact a pastiche of a normal relationship:

> Saturday afternoons in north London gave us a context in which we could be together. We could talk when we wanted, football gave us something to talk about (and anyway silences weren't oppressive), and the days had a structure, a routine. The Arsenal pitch was to be our lawn ... the Gunners Fish Bar on Blackstock Road our kitchen; and the West Stand our home.[5]

Significant here is the reconstruction of a domestic scenario within the context of a public arena. It is an example of what Yi-Fu Tuan has termed 'topophilia' – the installation of a specific location as containing a complex series of symbolic associations for the individual that initiates an emotional, and often devotional, relationship with that place.[6] The ritualistic return to Highbury functions as a therapeutic salve to the dislocation of family breakdown. Hornby projects his own desires for security and stability on the blank canvas of experience, creating the specific articles of domestic life – a lawn, a kitchen and, on a wider scale, the home.

An important feature of this father/son bonding experience is the strongly gendered context within which it takes place. Hornby accentuates the masculine inclusivity of the spectacle by excluding any female influence – his mother and sister are confined firmly to the home and, significantly, are never seen against an urban backdrop. Silverstone has pointed to the gendering of suburbia as a feminine domain[7] and others[8] have explored the extent to which women have been presented as 'naturally' inclined to the suburban lifestyle. In contrast to the male in suburbia, who desperately seeks escape and freedom (Medhurst cites Reginald Perrin as archetype), popular culture has portrayed women as emotionally predisposed towards the security and domesticity of the suburbs. Hornby perpetuates this stereotypical dichotomy. Football represents an escape into a masculine world from the overly feminised influence of the suburbs. The city becomes a space symbolically endowed with masculine qualities and the football stadium provides unfettered opportunity not only to express that masculinity, but also to learn what constitutes the limits of a gendered behaviour. Because suburbia offers him an identity based only upon what he perceives as feminine values, the escape to the city, as an affirmation of his masculine identity, becomes imperative.

Domestic crisis impels Hornby into football and simultaneously into a masculinised world, but his continuing obsession with Arsenal is fundamentally fuelled by the sense of inauthenticity and rootlessness that Hornby experiences in the suburbs. The distance between the suburbs and the city is continually foregrounded, such as in the suggestion that the 1960s 'took another seven or eight years to travel the twenty-odd miles down the M4 from London'.[9] Transforming himself into a 'naturalised' north Londoner through the identification of himself with the football club becomes an overt attempt to escape the implied mundanity of suburban life. The reasons behind his conscious metamorphosis are articulated in the following passage:

> The white south of England middle-class Englishman and woman is the most rootless creature on earth; we would rather belong to any other community in the world.... Hence the phenomenon of mock-belonging, whereby pasts and backgrounds are manufactured and massaged in order to provide some kind of acceptable cultural identity.... Ever since I have been old enough to understand what it means to be suburban I have wanted to come from somewhere else, preferably north London. I have already dropped as many aithches as I can – and I use plural verb forms with singular subjects whenever possible.... And what is suburban post-war, middle-class English culture anyway? Jeffrey Archer and *Evita*, Flanders and Swann and the Goons, Adrian Mole and Merchant Ivory, *Francis Durbridge Presents* ... and John Cleese's silly walk? It's no wonder we all wanted to be Muddy Waters and Charlie George.[10]

The cultural baggage that attends suburbia makes the experience of residence dispiriting and desperate. In order to escape this pernicious influence, the individual is required to recreate him or herself, fashioning an identity based upon falsity and wish-fulfilment. Any rebellion against the oppressive conformity of suburbia necessitates a compromise of the self and a blurring of the boundaries of identity. Hornby accuses the suburbs of perpetuating a cycle of falsity and imitation, reducing the 'Mockneys or the cod Irish, the black wannabees or the pseudo Sloanes'[11] to a form of schizophrenia.

Underpinning much of *Fever Pitch* is Hornby's paranoid fear that he will be discovered as a suburban interloper in north London and that his passion for the club is degraded by his physical distance from the stadium. A tension exists between his idealised identity, which is coherent, whole and culturally meaningful, and his actual identity, which is fractured, indefinite and problematic. By assuming the mannerisms of a north Londoner, Hornby attempts to circumvent his own perception of the debased quality of his support for Arsenal. The conscious transformation which he initiates is intended to produce a condition of, what Edward Relph has called, 'existential insideness'.[12] By locating Highbury and Arsenal as the nexus of his geographical, emotional and psychological existence, Hornby can be seen to be attempting to legitimise his adopted home as his actual home. In Relph's terms, Hornby strives to erect an authentic sense of place, which contrasts sharply with the inauthenticity of his suburban sense of place. In order to achieve an indisputable state of 'insideness', the process of identification requires the replacement of existing codes of identity with new parameters and terms of definition. It is significant that with the projection of an idealised home environment onto Highbury, the players and staff of the club become an extension of his family, and the fortunes of the team come to reflect upon the condition of his own family life. When the team loses, Hornby experiences a deep sense of personal betrayal as if a member of the family group had rejected him. This is particularly evident in the series of defeats incurred in cup finals, when the most intense expectation is replaced by an extreme sense of dejection. His father's pragmatic approach to defeat instils in the young Hornby a violent reaction in which he claims to have been betrayed three times, not only by his father but by the extended unit of his family – the team.[13] The implied reference to Christ's betrayal is not coincidental, Hornby is crucified on the cross of his own expectation, betrayed by those closest to him, and, because he has installed the team as part of his own self, betrayed by his own self.[14]

Such imagery evidences the extent to which Hornby's adoration of Arsenal becomes a form of self-examination. At regular intervals the narrator opines that to be a football fan demands the acceptance of a love/hate relationship with the game,[15] and for Hornby, 'fandom' enacts itself as a periodic oscillation between the acceptance and rejection of the self. The extrapolation of the team's failure onto the psychological condition of the supporter is normalised given the circumstances of identification whereby the team actually becomes part of the self. The symbiosis between individual and club is illustrated in a confrontation that takes place during Hornby's flirtation with a teaching career. Faced with a reluctant and taciturn student, the narrator attempts to appeal to the boy through reference to their mutual passion for Arsenal. The child's response is a sulky 'What do *you* know about it?'[16] at which Hornby explodes into a series of intricate questions about the club:

> 'Who scored for us in the `69 League Cup Final? Who went in goal when Bob Wilson got carried off in`72 at Villa Park? Who did we get from Spurs in exchange for David Jenkins? Who ...?' [*sic*][17]

In challenging Hornby's knowledge, the child effectively challenges his justification to life. Clearly Hornby feels that he needs to prove his relevance to Arsenal, partly because of his lingering perception of his distance from the club. Ironically, the distance is unconsciously reiterated by the student, placing emphasis on the age of Hornby as the alienating factor, a tactic which connects this displacement with that he felt at being geographically distanced from north London. Because Arsenal is so immanently conjoined to his sense of self, an attack on his knowledge of the club automatically infers a personal attack on his right to existence. The only way in which Hornby can refute such claims is by reeling off a series of data, which not only proves his interest, but also proves the historical longevity of that interest. In this response, Hornby constructs his own archaeology of the self, which taxonomically provides the basis for his continued existence. The distortion of his ego has brought about an inability to distinguish in his own mind between the boundaries of himself and the boundaries of Arsenal. Therefore, because he and the club are synonymously related, his own personal history can only be defined in terms of his relationship with the club.[18] Ultimately the only justification that he has for his life is a torrent of trivia questions, and his ability to answer them reinforces his self-worth.

The deliberate construction of a positive identity to counteract the negative pressure of his suburban origins informs this process of psychological projection. London is transformed into a vortex, which draws Hornby back to the centre with a ritualistic regularity. The journey becomes a quasi-religious ceremony in which his rootless and bland suburban self is converted in a rooted and defined persona. The lure of the city is seen as a temptation that Hornby cannot resist and to which he reacts passively, ensuring his complete identification of the urban condition with all things exotic and active. However, the sense of belonging that Hornby derives from his sojourns in the city is not unproblematic. The paralleling of his own fortunes with those of Arsenal, and the submission of his individuality to a corporate identity, are stringent attempts to construct an urban-dwelling alter-ego through which the suburban Hornby can live vicariously. The difficulties arising from this compromise revolve around his underlying sense of alienation even whilst within Highbury itself.

One area in which this ambivalence manifests itself is in his palpable sense of middle-class angst at his intrusion into a traditionally working-class game. The distance which exists between Hornby and Arsenal, and which is expressed very literally by their geographical rupture, also exists on a societal level and pivots on Hornby's perception of his class-isolation. A recurring concern in the book is the uncomfortable interaction between the working-class traditions of the game and a middle-class invasion of the stand in the period after the decline in hooliganism. Pervading *Fever Pitch* is the sense that the middle-class appropriation of the game is an insidious usurpation of a working-class bastion. Hornby feels that the middle-class supporter is, to some extent, always mimicking the 'traditional' fan but never belonging with the same degree of security. His impression of class extraneousness can be seen in his response both to the threat and to the actuality of violence, which he locates as emerging in a carnivalesque explosion from the lower-class sections of Arsenal's support.

His first encounter with hooliganism is when attacked by two black 'Secondary Modern'[19] boys who punch him and steal his scarf. His reaction is a momentary appreciation of the gulf which separates him, 'a wimp from the sticks'[20] from 'the planet Real Life, the planet Secondary Modern, the planet Inner City'.[21] This is superseded by a degree of shame and self-disgust which leads him to the conclusion that he deserves to be brutalised as part of the discourse of the experience of football.[22] Hornby always conceives his social position as ex-centric and fundamentally insignificant. To be middle-class means to be nothing definite or meaningful, and the overt parallel is drawn between the equivocal position of the middle class and the geographical liminality of the suburbs, positioned between the city and the country. Furthermore, the Secondary Modern inner-city boys are presented as having an undisputed claim to attack him, because they represent an underprivileged minority grouping for whom football has traditionally offered a means of social, or at least emotional, escape. Again, Hornby's presumptions bring to the fore his unspoken conviction that his support of Arsenal is illegitimate. He finds it impossible to reconcile his own social status with his conditioned response to the sociological function of the game as a form of community cement. Therefore, despite the subjugation of his own individuality to the influence of the team, his association with Arsenal has effected only an ambiguous sense of belonging.

Hornby's relationship with the hooligans and the working classes in general, is unresolved, and is characterised by a certain amount of moral fluidity. He sees the moment when he abandons the schoolboy's enclosure for the 'North Bank' (from where much of the violence emanates) as a rite of passage.[23] The younger Hornby revels in what he calls 'urban hooligan fantasies'[24] through chanting and intimidation, and as much as he disapproves of the excesses of violence, a sense of enclosure within a group whose identity is strongly demarcated, is irresistibly attractive to that part of him that yearns for a sense of community and belonging. Football offers him the opportunity to reclaim a form of urban, working-class past, which, to his mind, equates to meaning, purpose and definition. That it is a past which is entirely fictional and artificially generated limits the potential for complete identification. Ambivalence always characterises his reaction to the city and to Arsenal because, despite the wish-fulfilment of his fantasies, he cannot escape the circumstances of his past. One image is particularly appropriate for this sense of rootlessness. Describing the impact on football of the influx of a new middle-class audience in the early 1990s, he cites the atmosphere generated by the core traditional support as one of the prime attractions. However, with the influx of the new spectators, and the concomitant rise of ticket prices, the lower-class fan-base has gradually been eroded:

> Who'll make the noise now? Will the suburban middle-class kids and their mums and dads still come if they have to generate it themselves? Or will they feel that they have been conned? Because in effect the clubs have sold them tickets to a show in which the principal attraction has been moved to make room for them.[25]

Given his own background, this criticism of the new audience for football tends towards the self-reflexive. It encapsulates Hornby's contradictory relationship with Arsenal and with football in general. By his own definition, he becomes a parasite, feeding on a past and a present which do not belong to him, and which he feels he is slowly strangling through his continued involvement.

Ironically, *Fever Pitch* does contain a measure of resolution with Hornby's movement from being a consumer of Arsenal as product, to being a notional owner of the club through the purchase of a season ticket. This ticket guarantees him the same seat over the entire course of a season and represents the culmination of his determined project to belong in a concrete, definite way:

> What you're really doing, when you buy a seat season ticket, is upping the belonging a notch. I'd had my own spot on the terraces but I had no proprietorial rights over it.... Now I really do have my own home in the stadium, complete with flatmates, and neighbours with whom I am on cordial terms.... After a while, you stop wanting to live from hand to mouth, day to day, game to game, and you begin wanting to ensure that the remainder of your days are secure.[26]

The connection between Highbury and Hornby's home is reinforced by this process and it is noticeable that the projection of domesticity that he made as a child is actualised with the purchase of a small part of the club. Not only is he claiming ownership of the physical artefact of the stadium, but he acquires along with it a community that he describes as his neighbours. The identification that Hornby has fashioned with Arsenal can only become literal through a movement to the centre of the community. He thus becomes not an outsider, alienated by distance, age or class, but an active and indispensable part of the fabric of the club, financially and proprietorially identified with its interests. Regardless of the notional level on which this 'ownership' operates, Hornby manages to overcome his alienation, something that he also achieves by purchasing a house within sight of the stadium. By this action, Hornby is seen to surmount the most apparent contradiction in his claims to support Arsenal – his geographical distance from north London.

Buying a home in the area can only be read as a very literal attempt to circumvent criticisms of his loyalty. His urban thrall is complete; sated by a permanent return to the urban, an actualised pilgrimage to parallel his symbolic worship. The centripetal instinct that has drawn Hornby to London has become a permanent rejection of the centrifugal process of suburban sprawl. However, the imperative that has drawn him back to the centre has simultaneously driven others away from the urban environment. On moving into the area, he anticipates that a tight-knit (almost suburban) community of Arsenal supporters will have clustered around the stadium, but what he discovers is that any such community has collapsed and that the traditional localised support for a team has been superseded by a diaspora of Arsenal fans across the Home Counties. All he encounters around Highbury is transience, decay and apathy. His vision of a unified community, motivated by similar desires, all embraced by the beneficent social influence of Arsenal, is anachronistic. All that his nostalgic reminiscing reveals is the extent to which his sociological fantasy of a football team sprouting from the collective efforts of a locality, has become outdated. The dissolution of his utopia is a perfect metaphor for the impact of suburban expansion.[27] The desire to escape from the claustrophobia and social problems of the city suggests not just the denigration of the city, but also a simultaneous denigration of the suburbs. The centrifugal pressure away from the centre results in the collapse of traditional urban communities, destroying any coherent local identity. The dissipation of those communities over much wider suburban areas has the inevitable impact of diluting the positive identity of that group, and, in Hornby's view, creates a bland and atomised suburban middle class. *Fever Pitch* articulates the sociological history of the suburban diaspora. From a very limited, and autobiographical, perspective, the book juxtaposes the diametrically opposed spaces of the city and the suburbs. Hornby's account conforms to a conventionalised critique of the suburbs, but compares that with the futility of idealising a return to the urban as the centre of production, meaning and communal value.

Although its representation of suburbia is more oblique than *Fever Pitch*, *High Fidelity* emphasises the same issues of belonging and rootlessness which Hornby exorcised in his treatment of football. The novel's principal protagonist, Rob Fleming, is portrayed as a character without any defined sense of purpose or ambition, and without any coherent structure to his life. Fleming enacts the same journey from the suburbs to the city in search of both the anonymity of the urban environment, and the potential for self-direction. His absconding has less definite focus than Hornby's in *Fever Pitch*, lacking the symbolic centre which promises meaning and understanding. Fleming's motivations are far more nebulous but again construct the city as a nexus of activity and possibility in contrast to suburban predictability. The novel opens with condemnation of the identical nature of suburban towns and the consequently deadening impact that has upon the horizons of those born into those areas:

> I lived in Hertfordshire, but I might just as well have lived in any suburb in England: it was that sort of suburb, and that sort of park – three minutes away from home, right across the road from a little row of shops.... There was nothing around that could help you get your geographical bearings; if the shops were open ... you could go into the newsagent's and look for a local paper, but even that might not give you much of a clue.[28]

The reduction of suburban England to a single, architectural, cultural and psychological paradigm creates a clear polarisation between the city and its hinterland. The effect on the individual of growing up in suburbia is to make their geographical locality irrelevant, and home simply becomes part of a huge, homogenous wasteland without distinguishing features and without unique identity. Suburbia problematises the issues of home and belonging because such concepts demand inherent signification of their difference from the Other. The capacity to define 'home' in any coherent sense necessitates an ability to distinguish that which is not home; given the lack of distinction in suburbia, Hornby contends that such discrimination is impossible. The individual as a product of suburbia is therefore catapulted into an identity crisis where notions of roots and belonging become moveable and negotiable qualities. Home has a plethora of negative associations for Fleming, principally because of the perceived lack of change or development. The 'congealing gravy and *Songs of Praise* home'[29] is condemned for its immutability and timelessness, a metaphor for the stagnation of his parents' lives, and, on a wider scale, of middle-class suburban respectability. His antagonism derives from his unwillingness to accept the presence in himself of his suburban past. Like the narrator of *Fever Pitch* he deliberately distances his origins but is ultimately incapable of escaping them totally because they have conditioned his psychological reaction to the very concept of home. To a degree, he is trapped within a suburban *weltanshauung,* which inhibits his self-detachment from the world of his parents and consequently reminds him of his own

social background. Fleming confesses to the resistance of a
middle-class residue that he has been unsuccessful in eradi-
cating, a residue that ensures that his escape to the city is little more than a symbolic identification with an existence
which he cannot access:

> nobody ever writes about how it is possible to escape and rot –
> how escapes can go off at half-cock, how you can leave the
> suburbs for the city but end up living a limp suburban life
> anyway. That's what happened to me; that's what happens to
> most people.[30]

The fundamental hybridity of the suburban escapee is foregrounded in this admission. The life that Fleming plays out in
London is rooted in the performance of an idealised role but
the perpetual presence of the suburban within his consciousness queers the validity of his portrayal. More explicitly than
Fever Pitch, *High Fidelity* exposes the limitations of the process of
identification in which both protagonists indulge. To reject the
suburban in the self results in a form of self-alienation, for
although the suburban may be viewed as inferior, its influence
inhibits the creation of a home or an identity on any alternative level. His desire to belong leads him to erect complex structures of meaning which are intended to endow his life with
direction and security. The most overt exemplification of this
process can be seen in his history of emotional relationships.

In the same way that Hornby constructed a personal history
out of the trivia and clutter of Arsenal statistics, thereby providing some ballast for his identification, Fleming attempts to
solidify his nebulous feelings of belonging by constructing an
archaeological record of his past relationships. The novel's
opening section details his 'five most memorable split-ups'[31] in
a taxonomic process, which allows Fleming to define and
channel his emotions through specificity. These relationships
form a recurrent commentary upon the failure of his present
partnership, but more importantly, they function as a surrogate system allowing him to reminisce upon his past life
through the focus of that failed affair. These relationships act
as watersheds in his development, so that he is able to identify
a stage in his life through a specific partner. Because he has
consciously rejected his empirical past, it is necessary for him
to replace that with a chronologically ordered history that has
no connections with the mundanity of suburbia. These relationships provide him with a reference point from where he

can construct an identity and create a self which is not over-shadowed by the influence of his actual origins. However, that point of identification is fundamentally insubstantial and its ineffectiveness is revealed when he tries to contact his former partners. Far from providing him with fixed and stable points of definition from where he can confidently make assumptions about his own identity, these regurgitations of the past succeed only in destabilising his vision of his past self. In each instance he is made to appreciate either his own culpability in the breakdown, or his insignificance in the total course of his partners' lives. Given that he has founded his identity upon the basis of his importance to these people, to learn of his dispensability significantly undermines the stability of his self-construction. The virtual home that he has created, in which he feels himself to belong, and to be the central figure of importance, is revealed to be founded upon illusion.

His systematic ordering of relationships is not the only structure that he erects to defer knowledge of his rootlessness. His obsessive control of his record collection functions in a similarly reassuring, but ultimately empty, manner. Fleming's record collection represents a displacement of the self into an objectified, concrete reality, where the difficulties assailing that self can be simply resolved by recategorisation or reordering. In the aftermath of his separation from Laura, he reorganises the collection in order to satisfy his sense of individuality:

> I try to remember the order I bought them in: that way I hope to write my own autobiography, without having to do anything like pick up a pen. I pull the records off the shelves, put them in piles all over the sitting room floor, look for *Revolver*, and go on from there, and when I've finished I'm flushed with a sense of self, because this, after all, is who I am.[32]

This process replicates the ritualistic return to the past that is enacted in contacting former partners. The records represent a series of archaeological strata of the self and Fleming's excavation is designed to unearth and reaffirm the boundaries of that self. The details that are gathered around the individual provide the reference points for identity in the absence of an acceptable version of home. At one point Fleming describes clutter as 'the stuff that stops you floating away',[33] a significant metaphor for the absence of centre in the novel.

As an explicit parallel to the obsession with football displayed in *Fever Pitch*, Fleming's fetishisation of rock music and the concrete by-products of that industry, functions as the central site of signification in the novel. Music provides a channel of escape for Fleming, whether it is through the listing of favourite songs, the reorganisation of his record collection, or the application of sentimental song lyrics to his romantic disappointments. In each case, music provides a systemic structure through which his emotional instability can be both verbalised and therapeutically resolved. Fleming understands himself vicariously through second-hand emotions, reducing his emotional responses to the level of trite and clichéd sentiments, but nevertheless providing a grammar and vocabulary for the self that is otherwise absent. The inauthenticity of his emotional life is interpretable as a direct reflection of the inauthenticity of his sense of place. Because he lacks the solidity and stability of any concept of home, he is positioned outside the comfortable definability of both his familial background and of his adopted north London locale. Effectively he exists within a psychological no man's land; uncommitted to either lifestyle he is deprived of any independent and individual voice with which to express his liminality. His only recourse is to appropriate the language and sentiments of the world to which he wishes to belong.

By situating Fleming within the context of the music industry (albeit appropriately as a purveyor of second-hand records), Hornby has articulated further the fascination of the suburbs with the city, for it is through music that disaffected youth has traditionally sought to express its hatred of the suburban sprawl. As Simon Frith, Vicky Lebeau and Andy Medhurst have separately indicated, connections between rock, pop and punk music and urban, subcultural lifestyles are well established.[34] Punk's vitriolic invective against the Establishment and against conformist practices is displayed by Lebeau to have exploded out of the suburban ring around London. The anger expressed through its anarchic music counterpointed the staid, stolid banality of suburban attitudes, but, as Jon Savage has suggested of English pop music, beneath 'the surface ... you'll find a suburban boy or girl, noses pressed against the window, dreaming of escape, of transformation'.[35] Although the rhetoric of much postwar British popular music has been urban-oriented, its proponents and audiences have often been situated within what Medhurst calls 'the Gnome Zone'.[36] As Lebeau has said:

> Canvey Island, Woking, Harrow, Ealing, Bromley: here, outside London but not that far, punk was generated and sustained by the emptiness, the blankness, of the suburbs.[37]

In *High Fidelity*, Fleming absorbs the rhetoric of urban/suburban opposition and by situating himself within the music industry, he firmly stations himself as a suburban escapee; living out, on a permanent basis, the fantasy of metropolitan glamour. Surrounding himself by the appurtenances of a career in music enhances his conception of himself as an urbanite. The record shop and the collection thus become attempts at verisimilitude, indications of the depth of his association with the city, in some way attempting to project and reassure the onlooker – and Fleming himself – of the authenticity of his transformation. In the same way that football could be said to symbolise Hornby's access to a heightened form of 'real' experience, so Fleming's dalliance with the music scene, and his relationship with a songwriter/performer in particular, represent for him a quintessence of city life. They also articulate his desire to affiliate himself with traditionally inscribed working-class culture. Popular music as a means of literal and economic escape from deprived backgrounds is a well-established cultural phenomenon and it is no coincidence that Fleming is positioned within employment that firmly repudiates the careful and moderate norm of suburbia. Identification with the city, and the reconstruction of himself as a naturalised urban-dweller, motivate his decision to pursue a career that is historically connected to the lower strata of the class hierarchy. It is a parody of belonging, which situates the city and the working class as sites of meaning and identity. Experiencing a deep sense of loss arising from his middle-classness and suburbanity, Fleming fantasises about his displaced identity within the city providing the necessary context within which his self can become whole. Naturally, such wish-fulfilment is illusory and undermined by his enduring suburban values typified by his movement away from labour into capitalist ownership. It is significant that he owns the shop – *Championship Vinyl* – and employs two further members of staff. Such an arrangement removes him from the position of producer to that of owner-overseer and symbolically relocates him within the middle class from where he has tried to abscond.

Although the city represents a hyperreal distillation of suburban fantasies, the threat of exclusion from the metropolitan carnival is correspondingly intense. Because his continued acceptance within the urban context is dependent upon the convincing qualities of his performance, the tension of imminent disclosure prevails, evidenced by his uncomfortable relationship with his two employees. Characteristic of the

employer/employee dynamic in the novel is the periodic comparison of musical tastes and a competitive dialogue based
around musical knowledge. Again, the trivia of musical discourses figures prominently as a touchstone for the health of
the relationship between Fleming, Barry and Dick, but in addition, it enacts the problematical interplay between exclusion
and inclusion. In particular, between Barry and Dick there
exists a fundamental difference in taste which generates a pervasive sense of animosity between them. Assumptions about
character are underpinned by the musical preferences of that
individual being either acceptable or unacceptable to those
making the judgement. In a parody of adolescent tribalism
the tastes of their customers, and each other, are analysed,
and co-option into a circle of the *cognoscenti* either granted or
withheld. Much of this banter is implicit in their conversa-
tions, but percolating through these discussions is the assumption that one type of music is acceptable whereas another is
beyond the pail. Effectively this is another form of division
between forms of belonging and forms of exclusion. That
music which is peripheral or cultishly avant-garde becomes
qualitatively linked with the city as a site of innovation and
experimentation. To favour music which is fashionable or
mainstream is derided as evincing one's suburban sensibilities,
rooted in conformity and blandness. The way in which Rob,
Barry and Dick dismiss each other's preferences suggests their
own uneasy siting between the wider poles of acceptability
(the urban and rebellious) and unacceptability (the suburban
and clichéd) that the novel propounds.

The identification of the self with the city, the achievement
of a state of existential insideness, is continually disturbed by
Fleming's inability to eliminate that part of his persona that is
rooted in the Watford suburb. Unlike *Fever Pitch*, where Hornby
ultimately convinces himself of his north London indigenous-
ness by buying a stake in the area and in Arsenal, *High Fidelity*
proposes no such simplistic solutions to suburban rootlessness.
Fleming's pastiche of an urban-dweller is limited by his inability to see beyond the imperfections in his performance. Just as
the city defines the suburbs, so the suburbs provide a mode of
signification for the city, and Fleming is unmistakably suburban in his world-view. He typifies what Silverstone has called
'the suburban imaginary'[38] which, regardless of its proximity
or distance from the concrete reality of the suburbs, replicates
the anxieties and concerns of the middle-class mind. Fleming
is incapable of total identification with the rhythms of the city

because to be *of* the city would be no longer to install it as a fantastic Utopian ideal. The very process of identification, because of its self-consciousness, distances him further from authentic belonging. As Edward Relph states:

> Existential insideness is part of knowing implicitly that *this* place is where you belong – in all other places we are existential outsiders no matter how open we are to their symbols and significances.[39]

The insistence on unconscious belonging, which Relph proffers in this argument, countermands the foundations in identification which the protagonists of *High Fidelity* and *Fever Pitch* erect to distance themselves from the unpalatable knowledge of their origins. The determinism of place against which Fleming and Hornby contest undermines their best efforts at self-projection into idealised, urban Utopias. By consciously aligning themselves with alternative sites of belonging, they automatically negate the legitimacy of their new personae.

Searching for a transcendent authenticity, *Fever Pitch* and *High Fidelity* replicate through the narrative the dialogism that they install thematically. Hornby's writing displays a desperate search for a sincerity of narrative voice, a form of monological self-confidence, and yet his fiction and autobiography are characterised by his own internal polyphony. As a product of suburbia, he casts himself as hybrid and can thus express himself with no singular voice. His narratives represent a continual process of compromise by which the actual and idealised selves are brought into an uncomfortable alliance. The projection of home onto an already symbolically charged space results in a schism in identity whereby the two culturally inscribed lifestyles of the city and the suburbs are brought into opposition. The idealisation of the urban self from within the suburban consciousness can only ever exist as an idealisation, for the terms upon which that fantasy is created are rooted within the limits of the suburban world-view. The irony of Hornby's writing is that it inverts the sociological connotations of the urban/suburban dichotomy. Whilst the suburb has been installed in twentieth-century culture as the enclave of security and private space in opposition to the congestion and instability of the city, *Fever Pitch* and *High Fidelity* enunciate the imperative need to reclaim the urban as a space of individual and collective identity. Paradoxically, although they articulate a deep sense of loss at the destruction of metropolitan communities, they simultaneously acknowledge the anachronistic status of their fantasies of return. Ultimately the generation of suburbia is seen to have drawn parasitically upon the vitality of the city rendering London a blank canvas on which suburban daydreams can be safely enacted from a distance. As Simon Frith concludes:

> London, is not a place in which to live but a backcloth against which to imagine living.[40]

Notes

1. Simon Frith, 'The Suburban Sensibility in British Rock and Pop', in *Visions of Suburbia*, ed. Roger Silverstone, London, 1997, 270.
2. Roger Silverstone, 'Introduction', in *Visions of Suburbia*, ed. Roger Silverstone, 5.
3. Given that *Fever Pitch* can be most comfortably placed within the genre of autobiography, this essay will refer to the narrator as 'Hornby'. However such a policy should be understood to import the implied persona of Hornby as author and is not an indiscriminate collapsing of narrator and author.
4. Nick Hornby, *Fever Pitch*, London, 1993, 17.
5. Ibid., 18.
6. Yi-Fu Tuan, *Topophilia: A Study of Environmental Perception, Attitudes and Values*, New Jersey, 1974. Topophiliac responses to sporting stadia are common according to John Bale, and often form part of the discourse of supporter loyalty. The sanctification of the stadium reinforces the quasi-religious nature of the supporters' regular devotional returns, although in Hornby's case the identification is more clearly rooted in the symbolic connotations of home. See John Bale, 'Playing at Home: British Football and a Sense of Place', in *British Football and Social Change: Getting into Europe*, eds John Williams and Stephen Wagg, Leicester, 1991, 130–44.
7. Silverstone, 'Introduction', in Silverstone, ed., *Visions of Suburbia*, 7.
8. See Medhurst, 'Negotiating the Gnome Zone', in Silverstone ed. *Visions of Suburbia*.
9. Hornby, *Fever Pitch*, 16.
10. Ibid., 47–9.
11. Ibid., 49.
12. Edward Relph, *Place and Placelessness*, London, 1976, 50.
13. Hornby, *Fever Pitch*, 27.
14. The collapsing of the symbolic distance between the team and his father is important because it installs the team as a form of surrogate parent and reiterates the position of Hornby as an intrinsic product of that team. For a discussion of the parent/child relationship between the football club and supporter, see Rogan Taylor, 'Walking Alone Together: Football Supporters and their Relationship with the Game', in Williams and Wagg, eds, *British Football and Social Change*, 111–29.
15. Hornby, *Fever Pitch*, 30.
16. Ibid., 139.
17. Ibid.

18. At one point the process of identification extends beyond the psychological to the somatic, Describing Liam Brady, one of Arsenal's most celebrated players, he states that 'if you cut him he would bleed Arsenal'. (Hornby, *Fever Pitch*, 1993, 120–1.) In evidence here is the transgression of identity across the barriers of the body, revealing a form of abjection in which the external loyalty of the supporter is reflected by the internal constitution of the body's organs.
19. Hornby, *Fever Pitch*, 40.
20. Ibid., 41.
21. Ibid., 40.
22. Hornby undergoes an experience of symbolic emasculation in this attack and he openly admits to seeing the beating as a reflection of his inferior masculinity. Importantly he connects his suburban roots with his loss of pride, an implicit suggestion that he has been feminised by the environment in which he has grown up. Again, the dichotomy of urban activity and suburban passivity is reinforced by this incident.
23. Hornby, *Fever Pitch*, 74.
24. Hornby, *Fever Pitch*, 54.
25. Ibid., 77.
26. Ibid., 233.
27. The realignment of the spectacle of football in the aftermath of the Hillsborough disaster of 1989, with the concomitant embourgeoisement of the spectator market, parallels a pattern of suburban expansion. As Bale has argued, football has recently rejected its urban origins and become a significant part of the exodus to the peripheries of the city (Bale, 'Playing at Home', in Williams and Wagg, eds, *British Football and Social Change*, 134.) Like supermarket relocation, football has removed itself to its new middle-class audience and stadium construction is now largely focused upon green-field suburban sites, further divorcing the game from its urban and working-class traditions.
28. Nick Hornby, *High Fidelity*, London, 1996, 9–10.
29. Ibid., 113.
30. Ibid., 114.
31. Ibid., 9.
32. Ibid., 52.
33. Ibid., 211.
34. Frith, 'The Suburban Sensibility in British Rock and Pop', 280; Vicky Lebeau, 'The Worst of all Possible Worlds', 280–97; and Medhurst, 'Negotiating the Gnome Zone'; all in Silverstone, ed., *Visions of Suburbia*.
35. John Savage, 'Suede', *Mojo*, 3, January/February 1994, quoted in Frith, 'The Suburban Sensibility in British Rock and Pop', in Silverstone, ed., *Visions of Suburbia*, 271.
36. Medhurst, 'Negotiating the Gnome Zone', in Silverstone, ed., *Visions of Suburbia*, 240.
37. Vicky Lebeau, 'The Worst of all Possible Worlds?', in Silverstone, ed., *Visions of Suburbia*, 284.
38. Silverstone, 'Introduction', in Silverstone, ed., *Visions of Suburbia*, 13.
39. Relph, *Place and Placelessness*, 55.
40. Frith, 'The Suburban Sensibility in British Rock and Pop', in Roger Silverstone, ed., *Visions of Suburbia*, 274.

Chapter 9

The Sound of the Suburbs: the Idea of the Suburb in English Pop

D.J. Taylor

The suburbs, because of their presumed orthodoxy, exaggerate the extremities of mood and movement: the darkest alley in the seediest district of the biggest city will lack the sheer oddness of suburban neatness, where all that appears most settled conspires to make its own drama.

Michael Bracewell – *England's is Mine*

With its ultimate roots deep in Chicago blues, one might assume that English pop music was necessarily an urban phenomenon. In fact, this would be a substantial overstatement. For one thing, even before the 1967 'Summer of Love', with its sylvan overtones, 'Games for May' and perpetual Strawberry Fields, English pop had incorporated a distinct pastoral strain. Popular music was about bright lights, fast cars and big cities, but it was also about autumn almanacs and pipers at the gates of dawn. At the same time, more than one critic has made a convincing case for the centrality of the suburb. According to Simon Frith, the myths of pop culture are 'the product of suburban dreams, suburban needs'.[1] Certainly the most cursory glance at pop song titles of the past thirty-five years reveals a deep interest in the adjective 'suburban'. From Manfred Mann's 1960s 'Semi-detached Suburban Mr Jones' to

Siouxsie and the Banshees' 'Suburban Relapse' (1978) and the Skids' 'Sweet Suburbia' (1978), from the Members' 'Sound of the Suburbs' (1979) to Magazine's 'Suburban Rhonda' (1981) and beyond, pop writers have eagerly set out to explore suburban life and its supposed implications. Much of this has been ironic, sometimes downright contemptuous, occasionally almost the reverse. Again, as even the most assiduous pop theorist – an ever-expanding category – will be forced to concede, there is no single pop approach to the suburb. It can be something to embrace, something to flee from, something to regard with wary acceptance or a repository for virtue. There is even – something that might be expected – no particular agreement on what a suburb is or where it can be located yet, amid this multiplicity of styles and definitions can be found a beguiling range of perspectives on three-and-a-half decades of late twentieth-century English life.

The most obvious question to begin with is: from the point of view of the average rock writer, what is a suburb? Inevitably, a line of the kind pronounced by the American artist Jonathan Richman – 'We'll have a modern love, under suburban rain' – can be subjected to endless decoding before yielding up its intent, but when an English pop writer uses the word 'suburb' what does he or she mean? Somewhere halfway between city and country? Somewhere in the area bounded by the London postal districts and the M25? Somewhere else? To give an idea of the difficulties of definition, I should say that for the first nineteen years of my life I inhabited a supposedly archetypal suburban locale – a mile's walk in one direction took you to the centre of the city of Norwich, and a mile's walk in the other brought you to the beginnings of fields. Yet, I never imagined myself to be *suburban* in the conventional sense of the word. In Norfolk, twenty years ago, you lived either in the city or in the country: there was little sense of an intermediate zone. Unquestionably, to the average, and above average, pop lyricist the meaning of 'suburb' is wide to the point of vagueness. Blur's frontman Damon Albarn, for example, relocated in childhood from London to an Essex village on the margins of Colchester, is in no doubt that he is a suburbanite at heart. The explanation for his suburban fixations is quite straightforward:

> It comes from being born in London and then having a life transplant to Essex. Because my parents were slightly odd they really stood out, and I did as well. There were no blacks. The

whole village was full of people who commuted to London to work in banks.[2]

Blur's hymns to suburban emptiness were, consequently, 'a way of getting my own back on those people. If ever I have writer's block, I think of Essex'.[3] So the whole of Essex – for the most part, beyond the London overspill, a defiantly rural area – is a *suburb*? Obviously, in this explanation Albarn is codifying what he assumes to be suburban characteristics: a monoculture, commuting, the sense of a community without roots that has simply settled itself in a particular part of the country, whose emblematic focus, perhaps, is the daily train journey to and from London. One could make the same point regarding other recent centres of English suburban pop: Bromley, home of Siouxsie and the Banshees; Crawley, which spawned the Cure; Haywards Heath, where the principal components of Suede came across one another in the mid-1980s. Ambience, rather than location, is the key. Frith, again, has plausibly suggested that to most pop writers, 'suburb' is effectively the whole of south-east England outside London, an environment characterised by the snap of the car door, the returning train, lives lived out behind closed doors; a world which is as comforting to the old and the middle-aged as it is oppressive to their children. White, south-eastern English culture, in fact, dominated by the lure of the metropolis, which is both physically remote and easily attainable; somewhere to which one perpetually aspires but from which one is perpetually returning.

The suburban sensibility hereby defined is important both in itself and for its direct opposition to another, and intermittently dominant, English pop styling. Bracewell makes the point that the key sound of much recent English pop is the doleful *northern* voice (significantly, perhaps, the Beatles christened their publishing company 'Northern Songs'.) Whether brought to the listener by Lennon & McCartney, or, to move on into the last twenty years, Joy Division's Ian Curtis, Buzzcocks' and Magazine's Howard Devoto, The Smiths' Steven Morrissey or Pulp's Jarvis Cocker, such music emphatically did not reflect a suburban consciousness. Devoto has said that his early songs (the pieces collected on the first Magazine album *Real Life*) were written 'in rooms in cities'. Their preoccupations seem exclusively urban: crowds, motorcades, briefly glimpsed faces:

> 'Why are you so edgy, kid?'
> asks the man with the voice

> one thing follows another
> you live and learn, you have no choice
> I wormed my way into the heart of the crowd [4]
>   (Magazine, 'Shot By Both Sides')

Seeking to establish a context for these preoccupations, one turns inevitably to early- and mid-twentieth century literature – inevitably, because on the one hand literature has played a pivotal role in defining the English view of the suburb, and, on the other, many pop lyricists have consciously drawn on literary models. Albarn, for example, acknowledges a debt to classic suburban anatomists such as V.S. Pritchett. As with pop itself, no single response characterises British literature's attitude to suburbia. From the days of Gissing and Wells, the literary novel has been almost uniformly disparaging. By the 1930s, it seems fair to say, the suburb had become a byword for social uniformity, conservatism and spiritual deprivation. George Bowling, the hero of Orwell's *Coming Up For Air* (1939), a boy from the Thames Valley town of 'Lower Binfield' come to rest, or perhaps only to fester, in 'West Bletchley' on the western side of London, bleakly summarises his locale in terms which have come to represent the suburban archetype already quoted on the opening page of the Introduction to this volume.[5] Conformity (with dire warnings about the fate of nonconformists), fear, above all rootlessness – Bowling and his family have moved west from Ealing. What is the point of a place like Ellesmere Road, Bowling later wonders: 'Just a prison with cells all in a row. A line of semidetached torture-chambers where the poor little five-to-ten-pound-a-weeker quakes and shivers, every one of them with the boss twisting his tail and the wife riding him like the nightmare and the kids sucking his blood like leeches.'[6] Above all, perhaps, in these evocations of inter-war West London life rises the sense of a community arbitrarily set down, barely functioning according to received notions of communal life. Nick Jenkins, the narrator of Anthony Powell's *The Acceptance World*, waking up in a house situated somewhere off the Great West Road some time in the early 1930s (*The Acceptance World*, the third volume of Powell's *A Dance To The Music Of Time* is set nearly a quarter of a century before its 1955 publication date) is struck by the apparent unreality of his surroundings. Seeing the outline of other houses in the near distance, Jenkins diagnoses:

> a settlement of prosperous businessmen; a reservation, like those created for indigenous inhabitants, or wild animal life, in some region invaded by alien elements: a kind of refuge for

beings unfitted to battle with modern conditions, where they might live their own lives, undisturbed or unexploited by an aggressive outer world ... I felt miles away from everything, lying there in that bedroom: almost as if I were abroad.[7]

Although couched in Powell's characteristically glacial and impenetrable tones, Jenkins' reaction is essentially the same as Bowling's: this is an alien world, rootless and ultimately soulless. The sense of social superiority, dividing city man from his inferior suburban counterpart, is also strong. As Brian Howard, the co-model for Evelyn Waugh's arch-aesthete Anthony Blanche in *Brideshead Revisited* (1945), is supposed to have snapped at a policeman who demanded his name and address during a wartime raid on a Soho nightclub, 'I live in Mayfair. No doubt you come from some dreary suburb'.[8]

Not all the literature located in these bleak 1930s hinterlands expressed such elemental disgust. Betjeman's 'suburban' poems are much more ambiguous: mocking many of the features of Metropolitan Line life that depress Bowling and Jenkins, but detecting human quiddity, drowning effortlessly in a tide of communal and, of course, personal nostalgia. However, to another kind of writer – usually best-selling middle-brow novelists – the suburb could feature as a source of communal spirit and virtue. Ernest Raymond's *A Kilburn Tale* (1946) emphasises the advantages of a modest family life lived out at the heart of the 'Twenty Thousand Streets Under The Sky' which Patrick Hamilton offered as the title of his London trilogy of novels (*The Midnight Bell*, 1929, *The Siege of Pleasure*, 1932, *The Plains of Cement*, 1934). R.F. Delderfield's *The Dreaming Suburb* (1964) and *The Avenue Goes To War* (1970) have an even more optimistic focus – a vista of suburban life from the period 1918–45 ending with the marriage of a working-class veteran of the Great War to his middle-class neighbour and the symbolic destruction of garden fences. The suburbs, oddly enough, could also be a place to dream, even an environment conducive to the overthrow of class barriers. Each of these perspectives has some connection to the pop sensibilities formulated thirty or forty years later, from the interest in Orwell expressed by artists such as David Bowie and Paul Weller, to Albarn's recasting of Delderfield's title in the opening track of Blur's *The Great Escape* (1995), which begins with the words 'The suburbs they are dreaming ... '

If this – more or less – is suburbia, then some kind of definition needs to be applied to 'English pop'. Essentially my understanding of this occasionally protean noise is 'guitar-based popular music produced in the UK since the advent of the Beatles'. Chronologically, this divides up into perhaps four compartments: the period 1964–70, when, in the wake of the Beatles', the parameters of English pop music were being established by groups such as the Kinks, the Who and the Rolling Stones; a rather bleak early 1970s hinterland, stylistically dominated – at any rate in critical retrospect – by artists such as David Bowie and Roxy Music; the punk-fuelled 'New Wave' of 1976–80, more or less moribund by 1981–2 but whose ethic was perpetuated by the long-running 'Indie' movement and much of the rock/dance crossover of the late 1980s and early 1990s; and the resurgent 'Britpop' phenomenon of the mid-1990s, whose final descending fragments can be heard in the last Oasis album, 'Standing on the Shoulders of Giants' (2000).

Unsurprisingly, the deep vein of social comment probed by mid-1960s pop acts contained many a view of the suburb and suburban man. Almost without exception, the tone is ironic: Manfred Mann's 'Semi-detached Suburban Mr Jones' with its opening line 'So you finally got what you wanted'; the Kinks' acid portrayal of the contemporary Conservative archetype, 'Well-respected Man'. However, this is straightforward observation; perhaps the first significant pop performer with a considered sense of what 'suburb' might mean was David Bowie. Raised in Bromley, and a product of the Beckenham Arts Lab, Bowie has declared an interest in suburban styles and preoccupations for three decades, exemplified perhaps by his willingness to compose a soundtrack for the television adaptation of Hanif Kureshi's novel *The Buddha of Suburbia* in 1993. Bowie's early 1970s persona, 'Ziggy Stardust' from the 1972 album *Ziggy Stardust and the Spiders from Mars* and the following year's 'Aladdin Sane', slot neatly into Frith's roster of suburban myths and dreams: androgynous, appealing to both males and females, built on gesture and paradox, concealing – or occasionally failing to conceal – an underlying emptiness. If one wanted a locus for the suburban fixations of later 1970s pop it would be here in the south-west London sprawl originally colonised by Bowie. Bracewell makes the useful point that both the Sex Pistols' manager Malcolm McLaren and the designer of their record sleeves, Jamie Reid, studied at Croydon Art College. It was from Croydon that Reid's 'situationist newspaper', *Suburban Press*, was launched in 1970 (the cover of the first issue depicted a new semi-detached house; the fifth num-

ber bore a photograph of the newly-built Croydon flyover cap-
tioned 'Lo, a monster is born'.) The influence of Bowie, the Sex
Pistols and the south-western suburbs came together in the
group of teenagers known to music history as the 'Bromley
contingent': early followers of the Pistols, two of whose number – Siouxsie Sioux and Steve Severin – were to form the
nucleus of the punk group Siouxsie and the Banshees.[9] The
'myths and dreams' of the Bromley contingent were driven by
the lure of the city and the shabby Soho clubs where, under
McLaren's astute direction, the punk movement would take
root in the early part of 1976.

There are significant comparisons to be made. The New
York punk movement of 1974–76 that predated, and in many
cases informed, its UK equivalent [10] was self-consciously, if not
defiantly, urban in tone. Based around a handful of New York
clubs,[11] it had, as Jon Savage has pointed out, a manifest political dimension. The fenced-in quality of life under a near-
bankrupt municipal administration, repudiated by President
Ford, bred a close relationship between environment and
music. The gaze was inward rather than external: 'I want to
find myself, find myself a city to live in' in the words of Talking Heads' *Cities*. At first sight, the British New Wave of the late
1970s looks similarly city-obsessed. Perhaps the clearest indication of this lies in the regularity with which the metropolis
and its regions gets name-checked in key tracks of the period:
'London Girl' (The Jam), 'Fulham Fallout' (The Lurkers), 'I
don't want to go to Chelsea' (Elvis Costello), 'Up the
[Clapham] Junction' (Squeeze), 'A Bomb in Wardour Street'
(The Jam). Throughout the period, Outer London cast envious
eyes on the carnival of style and taste that supposedly existed
in the West End. In this search for specifically urban credentials, artists could often go to faintly absurd lengths. On The
Jam's first single (appropriately titled 'In The City') Paul Weller
announced 'I know I'm from Woking/ And you think I'm a
fraud/ But my heart is in the city/ Where it belongs'. Sham 69's
rabble-rousing 'Hersham Boys' featured the altogether risible
couplet 'Hersham boys, Hersham boys / They call us the cockney cowboys'. Hersham, as even the most charitable cartogra-
pher of Outer London may allow, is in Surrey.

At the same time, the suburban sensibility is present in
dozens of songs of the period. The Members' 'Sound of the Suburbs' (1979) specifically claims punk as a product and an
expression of suburban life; music for bored teenagers in high-
rise flats on the London fringe. Later Jam songs are about a

businessman taking the train into London to be presented with the sack ('Smithers-Jones', 1979), miserable housewives buying groceries in out-of-town shopping centres ('Private Hell', 1979). More subversively, perhaps, Siouxsie and the Banshees regarded the idea of suburban 'normality' as altogether misleading. Here the privet hedge and the permanently closed front door conceal all manner of private weirdness and frustration:

> I'm sorry that I hit you
> but my string snapped
> I'm sorry I disturbed your cat-nap
> but whilst finishing a chore
> I asked myself 'What for?'
> Then something snapped
> I had a relapse ... A Suburban Relapse.
> ('Suburban Relapse', 1978)

The singer goes on to wonder whether she should throw things at the neighbours, 'expose myself to stranger', or even 'kill myself ... or you?' This is an enduring theme in English pop's treatment of suburbia: the idea that the presumed repressions and miseries of suburban life give rise to a precariously concealed oddity. Blur's 'Stereotypes', with its account of wife-swapping parties behind the Essex lace curtains, mines a similar vein. Simultaneously, it was possible to find redemption in this halfway house between *rus* and *urbe*. 'Suburban Rhonda', a characteristically playful piece by one of the most interesting lyricists in English pop, Magazine's Howard Devoto, offers an almost ethical contrast:

> You urban vision of loveliness
> moving scenes of skin
> You understand the ways and means
> of city discipline
> a structured life in some girls' rooms
> mirror glass and light
> outside the landscape of power
> dreams around appetite.
> ('Suburban Rhonda', 1981)

Having sketched in the outlines of a world of 'city discipline', with its 'structured life' of mirrors, glass and light, the whole backing onto a 'landscape of power', Devoto then advises his subject: 'don't be so smart ... don't act so sharp ... you'll wreck your heart'. Urban sophistication, in other words, is won at a price. Without making too great an historical leap, there is a parallel in some of the early 17th century Caroline poets who anatomised the court/country divide, concluding that the authentic life lay in the Hampshire manor house rather than in the corrosive atmosphere of Whitehall.

In their varying degrees, these songs amount to comments about perceived aspects of suburban life and the suburb as an entity. Several critics, though, surveying the aftermath of the New Wave movement and its recrudescence in 'Britpop' have detected a specific suburban ambience at work, a dynamic that is not so much judgmental as simply integral. A band such as the Cure, born in the slipstream of punk and still going strong two decades later, have, according to Bracewell, managed to forge a musical expression of suburbia itself: 'a dense and repetitive sound, carrying a mesmeric dirge of infinitely trans- ferable songs, all of which sound as if they could go on for ever – like endless avenues, crescents and drives'. Certainly the gloomier end of the Cure's extensive repertoire – angst-ridden and yet curiously unspecific songs with titles like 'Faith', 'The Drowning Man' and 'One Hundred Years' – abet this view, full of abstract miseries and brooding atmospherics rather than particularity. Frith locates similar tendencies in Britpop icons Suede, finding in their lyrics a vague romanticism, a mood 'cre- ated by metaphor and simile' the whole realising a sense of alienation, the feeling of lives going nowhere, activity reduced to 'lying in my bed, lying in my head'. Blur, in contrast, offer a series of characters, short stories featuring tetchy, ill-at-ease suburban types: the denizens of 'Stereotypes', 'Ernold Same' liv- ing a repetitive life of work and domesticity, 'Tracy Jacks', a world-weary civil servant who eventually bulldozes down his house on the grounds that life is 'over-rated'. At the heart of Albarn's bleakly humorous vision of Essex life is a specifically literary context. Take, for example, the lyrics to 'Essex Dogs', subsequently reworked into a poem that appeared in one of Michael Horowitz's *New Departures* anthologies:

> Down rememberance [*sic*] avenue
> dogs somersault through sprinklers on summer lawns
> and on the plains of cement
> the english army grind their teeth
> in terminal pubs.[12]

As in 'The suburbs they are dreaming', with its nod to Delder- field, 'the plains of cement' reproduces the title of Patrick Hamilton's novel of 1934.

At the same time, there are mighty oppositions at work: here versus there; South versus North: *ersatz* versus *echt*. Set against the bleak urban noise offered by, say, Joy Division – whose epileptic Dostoevsky-fixated frontman Ian Curtis committed suicide – the Cure's suburban laments sound suspiciously factitious: 'armchair catharsis and safe self-hatred' Bracewell acidly concludes. Juxtaposed with self-consciously 'northern' competitors such as Oasis (Manchester) and Pulp (Sheffield), southern acts such as Blur and Suede have frequently been found wanting by exacting critics in search of that elusive pop beast, authenticity. The supposed rivalry between Blur and Oasis which dominated the music papers in late 1995 was founded on many of these oppositions – 'arty', novel-reading, 'mod' southerners versus down-to-earth northern rockers. Consequently, and in many ways, the typical 'suburban' pop song of the 1980s and 1990s is not merely an array of social observations, or the reflection of a specific south-of-England sensibility, but a kind of rueful complaint that the lyricist was born not in Liverpool or Manchester but in a London dormer town, a landscape of dull unease enlivened by the fugitive excitements of the railway track. The North/South divide is as much a feature of English pop as of postwar UK economics. Meanwhile, suburban themes and suburban obsessions continue to inform a wide range of contemporary pop – a process not without its incidental ironies. Reflecting recently on the demise of his solo career in the mid-1980s, the former Undertones singer Feargal Sharkey observed that he had 'run away from public life and gone to hide in suburbia'. To Sharkey, a Derry-born working-class Catholic, the contrasts of his adult existence may seem clear-cut, but for many of his musical contemporaries of the last twenty years, suburbia was merely the base camp from which they set out.

Notes

1. Simon Frith, 'The Suburban Sensibility in British Rock and Pop', in *Visions of Suburbia*, ed. Roger Silverstone, London, 1997, 269–80.
2. Interview in *Night and Day*, the review section of the *Mail on Sunday*, 7 January 1996.
3. Ibid.
4. Complete lyrics to Magazine's 'Shot By Both Sides' and 'Suburban Rhonda' are printed in Howard Devoto, *It Only Looks As If It Hurts: The Complete Lyrics 1976–1980*, London, 1990. Devoto's comments about his early songs being written in rooms in cities are made in a promotional

interview, produced as a seven-inch single and distributed with copies of the Luxuria album *Beast Box*, Beggars Banquet, 1990.

5. George Orwell, *Coming up for Air*, Harmondsworth, 1971, 13.

6. Ibid., 14.

7. Anthony Powell, *The Acceptance World*, London, 1967, 74.

8. Brian Howard's remark (made in the company of, among others, Guy Burgess) is quoted in *Brian Howard: Portrait of a Failure*, ed. Marie-Jacqueline Lancaster, London, 1968, 430.

9. Siouxsie, on her own admission, 'hated Bromley', thinking it 'small and narrow-minded'.

10. In particular through the influence of artists such as the New York Dolls, whom McLaren also briefly managed, the Ramones and Television.

11. 'This ain't the Mudd Club or CBGB's, I ain't got time for that now' Talking Heads would declare in an end-of-the-decade valediction in the 1979 single 'Life During Wartime'.

12. 'Essex Dogs' is printed in *The POW! Anthology*, eds Michael Horowitz and Inge Elsa, London, 1996, 10.

CHAPTER 10

KITSCH ON THE FRINGE: SUBURBIA IN RECENT AUSTRALIAN COMEDY FILM

Nicole Matthews

Equating Australia with suburbia seemed, during the 1990s, a logical way of understanding representations of the country circulating internationally on television screens, magazine covers and cinema billings. In Britain in particular, media representations of Australia tend to present it not as the exotic or feared 'other', but as a fundamentally similar place to the UK, but with more space, more cash and more opportunities for 'barbies'. Australian soaps like *Neighbours* and *Home and Away* were wildly successful, representing an affluent and almost exclusively white, Anglo-Celtic family life in the Australian suburbs. Soap stars like Jason Donovan and Kylie Minogue forged musical careers that started from and continued to play with their roles as suburban teenagers. The 1992 docusoap *Sylvania Waters*, which followed the lives and misdeeds of an affluent family in suburban Sydney was greeted with uproar when shown on British and Australian television. This representation of Australia as suburban stretches further back, to expatriate Australian comic Barry Humphreys' persona Edna Everage, Housewife Megastar.[1]

This overdetermined location of Australia as the suburbs of the globe is, on a literal level, understandable – it is one of the most urbanised countries in the world, with most people living in urban centres and their suburban fringes.[2] More metaphorically, John Archer points out the parallels between the position of the colony and of the suburb, each placed in opposition to the metropolis.[3] Representations of Australian suburbia in two internationally successful Australian films of the 1990s tell us something about the associations between suburbia and discourses of gender, sexuality, ethnicity and nation: *Strictly Ballroom* and *Muriel's Wedding*[4] each restate and rework discourses around suburbia.[5]

So, what will the expanded landscapes of suburbia in *Strictly Ballroom* and *Muriel's Wedding* allow us to see? Karl Quinn suggests that 'these films are motivated by an unacknowledged loathing of suburbia'.[6] At one level, these films reiterate long-standing associations between the suburbs and heterosexuality, whiteness, femininity and inauthenticity.[7] They offer a critique of suburbia through these well-worn connections. The way this comic critique is set up reflects on other critical visions of suburbia, which often hinge on a nightmarish picture of suburban femininity. There is something intriguing about the way the representations of Australia that are acceptable to the international market rest so firmly on these conventional associations.

Baz Luhrmann's 1992 release, *Strictly Ballroom* was described by Tom O'Regan as the Australian 'event' film of the early 1990s and credited with reviving the fortunes of the dance movie.[8] The film plays out an association between suburbia and artifice, articulated through representations of femininity. Its simple plot plays off accomplished ballroom dancer Scott Hastings (Paul Mercurio) and his white Anglo-Celtic family, obsessed with winning the Pan-Pacific Grand Prix Ballroom Dancing Championships, with the Spanish-Australian family of Fran (Tara Morice), which sustains a tradition of folk dancing. The two families are distinguished through the very different spaces in which they live. While the Hastings must drive to their bedroom suburb in that essential corollary of suburbia, the private car,[9] Francesca walks from dance practice to her inner city home. If suburbia is predicated on the distinction between (paid) work and home, the shop that fronts Fran's house and the railway sidings that flank it blur this distinction. Catherine Simpson argues that the back yard and especially the properly maintained lawn are a key trope of suburbia.[10] Instead of a lawn, Fran's family grows vegetables in the back yard – violating, as poet Ania Walwicz points out, the unspoken rules of Anglo-Australian propriety.[11] In contrast, a long dance sequence establishing the relationship between Scott Hastings and his father circles around that proud Australian invention, the space-gobbling and quintessentially suburban rotary clothes line.[12]

So how are those suburbanites, the Hastings ballroom dancing dynasty, represented in the film? They are performers, putting on a show not just on the dance floor but in the most intimate of relationships – between dance partners, husbands and wives, children and parents. Scott's mother, Shirley, strikes the keynote early on in the film. She faces adversity – Scott's refusal to dance approved by the Ballroom Dancing Federation – by putting her 'happy face on'. Scott draws on the same codes of performance when he instructs Fran to gaze intently into his eyes when they dance together, as if she were in love, but to remember that 'it's pretend'. The very family history of the Hastings is revised through performance. When a fraudulent history of the dance triumphs of Shirley Hastings and her mystery male partner is narrated to her son, the tale is acted out before our eyes in stylised choreography and costumes by characters prancing and primping in front of a painted backdrop and between stage curtains. This is family history rewritten into a fancy but two-dimensional performance.

The artifice of the Ballroom Dancing Federation and its members is especially marked in the costuming and style of the film. Almost all of the dancers we see in competition and at Kendall's studio, including Ballroom Federation heavyweights Les Kendall, Barry Fife and Ken Rayling, have platinum blonde hair in elaborate coifs, bouffants or comb-overs. The ultra blonde hair of the ballroom dancing contingent is precisely the shade that Richard Dyer argues is the marker of incontestable whiteness in stars like Marilyn Monroe.[13] The fakery involved in this white-blondeness is underlined in the character of Liz Holt (Gia Carides) whose dark hair is bleached blond and pulled into a levitating stiffly curled fringe. Carides is part of a well-known family of Greek-Australian actors and Baz Luhrmann in an interview has emphasised that he sought to cast her against public persona in this role.[14] Luhmann's casting of Carides emphasises the performative character not just of relationships but also of ethnicity.

The style of the film reiterates one of its central themes – the aspirational desires of the ballroom dancing fraternity and their willingness to bend the truth to achieve status and prestige. A neat image of this status-hungry fakery is presented to us when we see Liz and the equally dazzling blonde – and closet alcoholic – Ken Rayling bathing happily in a display spa in Ken's hot tub showroom. The spa, like the rotary clothesline, demands the space of the suburbs and this scene presents it, like bottle-blonde hair, as simply for display.

The fantastic, even grotesque, costumes donned by the ballroom dancers are perhaps the most obvious signifiers of the artifice and the effeminacy of ballroom dancing, with midriffs and chests, lustrous fabric, lime green feathers, spangles, lurid colours and fruit. One of the Federation's top dancers, Tina Sparkles, even reflects her gaudy costume in her name. The outfits and the rules of the Ballroom Dancing Federation reflect all the characteristics of suburbia according to its critics: 'inauthentic, banal, repetitive, tasteless, duped, a blot covering nature'.[15] Significantly, when Scott dances his own steps without an audience or rehearses 'authentic' Spanish folk dancing with Fran's father, he wears only his white singlet and dark trousers. The semiotics of the singlet – immediately identifiable in Australia, especially in its usual shade of blue, with male manual labourers[16] – underlines the contrast between the effete fakery of ballroom costumes and real masculinity to be found underneath or in the world of folk dancing. My reading of Scott's white singlet here is confirmed by the use of Paul Mercurio in an advertising campaign for the famous Australian clothing company, Bonds. Mercurio, wearing his white singlet, dancing in the ads alongside animated characters, is a more conventional 'Ocker', hypermasculine Australian style.[17]

The contrast between Scott's family and Fran's, between ballroom and folk dancing, between the white suburbanites and the Spanish-Australian inner-city dwellers is made mainly through the feminisation of the artifice of suburbia. Scott's father, cowed by pursuing his wife's ambitions at the expense of his own dreams, is a silent, passive figure throughout most of the film – a figure resembling the hen-pecked husband of the comic tradition.[18] Fran's father, on the other hand, is a powerful figure, who polices Fran's movements – including her dance moves – with a close paternal eye. Fran's grandmother is an imposing presence in the narrative – it is she who unbuttons Scott's shirt to reveal that white singlet, instructing him to feel the music in his heart, and quipping about his nice body in a Spanish he cannot understand. Nonetheless, the dance sequences, the centre of this film, emphasise not Fran's grandmother but her father. At one point, Scott and Fran's father play, through dance, the roles of matador and bull. Mercurio indicates in interviews that it is the parallel between Spanish dancing and the hypermasculine sport of bullfighting that first attracted him to the film.[19] So, on the one hand we have an authentic and paternalistic family, and on the other a fractured and self-deceptive one with a defeated father and a triumphant mother. The critique of suburbia in *Strictly Ballroom* is, in some ways at least, a critical commentary on families and especially fathers, who have lost their status.

The climax of the film reconciles the Spanish-Australian and the Anglo-Celtic families and the structures of establishment ballroom dancing and the authentic folk tradition, in a vision of Australian multiculturalism.[20] This reconciliation is staged (literally) when Scott and Francesca step outside of the rules of the Ballroom Dancing Federation to perform their original steps at the Pan Pacific Grand Prix. Like the fiesta at Fran's place, the final performance is participatory rather than competitive – at the very end the whole dance floor fills with dancing couples. Even Doug and Shirley Hastings, who have not danced together since 1968, come together on the dance floor. This reconciliation may be in the space offered by ballroom, but it is associated with the signifiers of ethnicity, masculinity and authenticity already established in the film. Fran wears her mother's dress and Scott a matador jacket, lent by Fran's father.[21] The authenticity of their dance is also guaranteed by the music that they dance to – or the lack of it. Just as at the fiesta, they are accompanied through part of their performance by simply the sounds of handclapping. This authenticity is underlined extratextually too, by the casting of Paul Mercurio, choreographer for the Sydney Ballet Company, and in the way that Mercurio's status was emphasised in publicity for the film.

The same staging of authentic inner-city life versus the fakeries of suburbia occurs in *Muriel's Wedding*. Where *Strictly Ballroom* judges suburban values by associating them with an inauthentic whiteness, *Muriel's Wedding* depicts suburbia as a place of claustrophobic gendered and sexual norms. Like *Strictly Ballroom*, however, the *bildungsroman* plotting of *Muriel's Wedding* links representations of suburbia intimately with music, costumes and performance. The first wedding of the film presents its central equation – marriage, and by extension heterosexual coupling – as fake. Muriel stumbles on Chook, the groom, having sex with his new bride's best friend in the laundry – an appropriately suburban location. Muriel's father arranges his extramarital affair by 'accidentally' meeting his mistress at restaurants, each time hailing her ritualistically: 'Deirdre, what a coincidence!' The increasingly elaborate lies Muriel tells to compile an album of photos of herself in wedding dress culminate in a marriage of convenience. Marriage to Muriel allows a South African swimmer to gain Australian nationality, evading the sporting boycott on South Africa and thus being able to compete in the Olympic games.

In the light of the links between whiteness, suburbia and fakery in *Strictly Ballroom*, it's interesting to note that it is a white South African who sets up Muriel's arranged marriage. On the other hand, the frank and free enjoyment of sex of Muriel's flatmate, Rhonda, has her bringing both black and white American sailors home for a night of highjinks. If a racialised geography of city and suburb in *Muriel's Wedding* is only hinted at, the association between suburbia and heterosexual marital couplings is clear.[22] The inner city in this film is a space for both unabashed (heterosexual) sex and real female friendship. Muriel leaves her adulterous and backstabbing female 'friends' behind along with Porpoise Spit's landscape of back yards and suburban streets when she moves to Sydney to share a flat with Rhonda. After Muriel decides upon her marriage of convenience the film returns to the terrain of suburbia. The setting of each part of the film underlines the association of suburbia with marriage and with lies.

Muriel's Wedding presents a much more critical view of the association of femininity and suburbia than *Strictly Ballroom*. Where Scott's mother represents all that is deceptive about suburbia, it's Muriel's father – local politician, adulterous husband, wheeler and dealer – who represents the parochialism and fakery of Porpoise Spit. The collapse of Muriel's mother's life is precipitated, in part, because she isn't able to carry off the smallest deception – not even getting away with an accidental lifting of a pair of cheap sandals. The moment of greatest pathos in the film is the death of Muriel's mother, significantly from an overdose of pills, a victim of what Betty Friedan called 'the problem that has no name' – the dissatisfaction of middle-class mothers trapped in suburbia.[23] Her unspoken final protest, setting fire to the back lawn, points the finger of blame not towards her husband or family, but at this symbol of suburbia itself.[24] However, if the film shows Muriel's mother as a victim of suburban hypocrisy rather than a perpetrator, Muriel's dad shares his sexual deceptions, his small-town horizons and his judgementalism with Muriel's Porpoise Spit 'friends'. *Muriel's Wedding* thus reiterates the association of feminine conformity with the suburbs.

As reviewers and interviewers note, this gaggle of vindictive girls is one of the film's most memorable visions of suburbia, particularly the opening scene with its vicious scrabbling for the bride's bouquet.[25] Images of the 'friends' feature prominently alongside pictures of Muriel in the photographs accompanying articles and reviews of the film. Intertextual factors spotlight Tania, the backstabbing newly wed, in particular. She is played by Sophie Lee, graduate of Australian soap *Flying Doctors* and Australian media celebrity of 1992.[26] Director P.J. Hogan locates Tania and her friends as, in essence, marking film's distinctiveness from Hollywood film-making – their removal from the centre of the narrative to the margins signals the different world view of this Australian film.[27]

As Jane Landsman remarks, 'Tania and her friends ... are 'hyperfemme' caricatures – drawing on a pastiche of Medusa-like wobbling headdresses, plastic-fruit Carmen Miranda dress-ups or overplayed femme fatale personae'.[28] As the reference to Medusa here indicates, Muriel's false friends could be discussed not just as ludicrous[29] but perhaps even grotesque[30] in their hyperfemininity. There are real similarities between the suburban norms of femininity here and the conformist ballroom dancing matriarchy in *Strictly Ballroom*, not least in the realm of costume. Tania's fruit headdress and coconut shell bustier would sit nicely alongside Tina Sparkles' ballgown with its 'wonderful fruit' and like Shirley Hastings, Deirdre Chambers sells cosmetics to young protégés. If there is a clearer thread of misogyny in *Strictly Ballroom's* imagining of suburban femininity, similar notions of femininity as pathology – 'narcissistic, envious, insincere, unjust and interested only in being loved'[31] are replayed in the bitchy suburban wives of *Muriel's Wedding*.

I have traced so far the well-worn association of suburbia with grotesque hyper-femininity in *Strictly Ballroom* and *Muriel's Wedding*. However, there is a missing element to this analysis. I have talked about style as a way of understanding representations of femininity, but this very same element of style pulls in the opposite direction to the argument I have made so far. The celebration of the music, costume and style of these films through their marketing and reception suggests a rather different view of suburbia.

The climax of *Strictly Ballroom* represents the triumph of the authentic, ethnically grounded dance of the *pasa doble* – in part, danced with no music at all. However, the credits roll to the sounds of the late 1970s John Paul Young disco hit 'Love is in the Air'; the song was rereleased as part of the promotion for the film, reviving JPY's fortunes in the charts. The video picked up on the excessive kitschery of the Hastings clan in its *mise en scène* and costuming. In the clip, the singer John Paul Young is accompanied not just by the romantic couple of the film but angels and other heavenly paraphernalia. The success of this song as the signature tune for the film and the circulation of the video underlined not 'authentic' Spanish inner-city life, but the visual elements of excess in the costumes, design and choreography of the film. The plotting of *Strictly Ballroom* may present a critique of the excesses, the effeminacy and the conformity of suburbia, but one of its key marketing tools, the theme song and its music video, recirculate and revel in that very excess.

The ubiquitous ABBA music in *Muriel's Wedding* has a similarly mixed set of meanings. Muriel's ABBA obsession characterises her life of lies in Porpoise Spit. When she starts her pursuit of the ultimate bridal photograph, she starts listening to ABBA again. On this evidence, ABBA seems to stand in for the self-deceptiveness of Muriel's fantasy life in suburbia. As she says to Rhonda:

> When I lived in Porpoise Spit I just stayed in my room for hours and listened to ABBA songs. Sometimes I'd stay in there all day. But since I met you and moved to Sydney I haven't listened to one ABBA song.

Inner-city living and genuine friendship take the place of ABBA, but there's an ambivalence here. ABBA might be central to Muriel's suburban self-delusions, but one of her first acts of revenge against her bitchy Porpoise Spit friends is a prizewinning karaoke performance, in the role of Frieda alongside Rhonda's Agnetha, of the aptly named ABBA tune 'Waterloo'. This scene is frequently mentioned in reviews and photographs as exemplifying Muriel and Rhonda's triumphant friendship.[32] Perhaps it is this moment that Muriel references when she goes on to say that she doesn't listen to ABBA anymore 'because my life's as good as an ABBA song – it's as good as Dancing Queen'. *Muriel's* director, P.J. Hogan, is certainly a fan: in interviews, he describes the 'love faxes' he sent to the band in the attempt to get permission to use ABBA songs in the film.[33] The film's celebration of ABBA is evidenced not just by the endorsement given to the film by the ABBA fanclub,[34] but also in the Australian ABBA tribute band Bjorn Again's performance at the film's Cannes Film Festival premiere.

One way of reconciling the negative representation of suburbia in these films with their celebration of suburban taste through costume, music and performance would be to draw on the notion of camp. The term 'camp' is frequently used when reviewers try to describe the style of *Strictly Ballroom*, *Muriel's Wedding* and other Australian films of this period.[35] David Hepworth's remarks are typical:

> No doubt a film student somewhere is already preparing his or her dissertation on the role of camp in the most recent flowering of Australian cinema. First *Strictly Ballroom*, then *The Adventures of Priscilla Queen of the Desert* and now *Muriel's Wedding* all flaunt the pink tulle underskirt covering the bony knees of Madame Oz.[36]

Moe Meyer has argued that camp is a form of parody, specifically by queers, of the dominant culture's originals. Camp thus allows a moment of queer visibility while 'piggybacking' on dominant ideologies. Meyer's account of camp as relying on an original certainly gives plenty of purchase on the use of music in the films.[37] We could see both Rhonda and Muriel's lip-synched performance of 'Waterloo' and Muriel's wedding, a performance of heterosexual union set to the strains of 'I Do, I Do, I Do'[38] as karaoke tributes to the ABBA originals. Other definitions of camp point to the way it emerges when objects of a previous moment of cultural production become available for rereading.[39] This emphasis on the nostalgia and 'failed seriousness' of camp can be similarly traced in both films' use of 1970s disco music.

Labelling *Strictly Ballroom* and *Muriel's Wedding* camp, as Thomas and other writers do, implies more than just describing their style. While some critics have viewed camp as blank parody, more recently queer and feminist theorists have seen camp as a critical resource. Describing these films as camp offers a reading of them, their style and the depictions of suburbia that are so central to their hyperbole of costume and music. According to this reading, such films can be seen not as a mobilisation of rather hackneyed representations of suburban femininity as conformist, ludicrous or even grotesque, but as critical rereadings of such representations.

Allan Thomas, starting from a discussion of *Priscilla Queen of the Desert*, makes explicit this celebratory reading of the camp style in these films. Thomas argues that we can see the use of camp style in Australian films as a way of articulating a progressive vision of Australian nationhood. He draws on Andrew Ross's definitions of camp:

Camp belongs to the history of the 'self-presentation' of arriviste groups. Because of their marginality, and lack of inherited
cultural capital, these groups parody their subordinate or
uncertain social status in 'a self-mocking abdication of pretensions to power'.[40]

Thinking through long-standing representations of Australia
as marginal to European and US 'centres' of culture, Thomas
argues that we can see a camp model of identity as present in
contemporary Australian cinema. *Muriel's Wedding* and *Strictly
Ballroom* both nostalgically embrace the styles of the unfash-
ionable 1970s – blue eyeshadow, satin and sequins – and by
drawing on these styles suggest Australia's distance from the
centres of taste and fashion.[41] If Australianness is characterised by the stylistic excess in such films, Thomas suggests,
camp style might serve to represent national identities as performative, as inauthentic.[42] There is an interesting alignment
here of Thomas's notion of camp Australian nationhood and
Homi Bhabha's argument that postcolonial subjects are
formed in the 'area between mimicry and mockery' of the
colonising culture.[43] Camp style could thus be seen as a
marker of marginality from both the originals of metropolitan
culture and the notion of a homogeneous, heterosexual
national identity.

There are a couple of problems with celebrating the double-
coded representations of suburban femininity in *Strictly Ballroom* and *Muriel's Wedding*. First, in moving from *Priscilla,
Queen of the Desert* to a discussion of its contemporaries,
Thomas leaves behind *Priscilla's* explicit (if depoliticised) references to gay men and queer culture. Neither *Muriel's Wedding*
nor *Strictly Ballroom* offer any gay or lesbian characters, despite
the critique of heterosexuality and the centring of female
friendship in the latter.[44] Meyer might argue that these films
are not in fact camp, since they bear no explicit markers of
queer culture. Instead, he might view them as, at best, containing an element of camp trace – a mark of queer uses of
camp that remains in mainstream culture. Alternatively, these
films could be described in the terms of Paul Rudnick and Kurt
Anderson 'heterosexual camp, Camp Lite'.[45]

More central to our discussion here of the gendered
metaphors underpinning representations of Australian suburbia is the problem of applying, in any simple way, models of
postcoloniality to settler colonies like white Australia. There is
a powerful argument to be made that white Australia should

be understood less as a postcolonial periphery and more as bearing the mantle of the colonial centre itself,[46] but Bhabha's central examples of such mimicry and mockery are the Indian administrative classes. MacAuley's education policy attempted to make these Indian elites English in sensibility, allowing them a place in the empire's chain of command.[47] Australia's status as both colony and coloniser presents, then, an even stronger argument for understanding white Australia as representative of Bhabha's 'mimic man'.[48] Reflecting this position, *Strictly Ballroom* and *Muriel's Wedding* mimic and mock discourses around suburbia in a way that suggests a point of view located both within and without suburbia, within and without the margins.

Bhabha's work suggests a problem with understanding the style of such Australian films as reflecting a take on global pop cultures from the fringe. The Camp Lite style of *Muriel's Wedding* and *Strictly Ballroom* presents Australia, yet again, as global suburbia. White Australian culture might present an example where this metaphor proves analytically useful. The spatial metaphor that equates the powerful with the centre and the marginal with the powerless is confounded by the suburbs. Suburbia may be literally on the margins of the metropolis but this is a margin of relative privilege.

Notes

1. See Stephen Crofts, '*The Adventures of Barry Mackenzie*: Comedy, Satire and Nationhood in 1972', *Continuum* vol. 10, no.2 (1996): 125, and John McCallum, 'Cringe and strut: comedy and national identity in postwar Australia', in *Because I Tell a Joke or Two: Comedy, Politics and Social Difference*, ed. Stephen Wagg, London, 1998, 206.

2. See Deborah Chambers, 'A Stake in the Country: Women's Experiences of Suburban Development', in *Visions of Suburbia*, ed. Roger Silverstone, London, 1997, 86.

3. See John Archer, 'Colonial Suburbs in South Asia, 1700–1850, and the Spaces of Modernity', in *Visions of Suburbia*, ed. Roger Silverstone, London, 1997, 27.

4. See Sandy George, 'The Knack and How to Keep It', *Screen International*, November 7 (1997a): 28.

5. For examples see Catherine Simpson, 'Suburban subversions: Women's Negotiation of Suburban Space in Australian Cinema', *Metro*, no. 18 (1999): 118; Karl Quinn, 'Drag, dags and the Suburban Surreal', *Metro*, no.100 (1994–5) 23; Angie Errigo, '*Muriel's Wedding* (review)', *Premiere*, vol. 3, no. 2 May (1995): 12; John Hartley, 'The Sexualisation of Suburbia: The Diffusion of Knowledge in the Postmodern Public Sphere', in *Visions of Suburbia*, ed. Roger Silverstone, London, 1997, 193; Tom O'Regan, 'Beyond

"Australian Film": Australian Cinema in the 1990s', *Continuum* online, http://wwkali.murdoch.edu.au/~cntinuum/index1.html (1997).

6. Quinn, 'Drag, dags and the Suburban Surreal', 24. See also Simpson, 'Suburban subversions: Women's Negotiation of Suburban Space in Australian Cinema', 31.

7. Simpson, 'Suburban subversions: Women's Negotiation of Suburban Space in Australian Cinema', 24, and Andy Medhurst, 'Negotiating the Gnome Zone: Versions of Suburbia in British Popular Culture', in *Visions of Suburbia*, ed. Roger Silverstone, London, 1997, 267.

8. O'Regan, 'Beyond "Australian Film": Australian Cinema in the 1990s'.

9. David Chaney, 'Authenticity and suburbia', in *Imagined Cities: Scripts, Signs, Memory*, eds Sally Westwood and John Williams, London, 1997, 143

10. See Simpson, 'Suburban subversions: Women's Negotiation of Suburban Space in Australian Cinema', 126.

11. Cited in Sneja Gunew, 'Denaturalizing cultural nationalisms: multicultural readings of Australia', in *Nation and Narration*, ed. Homi K. Bhabha, London, 1990, 99–120.

12. Simpson, 'Suburban subversions: Women's Negotiation of Suburban Space in Australian Cinema', 126.

13. Richard Dyer, *Heavenly Bodies: Film Stars and Society*, London, 1986, 42–43; see also Pamela Robertson, *Guilty Pleasures: Feminist Camp from Mae West to Madonna*, London, 1996, 36.

14. Ronnie Talor, 'Baz Luhrmann's *Strictly Ballroom*', *Cinema Papers* 88 (1992): 6–10.

15. Medhurst, 'Negotiating the Gnome Zone: Versions of Suburbia In British Popular Culture', in Silverstone ed., *Visions of Suburbia*, 267.

16. Crofts, '*The Adventures of Barry McKenzie*: Comedy, Satire and Nationhood in 1972', 134.

17. For a definition of 'Ocker', see Crofts.

18. Marion Jordan, 'Carry On ... Follow that Stereotype', in *British Cinema History*, eds James Curran and Vincent Porter, London, 1983, 319.

19. See *Premiere* 1992: 108.

20. O'Regan, 'Beyond "Australian Film": Australian Cinema in the 1990s', 5.

21. Mark Salisbury, '*Strictly Ballroom* (review)', *Empire*, no.4 (1992): 32.

22. See also Medhurst, 'Negotiating the Gnome Zone: Versions of Suburbia In British Popular Culture', in Silverstone, ed., *Visions of Suburbia*, 266.

23. Betty Friedan, *The Feminine Mystique*, London, 1965, 13.

24. Simpson, 'Suburban subversions: Women's Negotiation of Suburban Space in Australian Cinema', 126.

25. See Jan Epstein, 'Muriel's Wedding', *Cinema Papers*, no.101 (1994): 31; David Vallence, '*Muriel's Wedding* (review)', *Cinema Papers*, no.102, (1994): 69–70; O'Regan, 'Beyond "Australian Film": Australian Cinema in the 1990s', 5.

26. John Hartley, 'The Sexualisation of Suburbia: The Diffusion of Knowledge in the Postmodern Public Sphere', in Silverstone ed., *Visions of Suburbia*, 193–5.

27. Louise Wignall, 'The Extraordinary in the Ordinary: P.J. Hogan talks about *Muriel's Wedding*', *Metro*, no. 99, (1994): 31–4.

28. Jane Landman, 'See the Girl, Watch that Scene: Fantasy and Desire in *Muriel's Wedding*', *Continuum*, vol. 10, no. 2, (1996): 111–12.

29. Epstein, 'Muriel's Wedding', 31; Landman, 'See the Girl, Watch that Scene: Fantasy and Desire in *Muriel's Wedding*', 111.

30. O'Regan, 'Beyond "Australian Film": Australian Cinema in the 1990s', 8.

31. Landman, 'See the Girl, Watch that Scene: Fantasy and Desire in *Muriel's Wedding'*, 115–6.
32. For example see Allan Thomas, 'Camping Outback: Landscape, Masculinity and Performance in *The Adventures of Priscilla, Queen of the Desert'*, *Continuum* vol. 10, no.2, (1996): 97–110.
33. Kitty Bowe Hearty, 'Bride and Joy', *Premiere*, vol.8, no.3, (1995): 92.
34. Kristen O'Neill, 'Mamma Mia here we go again', *Premiere*, vol.2, no.12, (1995): 27.
35. For example see Vallence, '*Muriel's Wedding* (review)', 69; O'Regan, 'Beyond "Australian Film": Australian Cinema in the 1990s', 5; Pamela Robertson, *Guilty Pleasures: Feminist Camp from Mae West to Madonna*, London, 1996: 151; Kitty Bowe Hearty, 'Flirty Dancing: hot to trot', *Premiere*, vol.6, no.6, (1993): 30.
36. David Hepworth, '*Muriel's Wedding* (review)', *Empire*, no.78, (1995): 137.
37. For examples see: Errigo, '*Muriel's Wedding* (review)', 12; George, 'The Knack and How to Keep It', 19; O'Regan, 'Beyond "Australian Film": Australian Cinema in the 1990s'.
38. John Champagne, 'Dancing Queen? Feminist and Gay Male Spectatorship in Three Recent Films from Australia', *Film Criticism*, vol.21, no.3, (1997): 71.
39. Robertson, *Guilty Pleasures: Feminist Camp from Mae West to Madonna*, 5.
40. Cited in Thomas, 'Camping Outback: Landscape, Masculinity and Performance in *The Adventures of Priscilla, Queen of the Desert'*, 103.
41. See McCallum, 'Cringe and strut: comedy and national identity in postwar Australia', in Stephen Wagg, ed., *Because I Tell a Joke or Two: Comedy, Politics and Social Difference*, 206–7; Quinn, 'Drag, dags and the Suburban Surreal', 23–4.
42. Thomas, 'Camping Outback: Landscape, Masculinity and Performance in *The Adventures of Priscilla, Queen of the Desert'*, 105.
43. Bhabha, *Nation and Narration*, 86.
44. See Hilary Harris, 'Queer white woman as spectator', *Media International Australia*, no.78, (1995): 39.
45. Cited in Robertson, *Guilty Pleasures: Feminist Camp from Mae West to Madonna*, 120.
46. Jane Jacobs, *Edge of Empire: Postcolonialism and the City*, London, 1996: 23–4.
47. Bhabha, *Nation and Narration*, 87.
48. Ibid., 86.

NOTES ON CONTRIBUTORS

Peter Childs is Senior Lecturer in English at Cheltenham and Gloucester College of Higher Education. His primary areas of research are in post-colonial studies and twentieth-century literature. He has recently edited a reader on *Post-Colonial Theory and English Literature* (1999) for Edinburgh University Press and written the volume on *Modernism* (2000) in the New Critical Idiom series published by Routledge.

Gail Cunningham has taught at Oxford, Middlesex and the Open Universities, and is currently Pro Vice-Chancellor and Dean of the Faculty of Human Sciences at Kingston University. She has published widely on nineteenth- and twentieth-century fiction, and is at present preparing a book on New Woman novelists of the 1890s.

Simon Dentith is Reader in English at Cheltenham and Gloucester College of Higher Education. He has published widely on nineteenth- and twentieth-century culture, including, most recently, a book on *Society and Cultural Forms in Nineteenth-Century England* (Macmillan, 1998).

Lynne Hapgood is Head of English at The Nottingham Trent University where her main teaching and research interests are in late nineteenth-century and early twentieth-century English fiction. She recently co-edited *Outside Modernism: in Pursuit of the English Novel, 1900–1930* (Macmillan, 2000) with Nancy Paxton, and has published in a range of journals including

Literature and Theology and *Literature and History*. She is currently completing *Margins of Desire: the Suburbs in Fiction and Culture, 1880–1930* for Manchester University Press.

Dominic Head is Reader in the School of English, University of Central England. He has published books on the short story, Nadine Gordimer, and J.M. Coetzee. His current research interests include ecocriticism, and the future of English Studies. He is currently writing a survey of post-war British fiction from 1950–2000.

Daniel Lea is lecturer in literary studies at Liverpool John Moores University. His main areas of interest are contemporary British fiction, modernism and narratives of trauma. He has published on Martin Amis, Julian Barnes and J.G. Farrell, and is currently writing on George Orwell and modernist trauma narratives.

Nicole Matthews lectures in media and cultural studies at Liverpool John Moores University. Her book *Comic Politics: gender in Hollywood comedy after the new right* will be published by Manchester University Press in 2000. Her interest in gendered practices of the self has led to research on various forms of everyday television, including sitcom, reality T.V. and repeats.

Linden Peach is Professor of Modern Literature at Loughborough University. His research interests are in contemporary fiction, Virginia Woolf and her historical context, the modern Irish novel, and Welsh writing in English. He is currently researching the representation of crime and deviancy in modern literature. His recent publications include *Virginia Woolf* (2000) and *Angela Carter* (1998). He has edited *Toni Morrison Contemporary Critical Essays* (1998) and a new edition of his book on Toni Morrison is forthcoming from Macmillan.

Joanna Price is Principal Lecturer in American Studies at Liverpool John Moores University. She has published essays about Richard Ford, post-modern American Jewish autobiographies, the Vietnam Veterans Memorial, and feminist theory. Her book *Understanding Bobbie Ann Mason* is forthcoming with the University of South Carolina Press.

D.J. Taylor is the author of four novels, most recently *English Settlement* (1996) and *Trespass* (1998), and two critical studies,

A Vain Conceit: British Fiction in the 1980s (1989) and *After the War: The Novel and England Since 1945* (1993). His biography of W.M.Thackeray appeared in 1999. He is currently working on a centenary biography of George Orwell.

Roger Webster is Professor of Literary Studies and Director of the School of Media, Critical and Creative Arts at Liverpool John Moores University. He has published on Thomas Hardy, working-class fiction, literary theory and the 1930s.

SELECT BIBLIOGRAPHY

Julian Barnes, *Metroland*, London, 1980.

Anthony Barnett and Roger Scruton, (eds), *Town and Country*, London, 1998.

John Carey, *The Intellectuals and the Masses,* London, 1992.

W. Spencer Clarke, *The Suburban Homes of London*, London, 1881.

Steven Connor, *The English Novel in History, 1950-1995*, London, 1997.

T.W.H Crosland, *The Suburbans*, London, 1905.

H.J. Dyos, *Victorian Suburb: A Study of the Growth of Camberwell*, Leicester, 1961.

A. Conan Doyle, *Beyond the City: An Idyll of a Suburb*, London, 1912.

Arthur Edwards, *The Design of Suburbia: a Critical Study in Environmental History*, London, 1981.

Mike Featherstone, *Consumer Culture and Postmodernism*, London, 1991.

Robert Fishman, *Bourgeois Utopias: The Rise and Fall of Suburbia*, New York, 1987.

Joel Garreau, *Edge City: Life on the New Frontier*, New York, 1991.

David Harvey, *The Condition of Postmodernity*, Oxford, 1990.

Alan A. Jackson, *Semi-Detached London: Suburban Development, Life and Transport, 1900–39*, London, 1973.

Jane Jacobs, *Edge of Empire: Postcolonialism and the City*, London, 1996.

Flint, Kate (1986) 'Fictional Suburbia' in *Literature and History* vol.8, no.1, (1982): 67–81.

C.F.G. Masterman, *Condition of England*, 1909, London, 1960.

David Meadows, *Nattering in Paradise: Suburbia in the 1980s*, London, 1988.

Paul Oliver, Ian Davis and Ian Bentley, *Dunroamin: The Suburban Semi and its Enemies*, London, 1981, rev. 1984.

J.J. Palen, *The Suburbs*, London, 1995.

J. Phillips and H. Barrett, *Suburban Style: The British Home 1840–1960*, London, 1987.

C.B.Purdom, *The Building of Satellite Towns*, London, 1935, 60.

Edward Relph, *Place and Placelessness*, London, 1976.

J.M. Richards, *The Castles on the Ground: The Anatomy of Suburbia*, London, 1973.

Miranda Sawyer, *Park and Ride: Adventures in Suburbia*, London, 1999.

Rob Shields (ed.), *Lifestyle Shopping: The Subject of Consumption*, London and New York, 1992.

Roger Silverstone (ed.), *Visions of Suburbia*, London, 1997.

F. M. L. Thompson, *The Rise of Suburbia*, Leicester, 1982.

David Thorns, *Suburbia*, London, 1972.

Yi-Fu Tuan, *Topophilia: A Study of Environmental Perception, Attitudes and Values*, New Jersey, 1974.

Raymond Williams, *The Country and the City*, London, 1973.

P. Willmott and M. Young, *Family and Class in a London Suburb*, London, 1960.

INDEX

ABBA, 180
  'Dancing Queen', 180
  'I Do, I Do, I Do, I Do, I Do', 181
  'Waterloo', 180, 181
Adventures of Priscilla Queen of the Desert,
  The, 181, 182
Albarn, Damon, 162–3, 164, 165, 169
alienation, 72, 79, 83, 84, 99, 122, 129,
  130, 131, 146, 147, 149, 152, 165
America, 6, 63, 104, 109, 111, 113, 117,
  125, 130
  American, 10, 100, 109, 112, 114, 122,
  125, 132, 133, 135, 136, 138, 162, 178
  American Dream, the, 128
Amis, Kingsley, 72
  Lucky Jim, 72
anarchy, 123, 154
Anderson, Kurt, 182
Anglo-Australian, 174
Anglo-Celtic, 173, 174, 177
Anglo-Indian, 95
Anglophile, 95
anomie, 101
Archer, Jeffrey, 144
Archer, John, 174
The Architect, 93
Arsenal Football Club, 7, 11, 142, 143,
  144, 145, 146, 147, 148, 149, 150,
  152, 156
Arts and Crafts, 7, 15–16, 17, 18, 20, 22,
  23, 24, 26, 27, 28, 29, 55
Asia, 133
Australia, 6, 12, 173, 176, 182, 183
  Australian, 11, 175, 176, 177, 179, 181,
  182, 183
avenues, 6

Baden-Powell, 42
  Boy Scout movement, 42

Baldock, 28
Balham, 37
Ball, John Clement, 92
Baltimore, Anne Tyler, 126
Balzac, 5
Barker, Paul, 73
Barnes, Julian, 8, 77–8, 93
  Metroland, 77–8, 93
Barstow, Stan, 8, 72
  A Kind of Loving, 72
Barthelme, Frederick, 126, 134
Baudrillard, Jean, 6, 133
BBC, the, 141
Beatles, the, 163, 166
Beckenham, 101, 103, 166
Bedford Park, 23
Bellamy, Edward, 17
  Looking Backward, 17
Bennett, Arnold, 5, 13n8, 61, 66–8, 69, 93
  A Man from the North, 5, 13n8, 66–8, 69
Berne, Suzanne, 109–10, 112, 113, 115,
  116, 117, 119–20
  A Crime in the Neighbourhood, 10,
  109–10, 112, 113, 115
Besant, Walter, 46, 51
Betjeman, John, 5, 27–8, 165
  Collected Poems, 27
  Metroland, 5
  Mount Zion, 27
  'Slough', 5
Bhabha, Homi, 100, 182, 183
Bildungsroman, 86, 177
Bjorn Again, 180
Blackwood's Magazine, 35
Blur, 162, 163, 165, 168, 169, 170
  'Ernold Same', 169
  The Great Escape, 165
  'Stereotypes', 168, 169
  'Tracy Jacks', 169

body, 8, 121
Boer War, the, 41
Bohemian, 104, 105, 120
Bombay, 95, 99
Bonds, 176
Booth, Charles, 32, 41, 47–8
boundaries, 11, 120, 122, 125, 141, 144, 146, 153
Bournville, 25
Bowie, David, 5, 11, 83, 84, 104, 165, 166, 167
    Ziggy Stardust, 166
Bracewell, Michael, 161, 163, 166, 169, 170
Braine, 86
Brecht, Bertolt, 116
Brinkmeyer, Jr., Robert H., 134
Britain, 72, 73, 81, 92, 93, 94, 95, 96, 100, 106, 119, 173
    British, 79, 81, 83, 91, 92, 94, 95, 102, 103, 105, 109, 112, 114, 141, 154, 164, 167
    British Asian, 9, 86, 97, 106
    British India Society, 92–3
Brixton, 66
Bromley, 11, 83, 101, 103, 154, 163, 166, 167
Bromstead, 56
Bryson, Bill, 4, 13n6
    Notes from a Small Island 4, 13n6
Builder, The, 40, 44–5
Bull, John, 94
Bullock, Shan, 93
Buzzcocks, 163

Cadbury, 25
Cairo, 131
Calais, 4
Camberwell, 55, 63, 64
Camden Town, 34
camp, 11, 12, 181–2
Cannes Film Festival, 180
Canvey Island, 154
Cardiff, 95
Carey, John, 53, 54
    The Intellectuals and the Masses, 53
Caribbean, 94, 96
carnivalesque, 147, 155
Caroline, 169
Carpenter, Edward, 22
Catholic, Roman, 115, 170
Chaudhuri, Amit, 92, 96
    Afternoon Raag, 96
Chaudhuri, Nirad, 94–5
Chekov, Anton, 2
Chesterton, G.K., 66
Chicago, 136, 161
Christianised, 46
Cincinnati, 112
city, 2, 3, 4, 5, 6, 7, 8, 10, 11, 31, 32, 33, 34, 35, 39, 40, 41, 42, 43, 45, 46, 54, 60, 73, 74, 79, 82, 84, 92, 93, 95, 97,
    99, 110, 111, 120, 121, 122, 125, 134, 141, 142, 144, 147, 148, 150, 151, 152, 154, 155, 156, 157, 158, 161, 162, 165, 167, 168, 174, 176, 177, 178, 180
cities, 8, 17, 92, 96, 125, 161, 163
The Citizen, 33
Clapham, 29, 34, 40
Clarke, W. Spencer, 33–4
class, 2, 6, 7, 10, 20, 29, 30, 31, 33, 34, 35, 37, 38, 40, 41, 42, 43, 44, 47, 48, 58, 61, 69, 75, 83, 86, 92, 100, 102, 105, 120, 127, 128, 142, 147, 149, 155, 165, 183
    aristocracy, 43, 46, 63, 71
    artisan, 36
    blue collar, 37
    bourgeois, 6, 71, 77, 83, 111
    lower middle class, 36, 38, 45, 96, 97, 103, 120
    middle class, 10, 24, 33, 35, 36, 37, 39, 42, 43, 44, 45, 46, 47, 48, 52, 54, 65, 66, 71, 83, 93, 97, 104, 111, 113, 114, 134, 144, 147, 148, 150, 151, 152, 155, 156, 165, 178
    proletariat, 83
    subclass, 102
    underclass, 96, 101, 133
    upper class, 2
    upper middle class, 35, 59, 120
    working class, 2, 24, 33, 34, 35, 36, 38, 43, 45, 46, 47, 72, 96, 142, 147, 148, 155, 165, 170
Clausen, Christopher, 112–13
Cleese, John, 144
Cocker, Jarvis, 163
Colchester, 162
Collini, Stefan, 81–2
colonial, 7, 9, 92, 95, 99, 183
    colonialism, 2, 42
    colony, 2, 91, 93, 174, 182
    colonisation, 11, 182
    colonised, 8, 96, 104, 166
commercial, 7, 26, 73, 74
    commercialism, 28
commodification, 2, 6, 83, 128, 130, 132, 133
    commoditization, 126, 133
Commonweal, 16
community, 9, 10, 11, 20, 43, 47, 73, 74, 75, 79, 91, 92, 95, 96, 101, 111, 121, 122, 126, 132, 135, 144, 148, 149, 150, 158, 163, 164
Conan Doyle, Arthur, 32, 68, 112–13
    The Hound of the Baskervilles, 112–13
    Beyond the City, 68
Connor, Steven, 86
consumer, 5, 9, 10, 126, 127, 128, 129, 131, 132, 133, 137, 138, 149
    consumerism, 2, 6, 7, 127, 131, 133, 134
    consumption, 6, 11, 82, 129, 130, 133

Contemporary Review, 41
Corinthian, 44
Cornwell, Patricia, 111, 112, 121
  Body of Evidence, 111, 121, 122
  Postmortem, 111–12
Costello, Elvis, 167
  'I don't want to go to Chelsea', 167
country, 2, 3, 4, 5, 10, 54, 81, 92, 93, 101,
  113, 121, 122, 123, 134, 141, 148,
  162, 163, 169, 173
  countryside, 42, 43, 55
Country Life, 25
Cowper, William, 52, 69n2
Crawley, 163
credit card, 6
crime, 10, 109, 111, 112, 114, 115, 116,
  118, 119, 120, 122, 123
Crosland, T.W.H., 52, 54–5, 59–60, 68
  The Suburbans, 52
Croydon, 81, 166, 167
cultural, 2, 3, 5, 54, 58, 63, 69, 75, 82, 83,
  87, 91, 94, 97, 100, 102, 120, 126,
  127, 134, 141, 144, 145, 151, 155,
  157, 181, 182
  culture, 8, 9, 11, 33, 72, 74, 79, 81, 82,
  83, 87, 100, 101, 104, 111, 126, 128,
  129, 131, 132, 133, 137, 138, 141,
  142, 143, 157, 161, 163, 182, 183
Cure, the, 163, 169, 170
  'Faith', 169
  'One Hundred Years', 169
  'The Drowning Man', 169
Curtis, Ian, 163, 170
Curzon, Lord, 41

Dabydeen, David, 93
D'Arcy, Ella, 60
Daily Mail, the, 25
Darwinism, 113
Dawson, W.J., 45
deconstruct, 133, 134
defamiliarisation, 8, 10, 110, 134
degeneration, 21
Delderfield, R.F., 165, 169
  The Avenue Goes To War, 165
  The Dreaming Suburb, 165
denaturalisation, 134
Desai, Anita, 93
Devoto, Howard, 163, 168
Dexter, Colin, 119, 120
  The Silent World of Nicholas Quinn, 119
Dhondy, Farrukh, 94
dialogic, 12, 157
  dialogical, 5
Dickens, Charles, 93
  Great Expectations, 93
Didion, Joan, 130
Diski, Jenny, 116–18
  Nothing Natural, 116–18
diverse, 8
Divorced Men's Club, the, 10

domestic, 6, 33, 39, 40, 41, 46, 47, 54,
  60–5, 68, 73, 78, 111, 120, 121, 126,
  127, 143, 144, 149, 169
design, 6
Donovan, Jason, 173
Dorset, 118
Dostoevsky, 170
Dover, 4
Drabble, Margaret, 75, 86
Duncan-Sandys, Duncan, 100
Dyer, Richard, 175
dysfunction, 11, 118, 121
dystopian, 6

Ealing, 56, 154, 164
Easter, 135, 137
economic, 8, 33, 35, 36, 37, 43, 74, 84,
  134, 155, 170
  economy, 7, 126, 135
Edinburgh, 96
Edwards, Arthur, 32, 48n3, 71, 73
Eliot, T.S., 53
  The Wasteland, 53
Emechta, Buchi, 93
Emmett, J.T., 45
Empire, 41, 85, 91, 92, 103, 104, 183
England, 8, 9, 41, 42, 51, 71, 85, 92, 94,
  95, 97, 99, 100, 102, 103, 104, 105,
  106, 118, 151, 163, 170
  English, 6, 9, 21, 24, 33, 34, 38, 46, 53,
  55, 79, 81, 85, 86, 87, 92, 93, 94, 95,
  97, 98, 99, 100, 101, 102, 104, 105,
  106, 112, 114, 115, 119, 141, 154,
  161, 162, 163, 164, 165, 166, 168,
  169, 170, 183
environment, 5, 7, 21, 41, 55, 68, 69, 71,
  106, 109, 111, 113, 130, 131, 142,
  145, 150, 163, 165, 167
Essex, 42, 162, 163, 168, 169
ethnicity, 12, 87, 97, 102, 104, 174, 175,
  177
eugenics, 21
existential, 145, 156, 157

Fabian, 55
Faltskog, Agnetha, 180
family, 10, 12, 39, 40, 45, 46, 47, 54, 56,
  62, 64, 65, 81, 95, 96, 104, 105, 112,
  114, 115, 118, 121, 122, 127, 134,
  137, 142, 143, 145, 154, 165, 173,
  174, 175, 176, 177, 178
Featherstone, Mike, 128
feminist, 8, 28, 58–9, 128, 132, 181
First Garden City Company, 16, 22, 24, 25
First World War, the, 81
Fishman, Robert, 111, 125
Flanders and Swann, 144
Flint, Kate, 93
Flying Doctors, 179
football, 8, 41, 103, 142, 143, 144, 145,
  147, 148, 149, 150, 153, 155

Ford, President, 167
Ford, Richard, 10, 125, 126, 133–8
  Independence Day, 135
  The Sportswriter, 134–8
  'Walker Percy', 125
Forster, E.M., 95
  A Passage to India, 95
French, 4
Freud, Sigmund, 83
Friedan, Betty, 59, 178
  The Feminine Mystique, 59
Frith, Simon, 83–4, 141, 154, 158, 161,
  163, 166, 169
Fry's Turkish Delight, 104
Fulham, 61, 67

Gandhi, 103
garden, 2, 3, 7, 8, 25, 38, 42, 52, 54–5,
  56–7, 60, 93, 96, 165
Garden City, 7, 15, 16, 17, 18, 19, 21, 22,
  23, 24–5, 26–7, 28, 29
Gaunt, W.H., 22, 23
gay, 114, 115, 138, 182
Geddes, Patrick, 32
gender, 6,8, 12, 20, 39, 54, 58, 59, 63, 65,
  66, 69, 102, 127, 128, 143, 144, 174,
  177, 182
geographical, 2, 3, 4, 8, 10, 40, 51, 54, 71,
  72, 91, 94, 97, 110, 120, 145, 146,
  147, 148, 149, 151, 178
Ghosh, Amitav, 94
Gissing, George, 32, 43, 54, 57, 58, 61–66,
  68, 93, 164
  In the Year of Jubilee, 32, 63–6
  The Nether World, 43
  The Paying Guest, 58
  The Whirlpool, 61–3
Gnome Zone, the, 154
Golders Green, 15, 116
Good Friday, 135
Goons, the, 144
Great War, the, 165
Greek-Australian, 175
Greenwood, Frederick, 35–6
Grossmith, George & Wedon, 8, 38–9, 40,
  45, 46, 57
  Diary of a Nobody, 8
Gulf Coast, 134
Gunnersbury, 62
Gupta, Sunetra, 94

Hall, Stuart, 105–6
Hamilton, Patrick, 165, 169
  The Midnight Bell, 165
  The Plains of Cement, 165
  The Siege of Pleasure, 165
Hammersmith, 23
Hampshire, 169
Hampstead, 116
  Hampstead Garden Suburb, 15, 16, 20,
  23
Hardy, Thomas, 43

Jude the Obscure, 43
Harmsworth, 25
Harrison, Frederic, 32
  The Meaning of History, 32
Harrow, 65, 154
Hartley, John, 118
Harvey, David, 73
Haywards Heath, 163
hegemony, 3, 7
Hepworth, David, 181
Hertfordshire, 42, 151
Hightower, Lynn, 111–12
  The Debt Collector, 111–12
Hindu, 82
hippies, 120
history, 4, 5, 20, 71, 77, 78, 81, 91, 92,
  104, 111, 120, 126, 127, 132, 133,
  135, 137, 146, 150, 152, 155, 167,
  168, 175, 182
Hogan, P.J., 179, 180
  Muriel's Wedding, 174, 177–83
Hollywood, 179
Home and Away, 173
Home Counties, the, 11, 150
Hornby, Nick, 8, 10, 11, 142–57
  Fever Pitch, 8, 10, 11, 142–50, 152, 153,
  156–7
  High Fidelity, 10, 11, 142, 150–7
Horowitz, Michael, 169
  New Departures, 169
houses, 3,4
  boxes, 4, 23, 52
  bungalow, 81
  cottages, 18, 19, 23
  detached, 54, 56
  flats, 19, 116
  mansion, 81, 110
  semi-detached, 2, 4, 6, 19, 54, 72, 93,
  96, 109, 119, 122, 166
  slums, 22
  terrace, 19
  villas, 6, 54, 55, 60, 109
Housing Act, 26–7
Howard, Ebenezer, 15, 16, 17, 18, 19, 22,
  25, 27, 32
  Garden Cities of Tomorrow, 15, 16
Howard, 32, 68, 93
  The Smiths of Surbiton, 68
Humphreys, Barry, 173
  Edna Everage, Housewife Megastar, 173
hybrid, 9, 10, 99, 102, 134, 142, 157
  hybridity, 6, 9, 80, 86, 99, 101, 141, 152
hyper-reality, 6, 127, 155

Ibsen, Henrik, 2, 79
ideal, 10, 20, 26, 39, 42, 43, 74, 75, 110,
  111, 113, 114, 118, 121, 126, 134,
  145, 150, 157
  Ideal Homes Exhibition, 25
  idealism, 6, 12, 74, 104, 119, 152, 157
  idealistic, 7, 73,
  idyllic, 6

identity, 4, 5, 6, 9, 10, 76, 80, 84, 85, 86, 87, 92, 94, 98, 99, 100, 101, 102, 103, 104, 106, 120, 127, 132, 135, 137, 141, 142, 144, 145, 146, 147, 148, 150, 151, 152, 153, 155, 157, 182
identities, 9, 31, 79, 102, 117, 133, 182
ideological, 4, 7, 71, 79, 127, 130, 133, 134, 135, 138, 181
Idol, Billy, 83, 104
Illinois, 131
immigrants, 7, 35
immigration, 100
imperialism, 21, 41, 92, 93, 95, 96, 105, 106
Independent Labour Party (I.L.P.), 28–9
Indian, 9, 86, 87, 92, 93, 94, 95, 97, 98, 100, 101, 102, 103, 105, 106, 183
individual, 6, 22, 82, 115, 126, 135, 143, 144, 145, 151, 153, 154, 156, 157
individuality, 4, 66, 81, 147, 148
industrialisation, 7, 48
interstates, 127
Ireland, 115
Irish, 115, 145
Italian, 4
Ivory, Merchant, 144

Jackson, Alan, 116
Jackson, Holbrook, 15, 16, 26
Jam, The, 167–8
'A Bomb in Wardour Street', 167
'In The City', 167
'London Girl', 167
'Private Hell', 168
'Smithers-Jones', 168
Jefferies, Richard, 42–3, 44
Jenkins, David, 146
Jesus Christ, 137, 145
jingoism, 103
Joy Division, 163, 170

Kanga, Firdaus, 92, 94, 95–6, 105
Heaven on Wheels, 94
Kaleta, Kenneth, 87
Kensington, 100
Kentucky, 127, 132, 133
Kilburn, 20
Kinks, The, 166
Kipling, Rudyard, 103
The Jungle Book, 103
Knight, Stephen, 113
Kureishi, Hanif, 5, 82–87, 92, 98, 99–102, 166
The Buddha of Suburbia, 8–9, 82–6, 98, 99–102, 166
'The Rainbow Sign', 100

Lamming, George, 93
Lancashire, 23
landscape, 3, 10, 34, 109, 111, 123, 127, 136, 168, 170, 174, 178
Landsman, Jane, 179

Langman, Lauren, 130
Larkin, Philip, 78
law and order, 10, 113
lawn, 7, 112, 113, 122, 143, 169, 174, 178
Leavis, Q.D., 4, 13n7
Lebeau, Vicky, 154
Lee, Sophie, 179
Lee, Vernon, 59
Leigh, Mike, 2, 93
Abigail's Party, 2, 93
Lennon, John, 163
lesbian, 105, 182
Letchworth, 15, 16, 17, 18, 19, 21, 22, 23, 24, 25, 28, 29
Lever, 25
Levy, Amy, 59
lifestyle, 6, 130
Lincolnshire, 36
Liverpool, 92, 96, 170
Lloyd George, David, 28
London, 3, 4, 11, 16, 25, 27, 31, 40, 41, 43, 44, 45, 47, 51, 53, 54, 62, 63, 65, 73, 75, 77, 78, 82, 83, 85, 87, 92, 93, 95, 96, 99, 101, 103, 105, 109, 116, 141, 142, 143, 144, 145, 146, 149, 150, 152, 154, 156, 158, 162, 163, 164, 165, 166, 167, 168, 170
London Bridge, 101
London County Council, 32
London Indian Society, 93
Londonderry, 170
Low, Sidney, 8, 41, 42
Luhrmann, Baz, 174, 175
Strictly Ballroom, 174–83
Lurkers, The, 167
'Fulham Fallout', 167
Lynch, David, 79
Lyngstad, Anni-Frid, 180

McCartney, Paul, 163
McEwan, Ian, 76
McLaren, Malcolm, 166, 167
Madame Tussaud, 97
Magazine, 163, 168
Real Life, 163
Maidenhead, 11, 142
Manchester, 23, 25, 36, 170
Manfred Mann, 161, 166
'Semi-detached Suburban Mr Jones', 161, 166
Maryland, 132
Marx, Karl, 83
Mason, Bobby Ann, 10, 126–33, 138
'Coyotes', 128–9
In Country, 132–3
'Piano Fingers', 129
'The Secret of the Pyramids', 130–1
'Shiloh', 126–7
Mason, Simon, 79–81
Lives of the Dog-Stranglers, 79–80
Masterman, C.F.G., 32, 34, 42, 47
The Condition of England, 32

Masters, John, 102
  Bhowani Junction, 102
Mayfair, 165
Mayhew, Henry, 92
Mearns, Andrew, 33
  The Bitter Cry of Outcast London, 33
Medhurst, Andy, 143, 154
Medusa, 179
Mehta, Gita, 100
  Karma Cola, 100
Members, the, 162, 167
  'Sound of the Suburbs', 167
  'Suburban Rhonda', 162
Mendes, Sam, 2
  American Beauty, 2
Mercurio, Paul, 176, 177
metroland, 9, 92, 94, 106
  metropolitan, 10, 54, 59, 63, 65, 66, 72,
    73, 82, 87, 91, 92, 106, 142, 155,
    157, 163, 165, 167, 174, 182, 183
Meyer, Moe, 181, 182
Midlands, the 75, 115, 119
Milton, John, 51
Milton Keynes, 73
Minogue, Kylie, 173
misogyny, 179
Mississippi, 131, 135
Mo, Timothy, 93
Mohanti, Prafulla, 94, 95
  Through Brown Eyes, 94, 95
Monroe, Marilyn, 175
Morris, William, 7, 8, 15, 16, 17, 19, 20,
    21, 22, 23, 28, 29, 32, 41
  News from Nowhere, 15, 16, 19, 29, 32
Morrissey, Steven, 163
Morton, H.V., 3–4, 13n5
  In Search of England, 3–4, 13n5
Muller, Marcia, 120–1, 122
  There's Something in a Sunday, 120–1,
    122
multicultural, 9, 85, 87, 177
Munt, Sally, 121
music
  blues, 161
  dance, 166
  disco, 181
  hymns, 163
  Indie, 166
  New Wave, 166, 167, 169
  popular, 9, 82, 83, 99, 141, 154, 155,
    161, 162, 163, 164, 165, 166, 168,
    170
  punk rock, 9, 82, 83, 84, 99, 154, 166,
    167, 169
  rock, 11, 83, 142, 153, 154, 162, 166
Muslim, 101
myth, 11, 46, 83, 94, 103, 125, 126, 133,
    134, 135, 136, 138, 161, 166, 167

Naipaul, V.S., 94, 96
  The Mimic Men, 96
National Front, the, 95, 105

National Trust, the, 81
Neighbours, 173
neighbourly, 10, 111, 112, 113, 114, 115,
    120, 130, 134, 135
New Jersey, 135
New Jerusalem, 22
New Right, the, 100
New York, 82, 84, 167
Newton, Ernest, 46
new towns, 17, 22, 73, 74–5, 76
New Woman, the, 8, 58, 59, 60, 68, 121
Nobbs, David, 93
  The Fall and Rise of Reginald Perrin, 93
Norfolk, 162
Northern Songs, 163
Northumbria, 81
Norwich, 162

Oasis, 166, 170
Olsen, Donald, 48
Olympic games, 178
omnibus, 3,4, 29
O'Regan, Tom, 174
organic, 20
Orpington, 100
Orwell, George, 1, 27, 28–9, 164, 165
  Coming up for Air, 1, 12n1, 164
  The Road to Wigan Pier, 29
Osborne, John, 75, 77
  Look Back in Anger, 75
other, 2, 134, 151, 173
  otherness, 4, 10, 115, 137
overdetermined, 173
Oxford, 96, 119

pacifist, 28
Paducah, 132, 133
Pakistan, 100
Parker, Barry, 19, 24, 25
Paris, 78
parochial, 10, 91, 93, 98, 106, 178
parody, 8, 76, 86, 103, 155, 156, 181, 182
pastiche, 143, 156, 179
pastoral, 161
Peyton Place, 111
Percy, Walker, 126
Phillips, Caryl, 93
Pinkney, Tony, 74
Pinner, 62
Port Sunlight, 25
postcolonial, 9, 86, 92, 93, 94, 95, 96,
    182–3
post-imperial, 86
poverty, 9, 32, 35, 95, 96, 97
Powell, Anthony, 164–5
  A Dance To The Music Of Time, 164
  The Acceptance World, 164–5
Powell, Enoch, 100
prejudice, 9, 69, 72, 75, 85, 86, 92, 97, 98,
    99, 100, 119
Presley, Elvis, 132
Pritchett, V.S., 164

producer, 5, 9
  production, 11, 126, 150, 181
public house, 3, 4
Pulp, 163, 170
Punch, 36–9, 40, 45
Purdom, C.B., 18, 19, 21, 22, 23–4, 25, 26, 27, 28
  The Building of Satellite Towns, 22, 24
  The Garden City, 18, 22, 23
  Life Over Again, 22
Putney, 34, 62

Quaker, 28
Quarterly Review, 45
queer, 181, 182
Quinn, Karl, 174

race, 9, 33, 41
  racial, 9, 101, 102
  racism, 9, 85, 98, 100, 101, 103, 105, 106
railways, 34–6, 38, 81, 120, 170, 174
Ramchand, Kenneth, 93
Raymond, Ernest, 165
  A Kilburn Tale, 165
Reagan, Ronald, 110
Redmond, Phil, 3
  Brookside, 3
regeneration, 7
Reid, Jamie, 166
Relph, Edward, 145, 157
Richman, Jonathan, 162
Ridge, William Pett, 93
Rivers, Joan, 132
road, 4, 24, 73, 93, 101
Roethke, Theodore, 136
  'Meditation', 136
Rolling Stones, the, 166
romanticism, 21, 169, 180
Rosebery, Lord, 41
Ross, Andrew, 181
Roxy Music, 166
Roy, Rajah Rammohun, 93
Rubin, David, 102
Rudnick, Paul, 182
rural, 5, 7, 17, 34, 41, 42, 43, 51, 54, 56, 59, 81, 128, 163
Rushdie, Salman, 93
Ruskin, John, 32, 39
Rutherford, Mark, 43
  Autobiography and Deliverance, 43

Sahara, 40
Saint Loe Strachey, J., 25
Salt Lake City, 136
San Francisco, 120
Savage, Jon, 154, 167
Sawyer, Miranda, 71, 91, 94, 97
  Park and Ride, 71
schizophrenia, 145
Scotland, 116
Second World War, the, 130

Selvon, Sam, 93
Severin, Steve, 167
Sex Pistols, the, 166, 167
sexuality, 12, 61, 75, 103, 116, 118, 174, 177, 178, 182
Sham 69, 167
  'Hersham Boys', 167
Shakespeare, William, 51
Sharkey, Feargal, 170
Shaw, Norman, 23
Sheffield, 36, 170
Shields, Rob, 130
shops, 3,4, 71, 82, 96, 130, 151, 155, 174
  mail-order catalogues, 136
  Sainsbury, 96
  shopping centres, 6, 73, 130, 134, 168
  shopping malls, 6, 10, 73, 110, 125, 127, 128, 130–3
  temples, 6
Sillitoe, Alan, 8, 72, 86
  Saturday Night and Sunday Morning, 72
Silverstone, Roger, 126, 134, 141, 143, 156
Simpson, Catherine, 174
Siouxsie and the Banshees, 83, 162, 163, 167, 168
  'Suburban Relapse', 162, 168
  Sioux, Siouxsie, 167
Skids, the, 162
  'Sweet Suburbia', 162
Sloane, 145
Slough, 28
Smiths, The, 163
social, 5, 54, 63, 68, 69, 71, 72, 74, 75, 76, 77, 78, 79, 81, 83, 84, 87, 91, 94, 111, 113, 114, 118, 119, 120, 123, 127, 134, 147, 148, 150, 152, 164, 165, 166, 182
  Socialism, 29, 39
  Socialist League, The, 16
society, 7, 9, 65, 66, 75, 86, 93, 100, 105, 123, 147
Soho, 165, 167
South Africa, 178
Southampton, 92
South Kensington, 37
space, 6, 8, 11, 12, 34, 39, 41, 44, 45, 69, 71, 92, 100, 110, 122, 123, 127, 134, 142, 144, 150, 157, 173, 174, 175, 176, 177, 178
spatial, 3, 8, 91, 98, 120, 126, 130, 183
Spanish, 176, 180
  Spanish-Australian, 174, 176, 177
Spectator, The, 25
Spigel, Lynn, 114
Springsteen, Bruce, 133
  Born in the U.S.A., 133
Squeeze, 167
  'Up the Junction', 167
Standard, The, 42
St John's Wood, 36
Stratford, 96
students, 120, 146, 181

subjectivity, 4, 6, 100, 126, 130, 133
  subjective, 10
Suburban Press, 166
Suede, 83, 163, 169, 170
Surrey, 42, 167
Sussex, 122
Swift, Graham, 93
  The Sweetshop Owner, 93
Syal, Meera, 92, 97, 98, 99
  Anita and Me, 97–8, 99
  Life Isn't All Ha Ha Hee Hee, 99
Sydney, 109, 173, 178, 180
  Sydney Ballet Company, 177
Sylvania Waters, 173
Symons, Julian, 114, 118, 121
  Something Like a Love Affair, 114, 118,
    121, 122

Talking Heads, 167
  Cities, 167
technoburb, 10, 125
television, 3,5, 72, 82, 87, 127, 130, 132,
    166, 173
  soaps, 12, 76, 87, 105, 173, 179
terrain, 100, 178
territorial, 7, 31, 40
Thames Valley, 164
Thatcher, Margaret, 95, 105
Thomas, Allan, 181–2
Thompson, F.M.L., 52
  The Rise of Suburbia, 52
time, 6, 12, 135
Times, The, 36
Tolstoy, Leo, 22
topophilia, 143
Tory, 36
Tottenham Hotspur, 146
tradition, 4, 5, 55, 74, 82, 112, 128, 130,
    135, 141
Trafford Park, 22, 23
transculturation, 99
travelogue, 4
Trevelyan, G.M., 81
  English Social History, 81
Trevor, William, 115–16
  Felicia's Journey, 115–16, 117
Trojan horse, 116
Tuan, Yi-Fu, 143
typologies, 141

Undertones, the, 170
uniformity, 8
Unwin, Raymond, 16, 17, 18, 19, 20, 21,
    22, 23, 24, 25, 26–7, 29
  Town Planning in Practice, 16, 17, 19, 21
urban, 5, 11, 17, 41, 42, 43, 46, 71, 73,
    74, 87, 93, 96, 99, 104, 112, 122,
    141, 142, 143, 147, 148, 149, 150,

154, 155, 156, 157, 161, 163, 167,
    168, 170, 173
U.S.A., 100
utopia, 11, 46, 75, 150
  utopian, 6, 15, 18, 19, 20, 22, 25, 27,
    29, 30, 74, 157

Vietnam Veterans Memorial, 132, 133
Vietnam War, the, 132, 133
  Vietnamese, 132
violence, 6, 64, 79, 80, 111, 147, 148
vista, 4

Wain, John, 72
  Hurry on Down, 73
Wales, 51, 61, 73
Walters, Minette, 118–19, 121, 122
  The Breaker, 118–19, 121, 122
Walwicz, Ania, 174
Washington D.C., 110, 120, 132
Watergate scandal, 111
Watford, 156
Waugh, Evelyn, 87, 165
  Brideshead Revisited, 165
Weldon, Fay, 93
  Life and Loves of a She-Devil, 93
Weller, Paul, 165, 167
Wells, H.G., 8, 32, 41, 53, 54, 55, 56–7,
    101, 164
  Ann Veronica, 32, 56
  Anticipations, 32
  The New Machiavelli, 8, 53, 56–7, 101
  Tono-Bungay, 56, 58
weltanshauung, 151
Welwyn Garden City, 19, 21, 25, 27, 28
West Bletchley, 1, 164
West Indian, 93
West Midlands, 99
Whitehall, 169
Who, the, 166
Williams, Raymond, 3, 13n4, 73–4
  The Fight for Manod, 73–4
Williams, Nigel, 76, 77, 93
  The Wimbledon Poisoner, 76, 93
Wilson, Angus, 8, 75–6, 77
  Late Call, 8, 75–6
Wilson, Bob, 146
Wimbledon, 62, 77
Woking, 154
Woolf, Virginia, 79

xenophobia, 97

Young, John Paul, 179–80
  'Love is in the Air', 179

zone, 4